LATINO
CHRONOLOGY

Latino Population in the United States

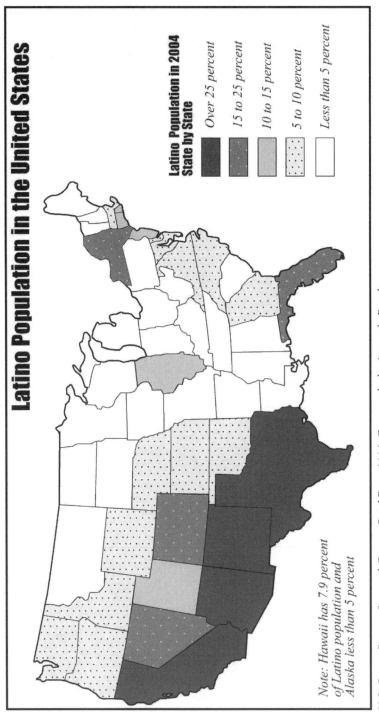

Latino Population in 2004 State by State

- Over 25 percent
- 15 to 25 percent
- 10 to 15 percent
- 5 to 10 percent
- Less than 5 percent

Note: Hawaii has 7.9 percent of Latino population and Alaska less than 5 percent

U.S. Census Bureau, State and County QuickFacts, 2004. Cartography by Armando Portela.

LATINO CHRONOLOGY

CHRONOLOGIES OF THE AMERICAN MOSAIC

D. H. Figueredo

GREENWOOD PRESS
Westport, Connecticut • London

Library of Congress Cataloging-in-Publication Data

Figueredo, D. H., 1951–
    Latino chronology : chronologies of the American mosaic / D.H. Figueredo.
        p. cm.
    Includes bibliographical references and index.
    ISBN-13: 978–0–313–34154–0 (alk. paper)
    ISBN-10: 0–313–34154–0 (alk. paper)
    1. Hispanic Americans—History—Chronology.   2. Spain—History—
Chronology.   3. Latin America—History—Chronology.   I. Title.
    E184.S75F543   2007
    973'.046800202—dc22   2006100435

British Library Cataloguing in Publication Data is available.

Library of Congress Catalog Card Number: 2006100435
ISBN-13: 978–0–313–34154–0
ISBN-10: 0–313–34154–0

First published in 2007

Greenwood Press, 88 Post Road West, Westport, CT 06881
An imprint of Greenwood Publishing Group, Inc.
www.greenwood.com

Printed in the United States of America

The paper used in this book complies with the
Permanent Paper Standard issued by the National
Information Standards Organization (Z39.48–1984).

10 9 8 7 6 5 4 3 2 1

The publisher has done its best to make sure the instructions and/or recipes in this book
are correct. However, users should apply judgment and experience when preparing recipes,
especially parents and teachers working with young people. The publisher accepts no
responsibility for the outcome of any recipe included in this volume.

To my wife and friend Yvonne and to my son Daniel and daughter Gabriela: they give meaning to the chronology of my life.

CONTENTS

Preface   ix
Introduction   xi
Abbreviations   xiii

Prehistory   1
First Century through Fourteenth Century   5
Fifteenth Century   9
Sixteenth Century   13
Seventeenth Century   25
Eighteenth Century   31
Nineteenth Century   39
Twentieth Century   65
Twenty-First Century   125

Glossary   133
Bibliography   139
Index   147

PREFACE

The chronology begins centuries before Columbus's arrival in 1492 and ends with the election of Senator Bob Menendez in November 2006. The intent is to identify major moments in Latino history across disciplines and across countries. I know as I write this that there are moments, events, personages, that I missed. No one else should be blamed but me, a victim of not having "world and time enough."

Throughout the text, there are sidebars that emphasize or highlight particular historical incidents. For example, there are two sidebars that accompany the discussion of the battle of the Alamo in 1836: one sidebar illustrates the Mexicans' brutality on the Texians, as Texan-Americans called themselves at the time, and the second sidebar depicts the brutality inflicted upon the Mexicans by the avenging Texians. With a couple of exceptions, the sidebars consist of passages from literary works, histories, sociological tracts, and popular culture. The sidebars will, hopefully, serve as pointers to cited sources and other works on Latino history. A bibliography at the end includes sources that I used and checked as well as DVDs and videos that I watched as I worked on this project.

The entries are arranged chronologically by date, and alphabetically by topic within individual years. The rich history of the Latino people is covered in over 40 subject areas, including arts, education, employment, health, immigration, language, legislation, media, and religion. Subject categories are indicated by abbreviations, such as POLI for politics, and EXPL for exploration. A list of subject abbreviations is located in the front matter for easy reference. Words in Spanish are used when necessary; however, the English translation follows.

In this chronology, I used the term Latino rather than Hispanic. The first designation allows for gender, thus providing variety within the text. It is also a term preferred by most people in academia and since that is my environment, I use the expression in conversation with my colleagues; therefore I thought it fitting to follow suit in this endeavor. While Latino and Hispanic both carry political connotations—Hispanic is conservative, Latino is liberal—that is certainly not the case with my usage. There is no political message in my preference for the word Latino.

The information in this volume comes from hundreds of sources, conversations with scholars and researchers, feature films and documentaries, CDs, pamphlets, oral histories, and personal knowledge. Many individuals shaped this book; some know they did, and others do not: Ruby Acosta, Frank Freyre, Salvador Güereño, Roger Hernández, Peter Johnson, Nicolás Kanellos, William Luis, Luis Martínez Fernández, Alfredo Massip, Armando H. Portela, Asela Rodríguez de Laguna, Pamela Maria Smorkaloff, and many friends from SALALM—Seminar on the Acquisition of Latin American Library Materials.

Many libraries were used for research, including the Ateneo Puertorriqueño, Center for Puerto Rican Studies at Hunter College, the Davies Library at University of Santa Barbara, the Otto Richter Collection, University of Miami, the Firestone Library, Princeton University, Rutgers University Libraries, and the St. Petersburg Library, Florida.

Thanks to my very patient editor, Mariah Gumpert, Acquisitions Editor, and the staff at Greenwood Press, always helpful. Gratitude and love to my joyful family: my wife Yvonne and my children Daniel and Gabriela.

INTRODUCTION

When my son was in elementary school, a teacher, who was explaining to the class the factual basis of the popular Disney film *Pocahontas,* described how the fort that Captain John Smith and his men erected became the first European settlement in the United States. Having visited St. Augustine the previous summer, where enthusiastic tour guides claimed how their city was the first permanent European settlement in the country, my son observed that the honor did not belong to Jamestown but to St. Augustine, to which the teacher responded by reaffirming his statement: "No, Jamestown was the first." Confused, my son related the event to me later on in the evening. I handed him a pamphlet we had picked up in St Augustine that announced in bold letters: St. Augustine, 1565. I suggested to him that if he wanted to, he could share the flyer with the teacher. The following day, my son did and the teacher replied, "It wasn't really a city, you know."

Relating this account is not a blaming act, though there is the potential to say that I'm pointing my finger at that teacher, now retired from the district. The incident illustrates that certain teachers who attended college in another era were not exposed to historical events that we now see as important but that were, for a long time, presented as trivial. The old observation about there being no survivors at Little Big Horn is sufficient proof of that mentality: Yes, there were survivors, the Native Americans. Once historians accepted the reality that there were other folks besides the white members of the 7th Cavalry, then other ways of looking at that famous battle appeared in books and documentaries. So, yes, my son's former teacher responded with a set of knowledge he had picked up at a time when U.S. history referred only to the adventures of British colonialists and their American subjects.

That has changed now. Still, there are people who are not fully aware of the early presence of Spanish conquistadores on American shores and of the proud Mexicans who, along with Native Americans, forged the American West before the likes of Billy the Kid, Wyatt Earp, and Buffalo Bill Cody learned to walk. This is where this chronology might serve a useful purpose.

The chronology begins before there was an America, before the appellation *La América Latina,* Latin America, was coined. The reader might wonder why bring the Roman empire in Spain and the crossing of the Alps by Hannibal into the picture along with the establishment of powerful kingdoms in Kenya and Nigeria. But these mighty events, of so long ago and so removed from the Americas, were leading the participants, and their descendants, into a new world, propelling them east across the Atlantic. The invasion of Spain by the Muslims in the 700s provoked, seven centuries later, the reconquest of Spain by the Catholic monarchs, Queen Isabella and King Ferdinand, a conflict that served as training ground for

Spanish soldiers who learned the art of conquest, not by the word but by the sword. The same soldiers sailed with Columbus and his followers, serving victorious monarchs now looking for more victories and the creation of an empire, and the lessons they learned on the plains of Iberia they perfected in the valleys of México, the mountains of Perú, and the shores of Hispaniola. We call those soldiers *conquistadores*.

As the civilizations encountered by the Spanish perished at the hands of the Spanish, a new society emerged from the bloody intermingling of two worlds. And to that emerging world, there came another element, not by choice, the way the conquistadores came, and not armed with swords, but by force and in shackles: the African slaves. It all came together: Africa, ancient America, and Europe. The new world they formed was Latin America, and from Latin America sallied forth the peoples we call today Latinos.

Do Latinos know that their history is a long one, stretching into countless empires and domains? Many do, many do not. It is a sad realization that often students of Latino descent know so little of the land of their grandparents, and what they do know is often diminished by non-Latinos. There was a professor at an east coast university who was specializing in the study of a particular type of horse carriage, called *volante,* that was used in Cuba in the nineteenth century. Sharing his research with a colleague, this other fellow historian, the colleague, dismissed the research as too narrowed, too focused for universal value. The humor, if not the irony, in the anecdote is that the fellow historian who dismissed the volante had achieved recognition for his studies of the American stagecoach. The volante, that Cuban coach, was not important, but the American coach was.

But there are other Latinos—and I offer a tremendous *saludo* to the Chicano community in particular—who bask in the sunlight of their pasts. They know that what they are today is because of what they were yesterday, incarnating Spanish philosopher José Ortega y Gasset's assertion of "I am myself and my circumstances." The circumstances of Latinos in this country include the sword and the cross, Christianity and *Santería,* epic battles and books of epics, the guitar and the drums, cries of liberties and cries against oppression. That man landscaping a condominium development is the child of a Mayan mathematician who developed the spacing required for the creation of the zero in our numerical system. That woman sweeping the hallways of a luxury hotel is the spiritual daughter of a Mexican Baroque nun who penned poetry that championed early feminism. That man and that woman, and the thousands of Latino professionals in hospitals and in schools and in science and in politics, want you to know that they know they come from greatness and that such greatness makes their adopted country—or their original country in the case of Mexican-Americans—an even greater nation.

Thus this chronology comes from other lands and oceans, meeting on this space we call the United States. This chronology acknowledges, in an act of friendship and cordiality, that Latinos helped to create the United States and that they continue to do so, in the company of the many people who have come from all over the world to make of America still the greatest experiment in history.

ABBREVIATIONS

AGRI	Agriculture and Farming		MEDI	Medicine
ANIM	Animals		MIGR	Migration
ARC	Architecture		MILI	Military
ARTS	Arts, Crafts, Music		MUSI	Music and Dance
BIRT	Birth		OBIT	Obituary
BUSI	Business		POLI	Politics
CRIM	Crime		POPU	Population
CULT	Culture		RACE	Race Relations
ECON	Economics and Employment		REBE	Rebellion
EDUC	Education and Schools		RELI	Religion and Spirituality
ENVI	Environment and Nature		REVO	Revolts
EXPL	Explorations		SCIE	Science
FOOD	Food and Drink		SETT	Settlements and Villages
HEAL	Health and Disease		SHEL	Shelter and Housing
IMMI	Immigration		SLAV	Slavery
INVE	Inventions		SOCI	Social Organization
LAND	Land Cessions and Reservations		SPOR	Sports and Recreation
LANG	Languages		TRAD	Trade
LAWS	Laws and Legislation		TRAN	Transporation
LEGE	Legends and Storytelling		TREA	Treaties
LIT	Literature		WARS	Wars and Conflicts
MED	Media		WORK	Jobs and Employment

PREHISTORY

50,000–10,000 B.C.

ENVI. The Bering Strait, connecting Europe to the American continent, forms a land bridge during an ice age. There is a drop in sea level, facilitating the crossing.

MIGR. Asian hunters migrate to North America across the 56-mile stretch of the Bering Strait, and some continue on to South America. They are following mammoths and other large animals that have migrated to the New World. In time, they will break into numerous groups or people who populate Latin America. Many minor and major civilizations will rise and fall; some, like the Incas, the Mayas, the Mexicas, and the Toltecs, will leave major archaeological findings as evidence of their existence.

11,000 B.C.

INVE. Flint tools and possible remains of temples found in modern-day Perú demonstrate evidence of human culture during the period.

4000 B.C.

SETT. Evidence of early settlements in the area occupied by present day Ghana. Many of the slaves sent to Latin America between the sixteenth and nineteenth centuries come from areas in and near Ghana.

1500 B.C.

RELI. Important Mayan deities are Itzamna and Ix Chel, father and mother of all other gods, Chac, the rain god, and Kukulcan, the feathered

---

Encounters of the Deadly Kind

"These first emigrants [to ancient America] carried few diseases with them and found no humans in America, diseased or healthy. They lived, died, and bred alone for generation after generation, developing unique cultures and working our tolerance for a limited, native American selection of pathological microlife. When the isolation of the New World was broken, when Columbus brought the two halves of this planet together, the American Indian met for the first time his most hideous enemy: not the white man nor his black servant, but the invisible killers which those men brought in their blood and breath."

Source: Alfred Crosby, Jr. *The Columbian Exchange: Biological and Cultural Consequences of 1492.* Westport, CT: Greenwood Press, 1972.

serpent, god of the ruling caste. To honor these gods, annual festivals are held that include ritual offerings, sacrifices, and the imbibing of an intoxicating mead called *balche*.

SETT. Mayan Civilization appears in México, areas in Central America, and in Perú. The Maya are direct ancestors of many Latinos.

1200 B.C.–800 B.C.

RELI. Quetzalcoat is the feathered serpent god from whom the people of Mesoamerica, including the Mexicas/Aztecs, the Olmecs, and the Toltecs, believe themselves to have descended. For the Toltecs, the feathered serpent represents earth and vegetation and for the Mexicas death and resurrection. Stories abound that Quetzalcoat leaves the earth, promising to return one day. Latin American scholars of the twenty-first century would dispute the concept, explaining that it was an idea introduced into the culture by the conquistadores so that they could claim they were the returning god.

SETT. Olmec civilization flourishes along the gulf coast of México. The Olmecs are known for the construction of massive sculptures of huge round heads. Their disappearance is still a mystery, though some historians believe that the Olmecs probably assimilated with other cultures, such as the Toltecs, as they moved from one region to another in México and Central America.

1000 B.C.

ARTS. *La Dama de Eche*, the Lady of Eche, is sculpted by unknown Iberian artist(s). It is the sculpture of an Iberian beauty wearing a mantilla, painted red; a large tunic, painted blue; and loop earrings. Her face is long with oblong eyes and straight, thin nose atop small lips. The sculpture is unearthed in 1897 by farmers working on a hillside. Some scholars maintain the find is a fake but recent research validates the sculpture as originating during the Iberian conquest of Spain.

EXPL. Iberians, traveling from Africa, invade the south of Spain. The peninsula is named after their civilization.

EXPL. Celts travel to Spain through the Pyrenees. Iberians and Celts become ancestors of modern day Spaniards and part of the ancestral pool of Latinos.

814 B.C.

POLI. City of Carthage, Africa, is founded by Phoenicians. First a colony, Carthage evolves into a powerful state that replaces the Phoenician nation. The Carthaginians relocate to southern Spain.

500 B.C.

AGRI. The Taínos and the Caribs, inhabitants of the Caribbean, cultivate the yucca, a tubular plant related to the potato or the yam. They use a system known as *conuco*, where a chunk of the root is planted in a position parallel to the surface. The seedling is buried near the surface with enough space to allow the root to stretch out sideways. The conuco system does not need much water or much soil. The plant sprouts long, thick angular leaves that can survive the strongest of winds.

The Many Cultures of Spain

"The Spain that arrived in the New World . . . gave us at least half of our being," writes Mexican author Carlos Fuentes. He also reminds Spaniards that they themselves, like Latinos, are composed of many people and traditions: "Spain is not only Christian but Arab and Jewish, she is also Greek, Carthaginian, Roman, and both Gothic and Gypsy. . . . Spain embraces all of us: she is . . . our commonplace, our common ground."

Source: Carlos Fuentes. *The Buried Mirror: Reflections on Spain and the New World.* New York: Houghton Mifflin and Company, 1992, p.15.

ANIM. The Carthaginians use the elephant as a weapon similar to the twentieth-century tank. The African elephant is about eight to nine feet tall and as large as a small house. The Carthaginians covered the elephants' bodies with sheets of bronze and probably attached knives to their trunks. The size and smell of the elephants terrify horses, thus sending the Roman cavalry into a panic. When the Romans first see the elephants crossing the Alps, they flee for their lives. The elephant used by the Carthaginians is now extinct.

ARTS. Taínos practice an art form called *areyto*, which pays tribute to deities. Held in a field or a ceremonial plaza, the *areyto* is a combination of narration, poetry, singing, and dancing used to tell events from the past and comment on local developments, such as a birth or a death. *Areyto* also rallies the villagers into battle with rival families or other villages in times of war or conflict.

CULT. The Taínos believe in life after death. Personal objects, such as jewelry, are interred with the deceased.

EXPL. The Ciboneyes (also spelled "Siboneyes"), also known as the Guanahatabey, are the oldest group of Amerindians to arrive in the Caribbean, and they are the first that Columbus encounters in 1492. It is believed that that they are hunters and gatherers. They live in small loosely structured groups and are culturally assimilated by the Taínos.

EXPL. The Taínos, originating from the northeast of South America and Florida, arrive in the Caribbean, selecting the Bahamas, Cuba, Hispaniola (which includes Haiti and the Dominican Republic), Jamaica, Puerto Rico, and Trinidad as major places for settlements. They are one of the primary ancestor groups of many people from the Hispanic Caribbean.

EXPL. The Carthaginians, ancestors of the Spanish and Latinos, settle in the south of Spain. They first create a mercantile network but later on use the area as a war base to fight against the Romans. The Carthaginian port of Gádir, present day Cádiz, flourishes.

FOOD. The Taíno and Carib women prepare the yucca, a main staple of the Amerindians' diet. The yucca, a tubular root, is poisonous and cannot be eaten unless is boiled and drained of its juices. The women place the yucca on a platform and hammer it flat, forming a substance similar to bread. The yucca is still a popular food in twenty-first century Cuban and Puerto Rican cuisine.

LANG. The Carthaginians speak a Semitic language, similar to Phoenician, and use an alphabet similar to the Hebrew alphabet. The name Cádiz is a variation of the Carthaginian Gádir.

LANG. Numerous Taíno words from this period survive in twenty-first century Spanish and English usage. Some of the English variations are "canoe," "Haiti," "hammock," "hurricane," and "Jamaica."

POLI. The Taínos divide their island homes into provinces that are ruled by a chief, a *cacique*. The provinces are composed of villages that, in turn, are ruled by less powerful chiefs or subchiefs. The caciques officiate at ritualistic festivities and oversee ceremonial ball games. They also settle disputes.

POLI. The Carthaginians organize the south of Spain into cities and towns, including Acra-Leuca, possibly present day Alicante. When Romans invade Iberia, they incorporate the Carthaginian towns into Roman political structures.

POPU. The estimated combined population of Taínos and Caribs is anywhere from 225,000 to six million, though most historians prefer a figure closer to 300,000.

RELI. The Taínos have a spiritual and natural healer called a *bohuti*. The *bohuti* is admired and respected for his knowledge of the desires of the gods and his wisdom regarding the healing benefits of local plants. Taínos worship spirits known as "cemis" or "zemis," protectors of villages and people. Taínos also believe in the deities Yucahus, who embodies all that is good, such as pleasant weather, good crops, and happiness; and Juracan, who is responsible for strong winds and storms, flooding, and destruction. There are also evil spirits, called Maboyas, who hide in the forest and come out at night to hurt people. As part of their religious rituals, the Taínos induce a hallucinogenic state with tobacco and tobacco smoke during religious ceremonies.

RELI. The Carthaginians have three major deities: Baal or Melgart, god of the sun, the sky, and the city; Astarte or Baalat, goddess of the moon, earth, and sexual reproduction; and Adonis, god of vegetation. From these gods emerge other deities connected with particular functions, peoples, and places. It is believed that the Carthaginians practice human sacrifices.

SHEL. Taínos live in communities that range from one unit to many families, and towns that include a few to a thousand houses. The houses are called *bohíos* and are erected around ball courts or courtyards.

SPOR. The Taínos play a ball game called *batu*, which resembles volleyball. The objective of the game is to keep the ball from falling to the ground; however, hands can not be used to achieve this objective. The team that drops the ball loses.

WARS. Carthaginians and Romans battle each other for control of the Mediterranean, with the former using the Spanish southern coast as a base to launch attacks. It is a conflict, known as the Punic Wars, that lasts from 246 B.C. to 146 B.C. when the Carthaginians are incorporated into the Roman Empire.

218 B.C.

WARS. Hannibal, who has sworn eternal hatred of the Romans, crosses the Alps with his army, including elephants, and marches into Italy, defeating the Romans. Twenty years later, Rome regains its military strength and defeats the Carthaginians and Spain is, eventually, handed to the Romans. Because of the wars

with the Romans and later invasions of Spain by Vandals, very little is left of Carthaginian civilization in the Iberian Peninsula.

100 B.C.

POLI. City of Teotihuacán, located 20 or so miles north of present-day México City, is founded by the Teotihuacanos, who are possibly of Olmec origin. The city has more than 4,000 stone and mud brick buildings consisting of one floor and attached rooms, an ancient precursor of apartments. By the first century B.C., the city will be one of the largest in the contemporary world with over 125,000 inhabitants.

27 B.C.

CULT. The evolution of Roman-Iberian culture is manifested in the use of Latin by Iberian writers, the evolution of the Spanish language rooted in Latin, the introduction of Christianity, the construction of pagan temples and amphitheaters, and the building of aqueducts, bridges, and roads. Many of these structures still stand today. Roman architectural style is evident throughout Latin America.

LANG. The name España, Spain, evolves from Hispania, the name the Romans give to the Iberian Peninsula.

WAR. Roman forces conquer Iberia. The Roman presence in Spain will last seven centuries.

4 B.C.

BIRT. Seneca is born Lucius Annaeus Seneca in Cordova, Spain. He is a philosopher, dramatist, and statesman. His tragedies, which include *Hercules Furens* and *The Phoenician Women*, are performed in several languages throughout the modern world.

FIRST CENTURY THROUGH
FOURTEENTH CENTURY

1 A.D.

EXPL. Sailing down the Orinoco River, in South America, and across the Caribbean Sea, the Caribs arrive in the Caribbean. They build canoes that can seat 100 men.

SHEL. The Caribs, who are highly moveable, live in small villages or gatherings with other family members. They prefer to settle on hills, probably because such locations allow for a clear view of the landscape, a useful strategy in the event of combat.

WARS. The Caribs war on the Taínos and, it is believed by European historians, based on reports written by Christopher Columbus, that the Caribs practice cannibalism, especially of captured Taínos; this assertion would be widely disputed by Latin American archaeologists and historians in the late twentieth century. The weapons that the Caribs use are bows, poisoned arrows, spears, and clubs.

40

BIRT. On March 1, poet Martial is born in present day Calatayud, Spain. His poems describe living conditions and sexual mores during the Roman Empire.

65

OBIT. Seneca, Roman-Spanish philosopher and dramatist, commits suicide. He is accused of plotting against Roman emperor Nero, his former student.

102

OBIT. Spanish-Roman poet and satirist Martial dies in Rome at the age of 62.

200–900

ARC. The Mayas of Guatemala, Honduras, northern Belize, and Yucatán, México, direct ancestors of many people from Central America and México, build pyramid-like temples with long stairways at oblique angles, palaces with dozens of rooms, observatories, ball parks, and roads. In the twentieth century, archaeologists will identify at least 15 Mayan cities in the province of Yucatán alone.

ARC. The city of Chichén Itzá is built. The first half of the city, called Chichén Viejo, is constructed in Yucatán circa 400. The second half of the city is constructed circa 850. The city still stands today, located about three hours away, by bus, from the resort town of Cancún.

ENVI. The Yucatán peninsula is a large slab of limestone. The soil is thin and there are no rivers. There are pockets of wells and sink holes, called *cenotes,* throughout the peninsula. The city of Chichén Itzá is built around a giant well.

FOOD. Chocolate is first used as a drink by the Mayas. It is so popular that the beans are used as a form of currency. Centuries later, the bean will become a delicacy for the Aztecs.

INVE. The Mayas develop and use a version of the zero, indicated by a dot representative of a cocoa bean. The Mayas' counting system is based on 20; it includes counting with all the fingers

The Mayan observatory at Chichén Itzá, Yucatán. The Mayas developed the placement of the zero, a source of great pride for Latino scholars and teachers. Photo by Daniel A. Figueredo.

and toes. The numerical system is used for commerce and astronomical purposes. In the twentieth century, Peruvian teacher Jaime Escalante will encourage Latino students from the ghetto who are failing the subject of math by telling them that their ancestors invented the zero.

RELI. Cenotes, or sink holes, are of great importance to the Mayas, who sometimes offer human sacrifices to the cenotes by throwing the victims into the well or sink hole.

SETT. Mayan Civilization emerges in Guatemala, Honduras, northern Belize, and the province of Yucatán, México. There are two civilizations. The first civilization, which dwells in Guatemala, is known as the "sages." The second civilization is called the "warriors," and it consists of the merging of two groups, the Mayas and the Toltecs.

300

POLI. The Roman Empire is divided into the Eastern and Western Roman Empire. Spain is located within the Western Roman Empire.

537

WAR. The Visigoths, a Germanic tribe, conquer Spain. They set up a monarchy to rule over the entire peninsula.

Drinking Chocolate the Old Way

"chololatl or chocolate—which probably means bitter water, from xococ, bitter, and atl, water—was drunk cold and was made in the following way: The cacao beans were ground in a mortar with a few boiled grains of corn and mixed with water. This was beaten with a spoon or wooden whisk until it was well mixed and frothy. Before it was finally drunk from the jicara container, it was again beaten until it was frothy. Aromatic spices such as vanilla and . . . honey were often added."

Source: Manuel Lucena Salmoral. *America 1492: Portrait of a Continent Five Hundred Years Ago.* New York: Facts on File, 1990, p. 60.

711

WAR. The Moors, consisting of Arabs and other Muslims from the north of Africa, begin the invasion of Spain. Seven years later, except for the regions near the north of the peninsula, the Moors defeat the Visigoths and conquer Spain.

714

LEGE. According to legend, in the year 714 A.D., an unknown number of Catholic bishops and followers sail to the island of Antilla, somewhere in the middle of the Atlantic Ocean. They find cities so wealthy, the streets and walls are made of gold.

786

ARC. Architecture and interior design flourishes in Spain during the Muslim occupation. Construction begins on Cordova's *Mezquite,* or mosque, probably the most famous and splendid design from the era. The mosque contains 100 pillars in Roman and Visigoth styles. At the center lies the *Mihrab* with elaborate mosaics and arches. The Mihrab faces in the direction of Mecca.

SETT. The city of Córdoba is the center of the Muslim Empire in Iberia.

900–1000

LIT. The Muslim Empire in Iberia cultivates the writing of philosophy, producing such works as *El Regimen del solitario,* written by Avempace de Zaragoza, and the novel, *El viviente hijo del vigilante,* written by Abubéquer-Aben-Tofail, meditations on the concepts of utopia. Poetry is the preferred literary form, and it is believed that a genre of Arabic lyrical poetry known as *muwassahas* and another called *zéjel* are first introduced in Spain. These genres are the first manifestation of poetry in a romance language, thus serving as roots for the literature that would emerge from Spain and Latin America.

SCIE. In Spain, the Muslims replace the Roman numeral system with the Arabic system, invent algebra, and develop studies of geography, medicine, and pharmacy. The study of medicine is based on scientific findings and theories of the time rather than on superstition. Muslims describe how to use plants as medical treatments. The Muslims spread their knowledge throughout Europe.

SLAV. African Muslim aristocrats, military leaders, merchants, and traders begin to modify the practice of slavery from military loot to a commercial enterprise where traders can prosper from the sale or exchange of slaves.

987

WAR. From northern México, the Toltecs arrive in Yucatán and settle in Chichén Itzá, merging their culture with the Mayas. Some early archaeologists suggest that the Toltecs invaded Yucatán, but present-day scholars prefer the theory that the two cultures met, probably through commerce, and assimilated.

1000–1100

WAR. Christian regions in Iberia begin to rebel against the Muslims in Spain, with Castile, in northern Spain, becoming the strongest opponent.

1043

BIRT. Rodrigo Díaz de Vivar, known as El Cid, is born in Burgos, Spain. As a legendary Spanish champion who battles the Muslims he will become a historical and literary figure, representative of the bravery and cunning that the conquistadores will emulate in the Americas six centuries later.

1100–1325

AGRI. The Incas, living predominantly in Perú, sow and plant on the sides of mountains, creating terraces held by low walls.

ARC. The city of Tenochtitlán, present-day México City, is founded in 1325. It is built by the Mexicas, or Aztecs, on a lake, by creating canals and artificial islands by digging and piling up dirt from the bottom of the lake. Tenochtitlán has nearly 100 buildings, consisting of temples, palaces, schools, shops, and so forth.

FOOD. The Mexicas' staples includes tortillas and tamales. The tortillas are similar to puff pastry, and they are filled with green tomato and chili sauce. Tamales are made of dough and rolled into corn leaves; they are filled with turkey or dog meat as well as chili and avocado leaves. The tamales are boiled and served hot. Variations of these dishes are still in use today, even by some popular fast-food restaurants.

The Lake of the Valley of México

"Tenochtitlán rose in the midst of [a lake]. . . . Because of its location at the very bottom of the valley, it constantly received the nitrate soils washed down from the surrounding slopes by the rains . . . [and] although the lake was brackish, it was by no means lifeless. It teemed with fish, frogs, turtles, and algae that could be dried and rolled up to a cheeselike consistency, and billions of mosquito eggs that were skimmed off the lake's surface and beaten into a protein-rich paste. All of the [lake was] a stopover for the countless birds migrating from the north. . . . Ducks, geese, storks, and egrets were so abundant that they could be trapped by the dozen by simply setting up large nets."

Source: Jonathan Kandell. *La Capital: A Biography of Mexico City.* Random House: New York, 1988, p. 31.

LANG. The Incas speak the language of Quechua. Quechua uses a three vowel system—a, i, u—and most of the consonants found in the English and Spanish alphabets. In the twenty-first century, over 13 million people in Bolivia, Ecuador, Perú, and parts of Argentina, Chile, and Colombia speak the language. A few Quechua words in English include "alpaca," "coca," "condor," "llama," "pampa," and "puma."

LANG. The Mexicas, also called the Aztecs, speak a language called Nahuatl. This language uses vowels, which are pronounced in the same way vowels in Spanish are pronounced, and a handful of consonants: ch, m, n, p, tk, k, kw, w, and y. The combination tl dominates most words. Some Nahuatl words of common use in English include "avocado," "chocolate," "cacao," and "chili."

POPU. Between 150,000 and 300,000 people live in the ancient city of Tenochtitlán, founded by the Mexicas.

SETT. In 1111 the Incas, direct ancestors of Peruvians, settle in Cuzco, Perú.

SETT. The Mexicas roam throughout México after migrating from somewhere in the American Southwest. In 1325, the Mexicas found the city state of Tenochtitlán, present-day México City.

1236–1248

WAR. Córdova and Seville are reconquered from the Muslims by the Spanish. Granada emerges as a stronghold of the Muslim Empire.

1338–1390

ARC. The Alhambra is built in Granada, the last stronghold in Muslim Spain. This palace contains royal quarters, chambers, a bath, and a mosque with dozens of inner courtyards surrounded by rooms. Centuries later, the design of the Alhambra inspired the architectural designs of numerous buildings in the United States, including Flagler College in Florida and the Capistrano Public Library in California. Muslim motifs are popular with Latin American and Latino designers throughout the world. In neighborhoods in Miami, such as Coral Way, houses bearing Moorish arches and courtyards are popular.

FIFTEENTH CENTURY

1400–1430

SETT. The Inca Empire extends throughout Central America and north of Perú.

C 1440

ARC. Incas build the city of Cuzco using a workforce of 30,000 men. It is estimated that between 100,000 and 200,000 people live in the city. The city still stands today.

1451

BIRT. Amerigo Vespucci is born in Florence on March 9. Schooled in geometry, Latin, and literature, he develops a great interest in sailing to the Americas after Columbus's successful first voyage in 1492. His writings about the new continent, the first to describe the Americas to Europeans, make him a popular figure in Spain and will influence modern geography.

BIRT. April 22 marks the birth of Queen Isabella I, who will expel the Muslims from Spain, unite the peninsula, and sponsor Columbus's four voyages to the Americas.

BIRT. Cristoforo Columbus is born in Genoa, now part of Italy, either in late summer or early fall. In Spain the navigator will be known as Cristóbal Colón, and in the United States and England he will be called Christopher Columbus.

1452

BIRT. King Ferdinand is born on March 10. His marriage to Queen Isabella will begin the unification of Spain. He will expel the Muslims from Iberia, help to form the Spanish Inquisition, and sponsor Columbus's voyages.

1453

WAR. On May 29, Constantinople is taken by nearly 100,000 Turkish troops, signaling the rise of the Ottoman Empire and, more importantly, closing down the pathway between Europe and the Orient. This prompts European monarchs to seek other ways to reach China, India, and Japan to purchase silk, spices, and other products.

1460

BIRT. Birth of Juan Ponce de León, the first European to reach Florida.

BIRT. Birth of Nicolás de Ovando, first governor of Hispaniola, known for his use of harsh methods to colonize the Taínos of the Caribbean.

1466

BIRT. The last Mexica/Aztec emperor, Motecuhzoma, is born. Some accounts say he does not want to be emperor but inherits the position.

1469

POLI. On October 19, King Ferdinand of Aragon and Queen Isabella of Castile marry, combining their kingdoms into one. Their union, both political and romantic, allows them to unite most of Spain and to plan the expulsion of the Muslims, now based in Granada, from the peninsula.

1473

SOCI. In central México, the city of Tlatelolco is annexed to the city of Tenochtitlán, creating one of the great metropolises of the contemporary world. The two cities are separated by a lake but physically connected by a bridge. Similar to Venice in structure, the two cities use hundreds of canals as streets and avenues.

1474

BIRT. On July 7, Bartolomé de las Casas is born in Seville. He will become the protector of the Taínos and Caribs and will criticize Spain's ruthless conquest of the Americas.

1475

WARS. Birth of Francisco Pizarro, a Spanish conquistador who will murder Inca emperor Atahualpa, defeat the Inca empire, begin the colonization of Perú, and found the city of Lima. A man of courage, given to violence, he is representative of the Spanish conquistadores, who use the sword to carve up an empire for Spain.

1484

EXPL. Columbus conceives of a trip sailing west to reach Asia. He is influenced by the writings of geographer and mathematician Paolo dal Pozzo Toscanelli (1397–1482), who believed that between Europe and Asia there was an island, called Antilla, that could serve as way station to India and Japan.

1485

BIRT. Birth of Hernando Cortés, or Hernán Cortés, the daring Spanish conquistador who will defeat the Mexicas Empire with a handful of men. He becomes symbolic of Spain's ability to conquer Latin America by the use of audacity and brutal force.

EXPL. Unable to convince the Portuguese to fund a trip to the west to find Asia, Columbus moves to Spain where he hopes to obtain patronage from Queen Isabella.

1487

WARS. The Spanish army captures the Muslim city of Málaga, enslaving over 11,000 Moors for being belligerent and not being willing to surrender peacefully.

1490

BIRT. Alvar Nuñez Cabeza de Vaca is born in Frontera de Andalusia, Spain. He is the first chronicler of America and probably the first conquistador to identify himself with Native Americans.

1491

WARS. The Spanish army lays siege to Granada, the last bastion of the Muslim Empire in Spain. The army blockades the ports and isolates farmlands. A year later, the Muslims of Spain capitulate and the Spanish monarchs take possession of Granada. Now that Spain is basically united, although there are still a few minor Muslim possessions in the peninsula, Queen Isabella and King Ferdinand can afford to contemplate imperial expansion by considering Columbus's proposal to sail to the west to reach Asia.

1492

ANIM. At the time of Columbus's arrival on October 12, primarily small animals live in the Caribbean islands: a small dog that does not bark, bats, crocodiles—called *caimanes*—iguanas, snakes, turtles, and parrots. On the islands closer to South America, like Trinidad, there are some larger animals such as sloths, anteaters, tiger cats, raccoons, and small deer. In the sea and rivers, there are manatees.

EXPL. After traveling for 36 days and 2,400 nautical miles, Columbus and his three caravels—La Niña, La Pinta, and Santa María—reach the island of Samana Cay, or Watling's Island, on October 12. He then proceeds to the Bahamas, Cuba, and Hispaniola, marking a defining moment in world history. Out of Columbus's discovery or encounter of the so-called New World comes the painful birth of the present culture of the Americas. Opposing civilizations begin to clash violently with each other, pitting the indigenous

---

Christopher Columbus: A Modern Perspective

For many modern Latinos, Columbus is a symbol of capitalism and repression. In Italy and Spain, however, the navigator is representative of courage, faith, and persistence. There are different perspectives as well on his accomplishments. Columbus's detractors refer to his journey to the Americas as an accident, since he was seeking Asia and not a new continent. But Columbus's supporters applaud his genius in not only figuring how to travel west but how to successfully find oceanic currents and winds to take him back to Spain, a feat that had never been accomplished before. To his supporters, Columbus is indeed a great discoverer.

---

groups' fights for survival against settlers' imposition of their own culture, traditions, and power.

ENVI. The flora that Columbus encounters includes palm trees, orchards, oleanders, begonias, pineapples, guava trees, mamey trees, peanuts, corn, beans, squash, peppers, tobacco, yams, and yucca.

LEGE. Columbus is so overtaken by the new sights he sees that he reports spotting mermaids near his ships, though he complains the creatures are not as beautiful as expected. He also believes that there are natives on the islands with feet protruding backwards.

1493

AGRI. Columbus introduces sugar cane to Hispaniola, though the crop is not cultivated, since the Spanish settlers are more interested in mining gold. From this insignificant beginning, sugar cane and the sugar industry will be the most important source of income for Cuba from the nineteenth century onwards.

EXPL. After establishing a fort near Cap-Haitien, in Haiti, Columbus sails back to Spain on January 16. On October 13, sailing with a fleet of 17 ships manned by 1,000 men, Columbus embarks on his second voyage to the Caribbean. He reaches Dominica, Guadeloupe, Antigua, Nevis, St. Kitts, St. Croix, the Virgin Islands, and Puerto Rico.

REBE. The fort that Columbus had left in Cap-Haitien is destroyed by the Taínos, who are rebelling against the 40 Spanish sailors in charge

of the fort. All the sailors are killed in the struggle. The Taínos flee to the countryside. It is the beginning of the violent phase of colonization, forecasting tragic consequences for the Taíno population in the Caribbean.

1494

POLI. The Papal Bull of 1494 is signed by Pope Alexander IV, who is of Spanish origin. The bull divides the world in half from the North Pole to the South Pole. One half of the inhabitable—meaning no European presence—world is Portugal's to explore and conquer; the other half is for Spain.

1496

BIRT. Chronicler Bernal Díaz del Castillo is born in Medina del Campo, Spain. He will accompany Hernán Cortés in the conquest of México and will write a history of the event that is widely considered the best and most complete account of the destruction of the Aztec/Mexican Empire.

SETT. Santo Domingo, the first European city in America, is founded.

1498

EXPL. Columbus begins his third voyage on May 30.

POLI. Queen Isabella and King Ferdinand are growing disappointed with the absence of the promised gold from the New World. They realize that it is expensive to send ships and men to the Caribbean. They also see Columbus as a poor administrator, unable to persuade the Taínos to cooperate with the Spanish and unable to predict or control the natives' violent resistance against colonization.

1499

EXPL. Explorer Amerigo Vespucci reaches the gulf coast of Venezuela.

SLAV. Columbus introduces the *encomienda* system on the island of Hispaniola. Through this system, the native population is entrusted to a Spanish settler who will convert them to Christianity while forcing them to work for him. The encomiendas, also known as *repartimientos,* are rewards given to the settlers.

Sixteenth Century

1500

CRIM. In October, Columbus is arrested on the island of Hispaniola (present-day Dominican Republic and Haiti) by Francisco Bobadilla, a representative of the Spanish monarchy. Columbus is accused of forcing the Spanish aristocrats who came with him to the Caribbean to perform manual labor, of enslaving the Taínos, and of keeping gold for himself. In Spain, the sorry spectacle of Columbus in chains saddens Queen Isabella and King Ferdinand, who decide to dismiss the charges. The king and queen forgive Columbus and grant him permission for a fourth voyage.

EXPL. Rodrigo de Bastidas spots the Caribbean coast of present-day Colombia.

EXPL. Amerigo Vespucci sails down the east coast of South America. The exploration, which lasts until 1502, convinces Vespucci that America is a new continent and not India as Columbus believed. The series of letters Vespucci writes regarding the journeys are the first descriptions of the new continent.

LEGE. The 1500s mark the development of the "Black Legend," exaggerated British and Protestant accounts of how the Spanish behave in the Americas, with the intention of demonizing Spain and encouraging attempts to reduce Spanish dominion in the New World. The Black Legend portrays the Spanish as inferior, an attitude assumed first by the British and then the Americans, who apply a variation of the Black Legend to Mexicans during the nineteenth and early twentieth centuries. The Legend is partially created by Friar de las Casas, whose book, *Brevísima relación de la destrucción de las Indias,* depicts Spanish cruelty in the Caribbean.

The Evil That Conquistadores Do

"When the Spaniards arrived at the village and found the Indians at peace in their houses, they did not fail to injure and scandalize them. Not content with what the Indians freely gave, they took their wretched subsistence from them, and some, going further, chased after their wives and daughters, for this is and always has been the Spaniards' common custom in these Indies. . . . A Spaniard, in whom the devil is thought to have clothed himself, suddenly drew his sword. Then the whole hundred drew theirs and began to rip open the bellies, to cut and kill those lambs— men, women, children, and old folk."

Source: Bartolomé de las Casas. "The Horrors of the Conquest." In *The Borzoi Anthology of Latin American Literature.* Ed. Emir Rodríguez Monegal. New York: Knopf Publishers, 1977, p. 25.

MUSI. The conquistadores introduce the guitar to Latin America. The Spanish guitar has a long journey to the Americas, originating from a Moorish instrument called *guitarra morisca* and also the *guitarra latina* brought to Spain by the Romans. The morisca guitar is oval and the Latina has curved sides. The conquistadores play the guitar to accompany a type of folksong called romances or coplas. The romances narrate great heroic deeds from Spanish history while the coplas, consisting of two lines that rhyme, address love, religious, or nostalgic themes.

MUSI. Music begins to emerge as an important social and cultural development in the colonization of the Spanish Americas. In the cathedrals of Santo Domingo and México, among others, choir directors are hired to train potential choir members. Organists travel from Spain to play in the churches.

1501

SLAV. The first slaves are imported to Hispaniola. The slaves are from Africa but are taken to Spain to work for Spanish masters and thus speak Spanish. This signals the arrival of African slaves to the Americas.

1502

ARC. Construction of a Spanish city begins in Hispaniola. All Spanish cities and towns will follow a similar grid: a plaza or a central square, usually with a park, a church standing on one side of the plaza, and a city hall on the other side, often facing the church.

Houses radiate away from the central plazas, edging on narrow sidewalks with a large barred window and an enclosed courtyard.

EXPL. The Spanish explore Argentina.

EXPL. Columbus begins his fourth and final voyage to the New World on May 11, disembarking in Martinique and sailing along the coasts of Central America and the north of South America. He spends some time in Jamaica.

POLI. Mexica emperor Motecuhzoma ascends to the throne. In Spanish, he is known as Montezuma. He collects high taxes from his subjects, and the many nations that make up ancient México fear and dislike him. Motecuhzoma wars on his enemies, but there is potential for a major uprising against the Mexica empire. A soothsayer tells him he will be the last ruler of the Mexica empire.

SETT. On February 13, Queen Isabella and King Ferdinand send the first governor, Nicolás de Ovando, to the Caribbean. He sails to Hispaniola with 30 ships and 2,500 settlers, mostly aristocrats and nobles. On April 15, Ovando assumes command of the island.

1503

OBIT. The Taíno princess Anacaona suffers death by hanging. To crush her rebellion, which had kept the Spanish conquistadores at bay in the Dominican Republic for over a decade, Governor Nicolás de Ovando sends over 2,500 men to Anacaona's village and tricks her into a meeting. He then captures her and kills her followers.

POLI. The *Casa de la Contratación,* or House of Contracts, is created to control mercantilism in the colonies. Spain holds a monopoly in Latin America in which the emerging colonies can only trade with Spain.

SLAV. In Hispaniola, the encomienda system is institutionalized by governor Nicolás de Ovendo. The encomienda system is a form of slavery. It is a land grant given by the king to a Spanish settler. The settler, or encomendero, receives Amerindians to work in agriculture or in the mines in exchange for religious education.

1503–1507

EXPL. Explorer Amerigo Vespucci, the first to realize that America is a new continent, publishes letters describing the continent to Europeans. The letters make Vespucci a celebrity. To honor his work, mapmaker Martin Waldseemüller names the new continent America, producing a world globe and a large world map where the name of America appears for the first time.

1504

OBIT. Queen Isabella of Spain dies on November 26.

1506

OBIT. On May 20, Columbus dies at the age of 54. Present-day scholars do not know if Columbus ever realized that he encountered a new continent rather than a passage to Asia.

1508–1509

ARC. Basilica Menor de Santa María, the first cathedral in the Americas, is constructed in Santo Domingo, Dominican Republic.

EXPL. Ponce de León sails to Puerto Rico in search of gold. He becomes governor of the island but is removed from office because of his cruelty towards the Taínos.

1510

MIGR. Realizing that the Spanish colonialists in Hispaniola want to enslave the Taínos to work in gold fields or to plant food products, a chief named Hatuey and 400 of his followers relocate to Cuba, hoping to live in peace and away from the invaders.

RELI. Father Bartolomé de las Casas is ordained. A participant of the conquest of the Caribbean, he witnesses the abuses inflicted on the Taínos by his compatriots. Remorseful of his participation in such acts, de las Casas decides to dedicate his life to protecting the indigenous population. He will become a representative of the strong Catholic faith espoused and expressed by many Latinos.

SETT. Santa María del Darien, the oldest Spanish colony on the continent, is established in Panama.

1511

WARS. On December 21, Spanish soldiers and settlers arrive in Cuba under the leadership of Diego Velásquez de Cuéllar. Chief Hatuey and his men attack the invaders, using guerrilla warfare tactics.

1512

LAWS. Persuaded by Friar Montesinos's arguments, King Ferdinand enacts the Laws of Burgos to improve the lot of the Amerindian laborers. Taínos are to work only nine months out of the year and pregnant women are excused after the fourth month of pregnancy. The sons of chieftains are to be educated. These laws, however, are not enforced by the Spanish settlers in the Americas.

OBIT. Chieftain Hatuey is captured and sentenced to death at the stake on February 12. Before he is executed, a priest offers Hatuey communion and acceptance of Christ so that he can go to heaven. Hatuey asks if all white men go to heaven and when the priest replies "yes," the chief says "Then, I do not wish to go to heaven."

OBIT. In Seville, explorer and writer Amerigo Vespucci dies on February 22.

SLAV. In Hispaniola, Dominican Friar Antonio de Montesinos delivers a sermon condemning Spanish treatment of the Taínos and demanding their release from servitude. Influenced by the sermon, Bartolomé de las Casas decides to fight on behalf of the Amerindians.

1513

EXPL. Ponce de León sights the coast of Florida between March 27 and April 2. The name Florida alludes to the variety of trees, palms, and tropical flowers he spots inland.

1515

RELI. Father Bartolomé de las Casas is named "The Protector of the Indians" by the Spanish king.

1516

OBIT. King Ferdinand of Spain dies on June 23.

1517

EXPL. On February 23 Hernández de Córdoba disembarks in Yucatán. After encountering combat with the Mayan warriors, he dies of multiple wounds.

1518

OBIT. Nicolás de Ovendo, former governor of Hispaniola, dies in Madrid. He is responsible for the death of thousands of Taínos in the Caribbean.

SLAV. For the first time, slaves are shipped directly to the Caribbean from Africa. From the Caribbean, the slaves are distributed to other colonies and the United States. It is the beginning of the transatlantic slave trade.

1519

ANIM. As the Spanish conquer México and, later on, as they proceed north into the present-day American Southwest, they bring along their horses. The horses procreate and spread throughout the region. The indigenous people study the way the conquistadores ride the beasts and begin to imitate them.

EXPL. Alonso Álvarez de Pineda sails along the coast of Florida and proves it is not an island as originally believed. He sails into the Mississippi River and Texas.

EXPL. On March 4, Hernán Cortés arrives in México after sailing from Cuba with 10 ships, more than 500 soldiers, and 300 settlers. The indigenous population is overwhelmed by this floating fortress, which carries soldiers, the artillery, and especially horses, which they have never seen before. The Amerindians believe that a rider and a horse are one large creature. Nevertheless, they attack the intruders but are defeated by the Spanish. On April 19 after battling and defeating the residents of Tabasco, Cortés is given 20 slave women, including a princess named Malintzin. She becomes his lover and interpreter. Highly intelligent, she speaks Nahuatl and Maya and soon masters Spanish. Her knowledge of the ways of the Mexicas, which she passes on to Cortés, aids in his defeat of the Mexica Empire. Cortés and Malintzin, also known as La Malinche and Doña Marina, bear a child, Don Martín Cortés, probably the first *meztiso*—the offspring of a European/Amerindian union. There are at least three ways of understanding Malintzin and her role in the conquest of the Mexicas. One interpretation is that she simply joined the ranks of the conquistadores. A second approach is that by serving as an interpreter she helped to destroy an empire she disliked. A third possibility is that she fell in love with Cortés. Today, in México, the expression "Malinchismo" describes a person who betrays his/her own country and culture.

REBE. Taíno chief Enriquillo, also known as Guarocuya, rebels against abuses committed by the Spanish in Hispaniola. For the next 13 years he wars successfully on the conquistadores and in 1533 he is granted a pardon by King Charles V as part of a truce. The first Latin American rebel to deal successfully with the Spanish invaders, Enriquillo is the subject of one of Latin America's most popular novels, *Enriquillo,* written in 1879 by the Dominican Manuel de Jesús Galván.

WARS. On September 19, Hernán Cortés occupies the town of Tlascala, also called Tlaxcala, after fierce fighting with its defenders. He learns of a large and wealthy city—Tenochtitlán—in central México and discovers that México is ruled by the powerful Mexicas, whom the Tlascalans hate. Cortés forms an alliance with the Tlascalans. It is the beginning of a strategy the conquistador uses again and again, creating alliances with the different Amerindian groups that live between Yucatán and central México. From September to November, Cortés marches towards Tenochtitlán, subduing opposition as he penetrates México. His use of artillery, muskets, arrows, swords, and horses first terrifies his opponents and then beats them. One strategic approach to battle aids him. The Amerindians fight to capture slaves to be sacrificed later on or used for forced labor. They do not fight to kill and the sword they use is a blunted instrument. The Spanish use the sword that is pointed and sharp, enabling one conquistador to wound several attackers at once. On November 19, Emperor Motecuhzoma and Cortés meet. The Mexica ruler invites the Spanish conquistador into the magnificent city of Tenochtitlán. The emperor believes that Cortés is representative of a king and a god that are more powerful that the Mexica emperor and his gods. He offers himself as subject to the Spanish king. Cortés becomes the virtual ruler of Tenochtitlán, using Motecuhzoma as his puppet.

1520

EXPL. Portuguese navigator Ferdinand Magellan, sailing on behalf of the Spanish, sights the coast of Chile in his journey around the globe.

WARS. In May, after several months in Tenochtitlán, where Hernán Cortés has used emperor Motecuhzoma's hospitality as an opportunity to imprison the emperor in his own city and where Cortés has placed armed soldiers in key locations, Cortés travels to Yucatán to meet an expedition led by Pánfilo de Narváez. Narváez has been sent by Cuban governor Velásquez to arrest Cortés for leaving the island without the governor's permission. Cortés arrests Narváez instead and convinces the newly arrived 1,400 soldiers to join him in the conquest of México. In June, Cortés returns to Tenotichtlán to discover that the Mexica lords have rebelled against Motecuhzoma and the Spanish. On July 1, Motecuhzoma is wounded by a rock thrown at him by angry Mexica warriors.

Some accounts indicate that the wound caused the emperor's death. Other accounts suggest that the Spanish killed the emperor. On July 20, Cortés and his soldiers abandon Tenochtitlán. They are ambushed by Mexica warriors, losing 1,000 Spanish soldiers and the loot they were taking from the city. Spanish history refers to this event as *La Noche Triste,* the sad night. It is Cortés's first major defeat. Cortés retreats into the countryside and is protected by the Tlascalans, who despise the Mexicas more than the Spanish.

1521

HEAL. The first hospital in the Americas, Hospital de Jesús, originally the *Hospital de la Purísima Concepción de Nuestra Señora,* is founded in México City, nearly three centuries before hospitals are founded in the United States. Cortés conceives of the hospital as a facility to treat Spanish soldiers. The hospital stills stand today, serving the people of México City.

OBIT. In July, Ponce de León dies in Havana of wounds he received while fighting Amerindians in Florida. The conquistador had sailed from Puerto Rico and landed in Tampa. Contrary to popular legend, his objective was not finding the "fountain of youth," but gold.

WARS. Hernán Cortés attacks Tenochtitlán. His allies number nearly 50,000 Amerindians, including the Tlascalans. The Mexicas, under the leadership of Cuauhtemoc, Motecuhzoma's nephew, fight bravely. But they do not have water and food. The Mexicas are also suffering from smallpox, introduced by the Spanish conquistadores. On August 13 Tenochtitlán falls to Cortés. The Mexica/Aztec Empire is defeated.

1524–1527

SETT. Guatemala, Honduras, and Nicaragua are founded as part of the Kingdom of Guatemala.

1524

POLI. The Council of Indies is established by the Spanish monarchy to oversee the colonization of the Americas. The council advises the king, appoints church officials, and dictates who is allowed to travel to the New World.

RELI. The Spanish Inquisition arrives in México City.

1525

LIT. The importation of books is authorized to México City.

Amerindians, Not Cortés, Defeated the Mexicas

"How could so few conquistadores defeat so many Aztecs? The more lethal weapons of the Spaniards are often cited as the cause . . . [and] the Spaniards' guns and cannons, too, were deadly—when not misfired. Despite such advantages, however, the Spaniards found the Mesoamericans formidable adversaries once they adjusted to the European weapons. They were nearly overwhelmed by the Tlaxcalans and were lucky to make their alliance. . . . Not until the pre-Columbians divided, adding tens of thousands of native soldiers to the ranks of the Spaniards, did the Aztec empire suffer defeat."

Source: Lynn V. Foster. *A Brief History of Mexico.* Rev. ed. New York: Checkmark Books, 2004, pp. 59–60.

SETT. Santa María la Antigua del Darién, the first European city in the American continent, is founded in Colombia.

SETT. El Salvador, Central America, is founded by Diego de Alvarado after he defeats its natives.

1526

EXPL. Sailing from Hispaniola, Lucas Vásquez de Ayllón lands on the mouth of the Santee River, in present-day South Carolina, and explores parts of Georgia. He and 150 men attempt to establish a Spanish settlement but succumb to disease within the year.

1527

ENVI. Explorer and chronicler Alvar Nuñez Cabeza de Vaca publishes his book *La relación*, one of the earliest descriptions of the forces of a hurricane by a European in the New World. In the book de Vaca describes how the winds of a hurricane pick up a boat from the bay and toss it several miles inland: "We went into the woods, and a quarter of a league into them we found one of the ship's boats in some trees. Ten leagues from there we found the bodies of two persons from my ship . . . [who] were so disfigured from having struck the rocks that they could not be recognized."

1527–1528

WARS. Francisco de Montejo attempts to conquer the Mayas in Yucatán but is defeated. The Mayas, unlike the Mexica/Aztec, are loosely organized and there is no center of power for the Spanish to attack. Furthermore, Maya warriors attack at night and flee into the countryside. Montejo's soldiers desert him.

1527–1532

WARS. Civil war breaks out in Perú as two Inca kings and brothers, Huascar and Atahualpa, fight each other for complete control of the Inca empire. Huascar is supported by an Inca priest, while Atahualpa has the Inca army behind him. Atahualpa defeats his brother's army but spares his life. The military drain and political division that develops will help Spanish conquistador Francisco Pizarro in his ruthless conquest of Perú.

1528

EXPL. On April 12, Pánfilo de Narváez and 300 men land in Tampa and journey into the interior, leaving their ships behind. Due to poor provisions and constant attacks by Amerindians, the expedition fails. In September, the men attempt to sail to México by building barges. At sea, de Narváez drifts away and is never seen again. Eventually, only four men survive. One is the legendary Cabeza de Vaca.

1528–1536

EXPL. Cabeza de Vaca and three other men walk from Florida to Texas, traveling naked and barefooted. They travel through Arizona, New Mexico, and Texas. In February 1536, they meet with Spanish explorers in the north of México and are transported to México City. The stories they tell encourage explorations of the Southwest and the belief in the Seven Cities of Gold, or Cibola.

1531

EXPL. Francisco Pizarro arrives in Perú.

RELI. On December 9, a Chichimeca Indian named Juan Diego Cuauhtlahtoatzin reports that the Virgin Mary has appeared before him, speaking to him in Nahuatl. She asks for a church to be built on the Tepeyac Hill. Since the bishop Juan Zumarraga does not believe him, on December 12, the virgin instructs Diego to gather roses, which do not grow on the hill, and to take the flowers to the bishop as proof. When Juan Diego opens his poncho, where he has placed the roses, the imprinted image of the virgin appears. The Virgin of Guadalupe unites the Spanish and native Amerindian faiths, strengthening Catholicism in México. Today, in St. Patrick's Cathedral in New York, a chapel honors the virgin and the millions of Catholic Latinos of the United States. Juan Diego will be beatified on May 6, 1990 by Pope John Paul II in the Basilica of Santa María de Guadalupe, México City.

1532

SETT. Francisco Pizarro establishes a military camp in Perú in July. He learns that the Inca Empire is torn by a civil war.

The Virgin of Guadalupe, patroness of the Americas. An image of Our Lady of Guadalupe appears in St. Patrick's Cathedral in New York City. Courtesy of the Library of Congress.

WARS. After hearing about the arrival of Francisco Pizarro, the emperor Atahualpa, the winner of the Inca civil war, visits the city of Cajamarca to meet the conquistador. On November 16, Pizarro tricks Atahualpa into a meeting without weapons, then ambushes his troops. Pizarro captures the Inca emperor.

1533

OBIT. On August 29, Inca emperor Atahualpa is executed by Francisco Pizarro. The Spanish conquistador had captured and imprisoned the emperor in 1532. Negotiating for his release, the Inca had promised the Spanish a room filled with gold—and twice as much silver—in exchange for the emperor's release. Pizarro agreed, but once the treasure was in his possession he accused Atahualpa of killing his brother Huascar—against whom he had waged a civil war—and rebelling against the Spanish crown.

1535

MED. The first printing press in the Americas is assembled in México City, nearly a century earlier than the first printing press is set up in the United States in Massachusetts in 1604.

SETT. Pizarro founds the city of Lima, Perú on January 18. It is also known as *Ciudad de los Reyes,* City of Kings.

1536

SETT. On February 2, Buenos Aires, Argentina is founded by conquistador Pedro de Mendoza. Indigenous people attack settlers, who abandon the site in 1540.

1537

SETT. Asunción, Paraguay, is founded by Spanish explorer Juan de Salazar on August 15.

1538

EDUC. The Universidad Autónoma de Santo Domingo is established in 1538. It is the first university in the Americas, almost a hundred years before the founding of Harvard University.

SETT. On August 6, the city Bogotá, Colombia, is founded by Spanish conquistador Gonzalo Jiménez de Quesada after successfully warring on the Chibcha Indians in a region called Bacatá by the natives.

1539

EXPL. Fray Marcos de Niza travels through part of the Southwest, searching for the legendary Seven Cities of Gold, or Cibola. His search is inspired by exaggerated misinterpretations of Cabeza de Vaca's account of his travels throughout the Southwest, where rumors said he had seen cities built of gold.

EXPL. On May 18, Hernando de Soto sails for Florida from Cuba. He reaches Alabama, Georgia, South Carolina, and Tennessee.

1540

BIRT. Cristóbal de Llerena is born in the Dominican Republic and becomes one of the Americas' earliest playwrights. In 1588 his play *Entremés* depicts the sack of Santo Domingo by Francis Drake three years before. The work also criticizes how the local government dealt with Drake's attack. Llerena is one of the first writers in the Caribbean to be censored by the authorities.

EXPL. Traveling from México, Francisco Vázquez de Coronado leads 300 Spanish soldiers and 800 Amerindians into the southwestern part of the United States. Though he does not find gold or the legendary Cibola, the Seven Cities of Gold, he travels through Arizona, Kansas, New Mexico, Oklahoma, and Texas.

EXPL. Pedro de Valdivia reaches Chile and begins its conquest.

WARS. In July, explorer Coronado clashes against 200 Native Americans who see his entry into their village as an invasion. This is the first battle between Europeans and Native Americans in what would become the United States.

1541

EXPL. Explorer Coronado reaches the Texas panhandle. He encounters Pueblo Indians for the first time.

OBIT. On June 26, Francisco Pizarro is assassinated by the son of a rival conquistador who had challenged Pizarro's rule in Perú. Today, many Peruvians view Pizarro as a criminal who duped the emperor Atahualpa, stole his gold and silver, and murdered him.

SETT. Santiago de Chile is founded on February 12.

1542

EXPL. On September 28, sailing on behalf of Spain, a Portuguese sailor named Juan Rodríguez de Cabrilla discovers the bay of San Diego, California.

LIT. Explorer Alvar Nuñez Cabeza de Vaca publishes *La relación,* his account of his eight-year odyssey in the Southwest. Published 66 years before Captain John Smith's *A True Relation of Such Occurrences and Accidents of Noate as Hath Happened in Virginia Since the First Planting of That Colony,* it is the first book written about the land that would become the United States and the first European account of such American creatures as the buffalo.

POLI. The Viceroyalty of Perú is established to oversee the colonial administration of South America. Viceroys are directly appointed by the Spanish king and can virtually rule as monarchs. Inca cities are renamed with Spanish names. Perú becomes the principal source of wealth from South America to Spain.

Early Written Culture in Spanish

"The actual introduction of written culture into lands that would later become part of the . . . United States occurred early on . . . when in 1513, explorer Juan Ponce de León . . . recorded his travels in diaries. . . . [His] voyage of exploration represents the first introduction of a written language into what later became the mainland United States. From that point on, the history of literacy, books and writing . . . was developed by Spanish, mestizo and mulato missionaries, soldiers and settlers."

Source: Nicolás Kanellos and Helvetia Martell. *Hispanic Periodicals in the United States: Origins to 1960. A Brief History and Comprehensive Bibliography.* Houston, TX: Arte Público Press, 2000, p. 4.

SLAV. The New Laws are passed with the purpose of ending the encomienda system and reducing the power of encomenderos throughout Spanish America, especially in México where an elite class is emerging. The pattern of elite bureaucrats and rulers in Latin American politics is solidly established in Latin America.

1545

SETT. The Spanish found the city of Mérida, in the traditional Mayan territory of Yucatán, signaling the end of Mayan rule.

1548

SETT. La Paz, Bolivia is founded.

1550

AGRI. Spain introduces to Europe products from Latin America: potatoes, tomatoes, and tobacco, among others.

SLAV. The famous dispute between Father Bartolomé de las Casas and Spanish philosopher and theologian Juan Ginés de Sepulveda on whether or not Taínos are humans takes place. The former maintains that the Taínos are no different than the Spanish, have a soul, and can be converted to Catholicism. The latter maintains Taínos are barbarians who can serve useful purposes as slaves. Las Casas recommends the end of the encomienda system, a form of slavery, and the release of Taínos from forced labor. He also recommends that Africans, known for their ability to work hard, be exported to the Americas to replace Taíno labor.

1552

LIT. Father Bartolomé de las Casa writes *Brevísima relación de la destrucción de las Indias* (Brief History of the Destruction of the Indies), his account of the enslavement and annihilation of Taínos. It is one of the earliest books in Latin American history that attempts to bring about social change and justice. The volume is a precursor of a literary genre called *literatura comprometida,* or socially engaged literature. Favored by Latin American and Latinos writers, this genre has political as well as artistic objectives.

1553

EDUC. The Universidad de México is founded to teach settlers from Spain and their children as well as Aztecs of royal descent.

1555

WARS. The French corsair Jacques de Sores captures and burns Havana to the ground. European Powers—the Dutch, English, and French—use piracy to tease the Spanish crown and to make inroads in Latin America.

1559

EXPL. The governor of Florida, Tristán de Luna Arellano, explores present-day Pensacola. With 500 soldiers, 1,000 colonists, and 240 horses, he

---

Soccer, Ancient Floridian Style

"They arrange themselves twenty on a side and play the game in a brisk, athletic manner. The ball carrier handles it smartly and he plays such an effective game with his sure shots that we can state that he scores on each shot. They erect goal posts made from pine trees about seven feet tall and on top of this goal they place a figure. Suddenly the forty players dash to the field, commence playing, and the game had begun with a rush. . . . In Castille the hands are used in playing ball, but these Indians play ball with their feet. They propel the ball with their feet directly at the goal."

Source: Alonso Gregorio de Escobedo. "La Florida." In *Herencia: The Anthology of Hispanic Literature of the United States.* Ed. Nicolás Kanellos. Oxford: Oxford University Press, 2002, p. 46.

proceeds to present-day South Carolina and then Georgia. Unable to establish a settlement due to disease and poor supplies, Arellano chooses to return to México.

1562

SETT. Costa Rica is established.

1565

SETT. Admiral Pedro Menéndez de Avilés founds St. Augustine on August 28. It is the first permanent European settlement in the present-day United States, existing 21 years before the founding of Roanoke by the British.

WARS. On September 29, Admiral Pedro Menéndez de Avilés (1519–1574) decapitates 200 Frenchmen, sparing only those who are Catholic. He pronounces, "I do not this to Frenchmen but to heretics." The killings occur on an islet near St. Augustine that becomes known as "Matanzas," meaning massacre.

1566

BIRT. Martín de Arguelles is born in St. Augustine, Florida, the first child of Europeans born in the present-day United States, 21 years before the birth of the first child of English parents in North Carolina, Virginia Dare.

LIT. Friar Diego de Landa publishes *Relación de las cosas de Yucatán* (1566) which describes the hieroglyphics, customs, temples, religious practices, and history of the Mayans.

1567–1572

RELI. Jesuit missionaries travel to Perú and México, establishing missions for Amerindians. They teach the natives music, religion, and how to read. They also protect them from the conquistadores. By the 1700s, the Jesuits will have baptized over 700 Amerindians.

1569

LIT. Alonso de Ercilla y Zuñiga publishes *La Araucana,* one of the first epics about the Americas and its conquest. *La Araucana* deals with the bravery of Chilean natives fighting against the Spanish conquistadores.

1571

MEDI. In Spain, a physician named Nicolo Manardes writes a treatise identifying 36 medical conditions, such as headaches or blisters, that can be alleviated by the use of tobacco. It is the first advertisement campaign of sorts promoting the use of tobacco. The crop will become a major industry in Cuba and Hispaniola.

1572

OBIT. On September 24, the last Inca ruler, Túpac Amaru, who has been leading a war against the Spanish conquistadores, is captured and publicly executed.

1573

RELI. Franciscan monks reach Florida with the objective of establishing missions.

WARS. Francis Drake raids Panama. A privateer, a pirate who is licensed by a country or a government to conduct attacks on enemy nations, Drake embodies contemporary British hatred of the Spanish. Over the centuries, Latin American scholars maintain that British animosity against Spain, the British sense of superiority over the Spanish and the people of the Caribbean, and the conflicts between British Protestants against Spanish Catholics, helps to seed the racism expressed by Americans of Anglo origins in dealing with Latinos during the 1800s and 1900s.

1579

BIRT. On December 9, Martín de Porres is born, the son of a Spanish nobleman and a slave woman. At the age of 11 he will enter the Dominican Orders. He accepts menial jobs and when the order has difficulty maintaining the monastery, he suggests to his superior that they sell him as a slave and use the profits for the monastery. Over the centuries, this humble friar will become one of the most loved Catholic saints in Latin America.

1580

HEAL. In Puerto Rico, diseases such as smallpox wipe out most of the remaining Taíno population.

SETT. Buenos Aires, Argentina is founded for a second time. The city was first founded in 1536, but constant attacks from indigenous people and disease forced the original settlers to abandon the site.

1581

EXPL. On August 25 Friars Agustín Rodríguez and Francisco Sánchez Chamuscado reach New Mexico in the area of present-day Bernalillo.

OBIT. Chronicler and conquistador Bernal Díaz del Castillo dies without seeing the publication of his masterpiece, *The True History of the Conquest of New Spain*, in which he narrates his participation in more than 100 battles against the Mexicas and other Amerindians.

1582

LIT. Juan Ponce de León y Troche, grandson of explorer Ponce de León, writes the first history of Puerto Rico, *Memoria y descripción de la isla de Puerto Rico*, better known as *Memoria de Melgarejo*. The manuscript is finally published in 1864.

1585–1586

WARS. Francis Drake loots and destroys Cartagena, Colombia; Santo Domingo, Hispaniola; and St. Augustine, Florida.

1586

ARC. An Italian engineer named Juan Bautista Antonelli is contracted to draw plans and build the fortresses El Morro of Havana, El Morro of San Juan, and several other forts and garrisons throughout the Caribbean. Nearly five centuries later, the forts still stand gallantly, lending architectural beauty and character to the harbors in Havana and San Juan.

1590

POPU. There are about 200,000 Spanish colonizers in the Americas. As a group, they have founded over 250 European cities.

1593

EXPL. Francisco Leyva de Bonilla and Antonio Gutiérrez de Humaña travel to the region of present-day Sante Fe and Kansas. The two explorers fight with each other. Humaña murders Bonilla. Plains Indians attack the expedition and kill Humaña.

1598

ARTS. On April 30, soldiers who are members of Juan de Oñate's expedition, in New Mexico, entertain themselves by staging plays. It is believed that one of the soldiers is a playwright named Marcos Farfán de los Godos, who writes about the group's experiences in the Southwest.

Día de Acción de Gracias: Thanksgiving, Spanish Style

The first Thanksgiving took place in 1598 in New Mexico, a little known event of great significance to the people of New Mexico but forgotten by historians until recently:

"The New Mexico Hispanic Culture Preservation League lobbied the NM State Legislature to declare April 30th as the First Thanksgiving, and in 1999 succeeded. Each year, hence forth, the NMHCPL banquet commemorates the Thanksgiving ceremony held by the pioneers, led by Don Juan de Oñate—Adelantado, in 1598. The ceremony over 400 years ago was marked by a high Mass giving thanks to the Lord, a banquet shared with the local natives, and an original play written by Captain Farfán de los Godos."

Source: New Mexico Hispanic Culture Preservation League. http://www.nmhcpl.org/. Accessed August 30, 2006.

EXPL. Juan de Oñate explores the north of New Spain, present-day México. He leads the colonization of the southwestern part of the United States and claims New Mexico for the Spanish Crown.

RELI. To celebrate the settlement of New Mexico, explorer Juan de Oñate holds a high mass and invites the natives to join his troops in a thanksgiving meal. Today, residents of New Mexico consider this event the original Thanksgiving.

SETT. Santa Fe is founded by explorer Pedro de Peralta, who is appointed governor of the territory of New Mexico.

WARS. Spanish conquistadores put down an uprising of Auraco Indians in Chile. Arauco prisoners are enslaved. The war will last into the seventeenth century.

1599

POPU. There are about 200,000 Spanish conquistadores and settlers living in the Americas.

Seventeenth Century

1600

POPU. About 60 percent of the settlers in the Caribbean are white. The rest of the population consists of African slaves and surviving Taínos and Caribs.

SETT. Seven Franciscan missionaries and 70 colonists settle in San Gabriel, New Mexico. Some of the colonists bring sheep, introducing the animal to the region.

SLAV. Throughout the seventeenth century, an estimated 10 to 15 million slaves will be shipped to the Americas. The eventual sexual relations and marriages with whites and Amerindians will create the racially and ethnically mixed population that will be the dominant characteristic of Latinos in the twentieth century.

TRAD. Jean Nicot, a French diplomat and scholar, introduces tobacco to Parisian society. He names the leaf *Nicotiana Tabacum*. The early 1600s mark the beginning of a growing tobacco market in Europe and the American colonies.

1604

LIT. "La grandeza mexicana," or "Mexican Greatness," is published. The poem is written in celebration of México City by Bernardo de Balbuena, the bishop of Puerto Rico. His rich descriptions of the New World make him one of Latin America's first major poets.

1605

LIT. Miguel de Cervantes Saavedra publishes the first part of *El ingenioso Hidalgo Don Quijote de la Mancha,* commonly known as *Don Quijote.* The work will prove one of the world's great masterpieces and will influence major Latin American and Latino writers in the centuries to come.

1606

POPU. The Aztec/Mexica, Maya, and other Amerindian populations in México have dwindled from 11 million a century before to 1 million.

1607

SETT. Jamestown, the first English-speaking settlement, is established in the United States on May 13. Until late in the twentieth century, history textbooks in the United States describe Jamestown as the first American city, ignoring the founding of Spanish St. Augustine in 1565.

1608

LIT. Poet Silvestre de Balboa Troya y Quesada writes "Espejo de paciencia," inaugurating Cuban literature. It is one of the first literary works to depict a sympathetic portrayal of a black man: a slave who rescues a bishop and kills a hated pirate who is terrifying Cubans.

1609

LIT. Garcilaso de la Vega publishes *Comentarios reales*, Royal Observations, an account of Inca history and traditions. De la Vega is one of the few chroniclers of the era to sympathize with the conquered Incas.

The Daily Life of a Slave in the Americas, 1600–1850

Life as a field slave was generally brutal and short. Many planters, rather than encourage natural reproduction among the slaves, simply replaced slaves after they died as a result of the difficult working conditions. Many planters knew that their initial investment in the slave was paid off by the sixth or seventh year, so that anything after that was pure profit. The planters preferred to import replacement slaves rather than invest in health and sanitary conditions that would prolong the lives of their laborers. Conditions for a city slave were probably somewhat easier, because their labor was connected to a particular trade, such as carpentry, or a function, such as driving a coach. Where a skill or a talent was involved, sewing, for example, replacement was not as easy as replacing a sugar-cane cutter.

About 60 percent of the slaves on plantations worked in the fields. Field hands were placed in groups involved in planting, weeding, and cutting of sugar cane. The age and vigor, but not the gender, of the slave determined placement. About 10 percent of the labor force was employed milling and refining sugar and about 20 percent transported the cane to the sugar mill or the market. The rest worked in the house as servants. Women participated in all aspects of sugar production, excused only from work when they were pregnant and near labor.

Slaves were defined as both persons and property. They were to work as needed by the master and could be sold like a piece of furniture. Slavery was hereditary, usually through the mother's side, and slaves could be passed on to children as part of an estate. When the master was in financial arrears, the slave could be sold as payment.

Source: D. H. Figueredo and Frank Argota-Freyse. *A Brief History of the Caribbean.* New York: Facts on File, in press.

1610

LIT. Gaspar Pérez de Villagra, a member of Oñate's expedition, writes an epic poem about the exploration and settlement of New Mexico, *La historia de Nuevo México.*

TRAN. A supply route is established between México City and Santa Fe, New Mexico.

1612

LANG. In Florida, Friar Francisco Pareja studies the language spoken by the original inhabitants of the peninsula, the Timucuan. Father Pareja publishes two books on the subject, *Gramática y pronunciación en Timucuan* and *Guía confesional in las lenguas Timucuan y Castellana.*

1615

LIT. The second part of *El ingenioso Hidalgo Don Quijote de la Mancha* is published, 10 years after the publication of the first part.

1616

RELI. Several missions—La Misión de Santa Isabel, San Pedro de Athuluteca, and others—are established in present-day Georgia to convert the Guale Indians to Catholicism.

1620

SETT. From December 11 to December 20, Pilgrim emigrants from England scout and settle in Plymouth, drafting the Mayflower Compact to take possession of the territory.

> ### The Birth of the Child of the Latino Father
>
> "By the end of the 1500s, the basic contours of Latin American ethnicities were established. American, European, and African genes and cultures had begun to mix, creating rich potential for human diversity, but the violent and exploitative nature of the Encounter would sour the mix for centuries. . . . In the Caribbean region, Europeans and Africans took the place of the indigenous populations. . . . In Mexico and Peru, by contrast, Nahuatl and Quechua speaking societies . . . survived to be gradually transformed."
>
> *Source:* John Charles Chasteen. *Born in Blood and Fire: A Concise History of Latin America.* New York: W. W. Norton, 2001, p. 57.

> ### The Stench of Sacrificial Blood
>
> "There were some braziers with incense which they call copal, and in them they were burning the hearts of three Indians whom they had sacrificed that day, and they had made the sacrifice with smoke and copal. All the walls of the oratory were splashed and encrusted with blood that they were black, the floor was the same and the whole place stank vilely. . . . The walls were so clotted with blood and the soil so bathed with it that in the slaughter houses of Spain there is not such another stench."
>
> *Source:* Bernal Díaz del Castillo. *The Discovery and Conquest of Mexico.* New York: The Noonday Press, 1956, pp. 219–20.

1621–1624

BUSI. The Dutch West Indian Company, *West-Indische Compagnie,* is founded by the State General of the Dutch Republic to explore, conduct businesses, and settle in the Lesser Antilles. Their excursions eventually force the Spanish to concentrate on three islands: Cuba, Hispaniola, and Puerto Rico.

1626–1664

EXPL. The French establish three companies, the Compagnie de Saint Christophe, the Compagnie des Iles D'Amerique, and the Compagnie des Indes Occidentales, with the objective of colonizing the Lesser Antilles and reducing Spanish presence and power in the region.

1628

RELI. Three Cuban fisherman say the Virgin Mary has appeared to them during a storm on the high seas. As the men feared their boat would sink, the Madonna appeared over the water, floating on planks with the phrase "I'm the Virgin of la Caridad," and saving them from drowning. The men are representative of the Cuban people: one is from Spain, another is a native of Cuba, and the third is Afro-Cuban. The Virgin's skin is the color of copper. The Virgin will become the island's patron saint and will be worshipped on the island and in Florida, where many homes owned by Cubans will have a statue of her likeness on the front lawn.

1630

BIRT. Puerto Rico's first poet, Francisco de Ayerra Santa María, is born.

POPU. There are 1,000 Spanish colonists in Santa Fe. About 200 are Spanish and the rest are mestizos, of mixed European and Mexican Indian origin.

1632

LIT. The manuscript, *The True History of the Conquest of New Spain,* by conquistador Bernal Díaz del Castillo, is found and published in Madrid. The best chronicle of the conquest of México, the narrative reads like a novel. The combined fascination with the mystical and the fantastic, as well as the daily routines of the conquistadores in México, reveals an interest in spirituality that is characteristic of many Latinos and people from Latin America and Spain.

SETT. Buccaneers—pirates—settle in Tortugas, a small island off Hispaniola while the British do the same in Antigua and Montserrat. This marks the beginning of Spain's inability to exert full control over the colonies in the Caribbean.

1633

TRAN. A *Camino Real*, or "royal road," is constructed between St. Augustine, Florida, and St. Mark on the Gulf coast.

1634–1635

HEAL. Yellow fever ravages Guadeloupe where a French physician describes the disease for the first time.

SETT. The Dutch occupy Curaçao as an entry and departure point for slaves from West Africa. The French take over Martinique and Guadeloupe.

1646

RELI. In Puerto Rico, it is reported that the Virgin Mary has appeared over the horizon in the town of Monserrate. A small shrine is built on the spot, the *Ermita de la Virgen de Monserrate*. In the next century, there will be reports of several similar apparitions in Cuba and México.

1648

BIRT. Sor Juana Inez de la Cruz, one of the world's greatest poets and Latin America's first feminist, is born. Her most famous poem "Hombres necios" ("Foolish Men") is a protest against male chauvinism.

1659

RELI. On the west bank of the Rio Grande river, Franciscan monks establish a community in present-day Juárez.

1664

REBE. There are growing tensions between the Apaches and the Pueblo Indians and the Spanish and Mexican settlers. In New Mexico, the Spanish governor fears an uprising and orders a limit of Apaches and Pueblo Indians allowed into Spanish settlements and presidios.

1670

POLI. England and Spain sign the Treaty of Madrid, allowing England to keep territories that it had illegally taken from the Spanish. This signals the opening of the Caribbean to other European nations and the Spanish preference for the active colonization of three islands: Cuba, Hispaniola, and Puerto Rico.

1671

CRIM. British pirate Henry Morgan attacks and sacks Panama. News of the daring raid, the report that Morgan has massacred dozens of Spanish soldiers by locking them up in a cell and then blowing them up, terrifies Spain and Great Britain as well. European nations begin to contemplate the end of privateerism, a form of paid piracy on behalf of a nation.

REBE. After Apaches attack a wagon train making its way to Albuquerque, New Mexico, the governor orders a series of raids against the Apaches. The conflict will last for four years, ending with the Spanish retreating from New Mexico, overwhelmed by superiority in number and the Apaches' bravery.

1672

ARC. On October 2, construction of the San Marcos fortress in St. Augustine begins. The fortress is the oldest stone fortress in the United States.

1680

REBE. Pueblo Indians rebel against the Spanish conquistadores and settlers in New Mexico.

The First Cubanos in the United States

They were conquistadores born in Cuba who participated in De Soto's exploration of Florida: "[the] chronic landed all around them. They were wounded, but made their way to safety. They are the first natives of Cuba known to have set foot in North America."

Source: Alex Antón and Roger E. Hernández. *Cubans in America: A Vibrant History of a People in Exile.* New York: Kensington Books, 2002, p. 4.

Pirates of Great Britain

The immortalization of pirates as fun-loving scoundrels can be seen today at Disneyworld's Pirates of the Caribbean amusement ride, which depicts them running through burning towns drunk and in search of female companionship. This historical depiction of pirates is more common in the United States and the United Kingdom, since often the pirates covertly promoted English foreign policy aims and the victims were typically Spanish.

Source: D. H. Figueredo and Frank Argota-Freyse. *A Brief History of the Caribbean.* New York: Facts on File, in press.

The 2,000 settlers relocate to El Paso del Norte, Texas. Popé, the medicine man and chief of the Pueblo Indians, forbids the use of Spanish among the Pueblos and orders the bathing in the river of Indians who are Christians in order to reverse the effect of the Christian baptism ceremony.

1690

RELI. Alonso de León establishes a mission in Texas near the Neches River.

LIT. *Los infortunios de Alonso Ramírez*, by Mexican poet Carlos de Sigüenza y Góngora, is published. The first literary work to depict the picaresque adventures of a Puerto Rican character, the chronicle tells the true story of a man who is kidnapped by pirates and survives by his wit and bravery.

1691

RELI. Jesuit missionary Eusebio Kino explores Arizona, founds five missions in the Southwest,

and proves that Baja California is not an island but a peninsula.

SETT. Texas becomes a separate Spanish province of the Spanish empire in México.

1692–1725

CRIM. The golden age of piracy in the Caribbean begins. From this era emerges the romantic notion of pirates depicted in Errol Flynn films and in novels by Rafael Sabatini and Emilio Salgari.

POLI. Pirates practice the earliest form of democracy in the Americas. Each pirate has a vote and through a voting process, pirates elect captains, destinations, and assignments.

1693

EXPL. Admiral Andrés de Pez and scholar and writer Carlos de Sigüenza y Góngora study the topography, flora, and fauna of southeastern United States.

To Foolish Men

Stupid men who accuse
Women without reason,
Not understanding that you are the reason
Of the very thing that you blame

Source: Sor Juana Inés de la Cruz. "Hombres necios." In *Latin American Writers*. Vol. 1. Ed. Carlos A. Sole and Maria Isabel Abreu. New York: Scribners, 1989, p. 93.

SETT. Fearing Native American uprisings, Spain withdraws from Texas. Santa Fe becomes the capital of New Mexico.

1695

OBIT. On April 17, Sor Juana Inés de la Cruz dies. She is a Mexican feminist, nun, philosopher, and poet whose style is one of the best representations of the literary movement known as *El barroco*, or baroque.

1698

SETT. The community of Pensacola, Florida, is established by Andrés de Arriola with 200 men.

EIGHTEENTH CENTURY

1700

MUSI. Slaves dance and sing as they work, not because they are joyful but to escape the pangs of slavery. The music is based on tonal scales and the dancing consists of steps and swaying movements. When they are freed from work, the slaves also play drums to call on their gods and, sometimes, to communicate with each other. The white masters soon forbid the slaves from playing drums, fearing it could lead to insurrection.

RELI. Father Eusebio Kino establishes a mission in present-day Tucson, Arizona.

1702–1713

WARS. France and Great Britain fight for control of the North American continent in a conflict known as Queen Anne's War. The British capture St. Augustine. The war is part of the War of the Spanish Succession, in which Spain and France join forces against Great Britain, Germany, Portugal, and Holland.

1716

SETT. Spanish settlers from México and Spain return to Texas after leaving the state based on fear of the Pueblo Indians. The Spanish begin to establish missions to convert the natives to Catholicism. The first mission in Texas, Nuestra Señora de los Dolores de los Tejas, is founded near the banks of the Neche River.

1717

AGRI. The *Real Factoría de Tabacos*, the Royal Tobacco Factory, is established by the Spanish crown as a monopoly, forcing Cuban planters to sell to Spain all the tobacco produced on the island and restricting direct sales to other Spanish colonies. The planters rebel and in 1723, the crown executes 12 tobacco growers. As a result of the oppression many tobacco growers relocate to a region, known as Vuelta Abajo, in western Cuba (modern day Pinar del Río) to avoid the intrusion of the colonial government. As circumstance would have it, the growers find better soil for the cultivation of tobacco. The product produced, described as having a richer aroma, is now considered superior to the tobacco cultivated in other areas of Cuba and on other Caribbean islands.

1718

RELI. The mission in San Antonio, Texas, is established. This mission will become the site of the Alamo battle in the nineteenth century.

1721

RELI. The missions Nuestra Señora de Loreto, in Bahia, and Nuestra Señora del Pilar de los Adaes, near the site of the present border of Louisiana, are founded.

1721–1732

REBE. A series of rebellions take place in Paraguay against Spanish rule.

1722

MED. On January 1, *La gaceta de México*, the earliest true newspaper in Latin America, appears. Edited by Juan Ignacio María de Castorena, it comes out once a month and features business stories, religious editorials, and social commentaries.

1724

SLAV. Slave Francisco Menendez escapes from the Carolinas and reaches St. Augustine, Florida, where he converts to Catholicism and is granted his freedom by the Spanish authorities in the city. He joins the militia and rises to the rank of captain.

1728

ECON. Venezuela becomes a center for the cultivation of cocoa. Merchants from Europe violate the Spanish monopoly in Venezuela and journey to the colony to trade in cocoa. To end the contraband, Spain grants a Basque company, the Caracas Company, the rights to administer cocoa exports.

1733

SLAV. In Florida, Spanish authorities promise freedom to any slave who escapes from the British colonies and converts to Catholicism.

1738

SLAV. A community of runaway slaves, known as Maroons, builds Fort Mose in St. Augustine, Florida. Under the command of freed slave Captain Francisco Menendez, the fort houses over 100 runaway slaves. It is the first settlement of freed slaves in the United States.

1739

WARS. In October, The War of Jenkins' Ear formalizes hostilities between Great Britain and Spain over the land between South Carolina and Florida and Spain's monopoly in Caribbean trade. Spain believes that it is her right to board all ships sailing the Caribbean and to arrest and punish smugglers. England's position is that the oceans belong to all and that she has the right to defend herself from interceptors on the high seas.

1740

WARS. In May, General James Oglethorpe sails to Florida from Georgia with intentions of occupying St. Augustine. He lays a siege to the city but disorganization within the British soldiers and sailors leads to failure. The fort at St. Augustine, Castillo San Marcos, withstands the bombardment from Oglethorpe's artillery. Maroon slaves, under the leadership of Francisco Menendez, participate in the successful defense of St. Augustine.

1745–1763

WARS. Prussia, Great Britain with the American colonies, and Hanover are at war with Austria, France, Portugal, Russia, Sweden, Spain, and Saxony. The conflict, known as the Seven Years' War, the Pomerian War, and the French and Indian War, is the result of territorial disputes between France and Prussia as well as colonial conflicts between Great Britain and France over possession of North America.

Human Parts Lead to War

"As the story goes, [Captain Richard Jenkins' ear] was cut off, and he was told to take it to his King, and tell him that he would be treated in similar fashion if ever the opportunity offered. Jenkins appeared before the House of Commons with his tale. When asked what he thought when found himself in the hands of such barbarians, he produced his ear. . . . The Spaniards countered with the story of a certain noble Spaniard who had been made by an English captain to cut off and devour his nose."

Source: Eric Williams. *From Columbus to Castro: The History of the Caribbean*. New York: Vintage Books, 1984, p. 93.

1746

BIRT. In the province of Malaga, Spain, Bernardo de Gálvez is born on July 23. He will become one of the Spanish heroes of the Revolutionary War in the United States in 1776.

1749

REBE. On April 19, the first rebellion against Spain in Venezuela takes place under the leadership of a cocoa grower, Juan Francisco de León.

1750

BIRT. On March 28, Francisco de Miranda is born in Venezuela. He will lead the initial war of liberation from Spain in an attempt to form an empire called Colombia, composed of all of Spanish America from the Mississippi River to the tip of South America. He will also participate in the battle of Pensacola during the American Revolution, picking up military expertise he will employ in South America two decades later.

1751

SETT. San Francisco Xavier de Gigedo is founded on the south bank of the San Gabriel River, Texas.

1753

BIRT. May 8 marks the birth of Father Miguel Hidalgo y Costilla, leader of the Mexican war of independence in 1810.

1756

SETT. San Agustín de Ahumada, near Trinity River and Wallisville, Texas, is founded.

1757

SETT. Mission Luis de las Amarillas, north of Menard and on the San Saba River, Texas, is founded.

1762

FOOD. *Fufu*, mashed plantain cooked with lemon and garlic, grows in popularity in Cuba. It might be a variation of a recipe from West Africa. Some historians say that in Cuba the appellation comes from the way the slaves ask the British soldiers, who are occupying Havana, for food, accenting the vowels and dropping the consonants: "fu-fu."

SLAV. In the single year that the British occupy Havana, the slave presence increases with the arrival of 10,000 slaves distributed amidst 70 sugar plantations throughout the island. This boosts the sugar industry on the island from 10,000 acres of sugar canes before the arrival of the British to 160,000 less than two decades later.

SOCI. Free Masonry is established in Cuba and becomes popular throughout Latin America. In the United States, Cuban and Puerto Rican Masons

---

The Emergence of a Latin American Persona

"By the middle of the eighteenth century colonists were beginning to call themselves Americans [meaning from Latin America]. Two centuries in the New World had created a new man. Besides the intermixing of European and Indian and Negro, there were many other influences at work. The natural environment, forbidden and beneficent, the extraordinarily high mountains and the rain forests, the huge rivers, the tropical regions and the highlands, the plains and the valleys, the deserts and the coastal areas. . . . The rough frontier life, the daily contact with Indians and with Negroes . . . the physical isolation from Europe and its incessant wars: all this and more accounted for the emergence of americanos whose outlook was substantially different from that of the peasant, hidalgo, cleric, merchant or lord in a Spain long in the process of decay."

Source: Alberto Prago. *The Revolutions in Spanish America: The Independence Movements of 1808–1825.* New York: MacMillan, 1970, pp. 27–28.

will conspire against Spanish rule in the 1890s. In the 1960s, the extensive Cuban Masonry network helps new exiles assimilate into their new communities in Miami and New York City.

WARS. The largest armada ever to cross the Atlantic Ocean, under the command of Lord Albermarle, sails from England with intentions of capturing Havana. Two hundred ships bombard the city and in late summer 15,000 soldiers rush the El Morro fortress. The occupation of Havana by the British will alter the future of Florida and will even affect the course of the United States' war of independence by promoting anti-British sentiment in Spain and in the Caribbean.

1763

CULT. British officers are taken aback by Cubans' casualness, friendly manners, and sense of humor. The British are experiencing what Cubans and Puerto Ricans call *relajo* and *choteo*. Both indicate the ability to make light of tragic circumstances and to belittle the power of an oppressor by caricaturing and poking fun at the individual. *Relajo* and *choteo* will become tools of survivals used by Puerto Ricans and Cubans living in New York City during the twentieth century.

SLAV. Fearing the British will enslave the black residents of St. Augustine, Captain Francisco

---

Fufu: You'll Never Eat This at McDonalds!

Three large, medium ripe plantains
3 cloves of garlic, mashed
1/4 cup green onions
4 cups chicken stock
Juice of one lemon
Salt and pepper to taste
Pork meat with fat

Cut the ends off the plantains and discard. Slice each plantain into two-inch chunks and score the skin with a knife along one edge. DO NOT PEEL. In a large pot, add the plantains to the chicken stock. Bring to a boil, then lower heat, cover, and simmer until tender.

For meat, you need pork with plenty of fat—either well marbled or with a fat layer or both. We've had good luck with de-boned pork ribs. Or have the butcher cut something to order.

Whichever meat you use, you need to slice it into small pieces—approximately one inch square. Salt with a shaker and place in a large sauce pan. Add water to just barely cover. Bring to a boil and simmer, uncovered until all of the water has boiled away. Fry the pork pieces in the rendered fat just until brown, but NOT crispy! The meat should be tender and stringy.

Remove the meat. Sauté the garlic and onion in the rendered fat at medium temperature, three to five minutes. During the last minute add the lemon juice.

Remove the fully cooked plantains from the broth (do not discard the broth) and peel. Mash the plantains with a little of the broth—just enough to make a soft, thick paste—like mashed potatoes.

Mash together with the garlic and lemon and the fried pork. Salt and pepper to taste. Serve hot.

Source: "Three Guys From Miami." http://cuban-christmas.com/fufu.html. Accessed September 1, 2006.

Menendez, one of the builders of Fort Mose, the first African-American settlement in the United States, and dozens of freed slaves flee from Florida to Havana, Cuba.

TREA. With the signing of the Treaty of Paris ending the Seven Years War, Spain exchanges Florida for the city of Havana but receives from France the territories of Louisiana and the Mississippi.

1765

CULT. By preferring Spanish officials over *Criollos*, as the people born in Latin America of Spanish parents were called, a cultural and political schism evolves out of the Bourbon reforms being implemented in Latin America. It will become another factor leading to the wars of independence in the next century.

EXPL. Both Great Britain and Spain explore different areas of the Malvinas/Falklands on the south of the Atlantic Ocean. Both establish settlements on the island.

LAWS. Spanish Bourbon reforms increase taxes in the colonies, open up Latin American ports to other nations, reduce the Church's power by expelling the influential Jesuits, and place political control in the hands of peninsular administrators rather than Spanish officials born in Latin America.

1766

SETT. San Francisco is founded on September 16.

1767

POLI. Six thousand Jesuits are expelled from Spanish America by King Charles III as part of the Bourbon reforms. It is a political decision, not a theological one, based on the missionaries' influence over the Amerindians and their disputes with conquistadores' treatment of the natives in South America. The Jesuits' emphasis on education and opposition to violence slow down productivity in the colonies, a development resented by the Spanish crown.

1769

RELI. On July 3, Fray Junípero Serra establishes a mission in present-day San Diego. It is the first of 10 missions Serra will found throughout California. Father Serra converts nearly 7,000 Amerindians.

So Many Wars, So Large an Empire

Spain was involved in so many wars during this century that it debilitated its hold in the Americas, resulting in South American nations conducting wars of independence against Spain in the next century.

Eighteenth-Century Spain at War

1701–1715	War of Spanish Succession
1718–1720	War Against France and England
1727–1729	War Against France and England
1733–1738	War Against Austria
1739–1741	War of Jenkins' Ear
1740–1748	War of Austrian Succession
1756–1763	Seven Years' War
1779–1786	Participation in the American Revolutionary War
1796–1800	War Against England

Adapted From: Alberto Prago. *The Revolutions in Spanish America: The Independence Movements of 1808–1825.* New York: MacMillan, 1970, pp. 235–36.

RELI. The colonization of California begins, conducted by the Spanish.

WARS. Spain leads several military expeditions in the Southwest against the Apaches. One of the commanders is the future governor of Louisiana, Bernardo de Gálvez. His experiences in the war against the Apaches prepare him for participation in the American Revolutionary War six years later.

1776

REBE. On July 4, the United States declares independence from Great Britain.

SETT. Buenos Aires, the capital of Argentina, emerges as a strong commercial and cultural center. Much of the intellectual output of Latin America will emerge from Buenos Aires throughout the nineteenth and early twentieth centuries.

1777

POLI. A year after the United States declares its independence from Great Britain, Spain, resentful of losing Florida to the British and ongoing British harassment in the Malvinas/Falklands, sides with the Americans in the conflict. A merchant from Havana, Juan Miralles, travels secretly to North Carolina to represent the Spanish government before the Continental Congress. Miralles and General George Washington meet and become fast friends.

POLI. The Spanish governor of Louisiana, Bernardo de Gálvez, corresponds with such American patriots as Thomas Jefferson and Patrick Henry. Sympathizing with the revolutionary war, Gálvez secures the port of New Orleans so only American, French, and Spanish ships can enter it.

1779

FOOD. In the autumn, the governor of Texas, Domingo Cabello y Robles, sends more than 10,000 head of cattle to Gálvez and American rebels in the Southeast to help in the Revolutionary War.

WARS. Spain declares war on Great Britain on June 21. Plans are made for Spanish troops to attack Pensacola, Florida, and to march north to join the American rebels in Georgia. Spain names Bernardo de Gálvez, governor of Spanish Louisiana, commander of the Spanish troops in the Caribbean. Operating out of Cuba, Gálvez commands over 1,000 soldiers, probably the first army composed of Spanish, Cubans, Dominicans, Mexicans, and Puerto Ricans. Gálvez captures Baton Rouge and areas of the Mississippi.

1780–1782

REBE. Túpac Amaru II rebels against the Spanish authorities in Perú. When his peaceful protests against inhumane treatments of workers in the mines and textile factories are ignored by the governor of the region of Tinta, Perú, Túpac Amaru captures and kills the Spanish official. Two years later, the Peruvian leader is captured by Spanish forces. Amaru's rebellion is the first violent uprising against the Spanish in two centuries.

Eyewitness Account: Death of an Inca Warrior

"He was brought into the middle of the square and the executioner cut out his tongue. Then they unshackled his hands and feet and laid him on the ground. They tied four ropes to his hands and feet and fastened the ropes to the girth of four horses, which were led . . . in four different directions . . . the horses did not manage to tear him apart. . . . Finally, the commander, moved by compassion . . . ordered the executioner to cut off the head of Tupac Amarú, and this was done."

Source: Carlos Fuentes. *The Buried Mirror: Reflections on Spain and the New World.* Boston: Houghton Mifflin Company, 1999, p. 212.

Disease Changes the World of the Amerindians

"Epidemics caused demographic damage on a scale without historical precedent. In some regions, particularly those on the coasts fringing the Caribbean and the Pacific or in areas . . . where Spanish gold mining imposed special burdens on native peoples whole societies were wiped out in the passage of a few generations. . . . Repeated attacks by epidemics of smallpox, influenza, measles, typhus and other imported diseases not only had horrifying short-term damage . . . but they also inflected lasting long-term damage by undermining the social integrity, economic productivity and reproductive capacity of the communities."

Source: Anthony McFarlane. "Pre-Columbian and Colonial Latin America." In *The Cambridge Companion to Modern Latin American Culture.* Ed. John King. Cambridge: Cambridge University Press, 2004, p. 15.

1781

OBIT. Inca prince and Peruvian rebel leader Tupac Amarú, after fighting against the Spanish for nearly a year, is executed on May 18. He is beheaded in the presence of thousands of Incas and Spanish settlers. He will become a symbol of rebellion through Latin America. In the United States in the 1990s, rapper Tupac Shakur will adopt his name to honor the fallen Inca and to signal rebellion against racism.

REBE. *Comuneros*, or residents, of New Granada, Colombia, rebel against the Spanish authorities, who crush the rebellion. It is the beginning of independence struggles that will lead to war against Spain in the early nineteenth century.

SETT. On September 4, Los Angeles is founded as the Misión Nuestra Señora Reina de los Angeles.

WARS. On May 10, after a siege initiated in February, Gálvez and 4,000 soldiers capture Pensacola. The British retreat from Florida.

1783

BIRT. Simón Bolívar is born on July 24. He will become Latin America's greatest general and liberator.

LAND. Spain regains Florida from Great Britain.

MED. The Jesuits introduce the printing press to Colombia.

1784

HEAL. Over 300,000 Mexicans die from disease and malnourishment. It is a pattern of neglect in which elite families and member of the aristocracy live in comfort while the natives and poor Mexicans experience economic depravity. This pattern will continue into the twenty-first century, forcing many Mexicans to relocate to the United States.

1785

EDUC. The first integrated school in the United States opens in St. Augustine, Florida. White and black children attend classes together. It is also the first school in the United States to teach Spanish.

1786

OBIT. In México City, revolutionary war hero Bernardo de Gálvez dies of high fever on November 30. After the end of America's war of independence, Gálvez lived in Spain and then went to México to serve as viceroy. In the United States, his role in the Revolutionary War will be overshadowed by the French Jean Lafayette.

1789

LAWS. The Alien and Sedition Acts are passed, authorizing the president of the United States to expel immigrants deemed dangerous.

LAWS. The Naturalization Act of 1789 is passed. The act raises the residency requirements for American citizenship from 5 to 14 years. Historians believe that it designed to curb the growing power of Irish and French immigrants.

SETT. Mission San Elizario, 15 miles southeast of El Paso, Texas, is founded.

SLAV. In Puerto Rico, the Royal Decree of Graces of 1789 allows slaves to buy their own freedom.

1790

EXPL. The port of Valdez is named by the Spanish explorer Don Salvador Fidalgo.

SLAV. There are 50,000 slaves in Cuba.

1791

REBE. The Haitian Revolution begins on August 22. The conflict, lasting 13 years, will force many French and Spanish planters to relocate to Cuba and Puerto Rico. In Cuba, their presence will help develop the sugar industry.

1792

LIT. The poem "A la piña" ("ode to a pineapple") becomes popular in Havana. The ode is written by a military man and poet, Manuel de Zequeira y Arango. Considered Cuba's first poem, it celebrates Cuba's flora and fauna. In doing so, the poet takes pride in being Cuban and not Spanish. The poem is an early manifestation of a Cuban identity distinct and separate from a Spanish identity.

1797

WARS. In February, a British fleet of 17 ships and 8,000 soldiers defeat Spanish forces in Port-of-Spain, Trinidad. The British take over the island, signaling the beginning of the end of the Spanish empire in Latin America. Within a generation, Spain will lose all its colonies but Cuba and Puerto Rico.

NINETEENTH CENTURY

1800

ANIM. Millions of long-horn cattle, as well as horses, originally introduced in the 1500s by the Spanish conquistadores, roam the Southwest. To make a living, *vaqueros*, Spanish and Mexican horsemen, herd the animals from the Southwest to México. These highly talented and skilled horsemen are the original cowboys. As non-Mexican and non-Spanish settlers arrive to the Southwest, they imitate the riding style of the Mexican-Spanish cowboys.

ARTS. Throughout Latin America *tertulias* become popular. Tertulias are formal and informal literary salons where colonial society's elite meet to discuss literature and political matters. Through tertulias ideas for conspiracies are developed in cities like Havana, México, and San Juan, among others. Tertulias will remain popular beyond colonial times and will be transported to New York and Florida in the twentieth century as avenues for cultural affirmation and political activism of the Latino community.

CULT. Halfway through the century, Americans espouse the philosophy of Manifest Destiny, which promotes American superiority and continental expansion even if it means war.

MED. Hundreds of newspapers, consisting of at least one page but often more and distributed on a daily or a weekly basis, are published in Spanish throughout the Southwest, parts of Florida, New York, and Pennsylvania. In time, most of the publications would be lost, but in the 1980s a team of Latino researchers, under the leadership of scholar Nicolás Kanellos, would find rare copies of the newspapers to document their existence. Some of the newspapers include *El Misisipí* (1809), *La Gaceta de Texas* (1813), and *El Telégrafo de las Floridas* (1817).

Latinos and Newspapers

"From [colonial times] to the present, the Spanish-language newspaper has been a mainstay in Hispanic communities throughout the United States, preserving an advancing Hispanic culture and maintaining its relationship with the larger Spanish-speaking world. . . . Hispanic communities from coast to coat have supported newspapers of varying sizes and missions, from the eight-page weekly printed in Spanish or bilingually to the highly entrepreneurial large-city daily published completely in Spanish."

Source: Nicolás Kanellos and Helvetia Martell. *Hispanic Periodicals in the United States: Origins to 1960. A Brief History and Comprehensive Bibliography.* Houston, TX: Arte Público Press, 2000, p. 5.

Mexican vaqueros. The American cowboy learned the art of riding horses from the Mexican vaqueros who roamed the Southwest from the 1500s to the late 1800s.

MUSI. In Puerto Rico, *aguinaldos*, Christmas carols, become a popular art form. During December and early January, singers walk from house to house and neighborhood to neighborhood singing carols, a tradition that will remain popular through the twenty-first century and will be transplanted to Puerto Rican communities in the United States, where civic centers and schools schedule performances during the holidays.

SHEL. Large haciendas, built in the style of missions or even small fortresses, spread around the Southwest. The dwellings contain an enclosed courtyard, and many rooms one after the other, flanked by a corridor, a kitchen, and a large dining room. In the twentieth century, Hollywood films portraying the adventures of the imaginary Zorro will duplicate the hacienda setting.

1801

WARS. Toussaint L'Ouverture invades Santo Domingo, the Spanish side of Hispaniola. He abolishes slavery on the island. The Haitian ruler sets up a dictatorial regime. More than 2,000 Spanish and French planters relocate to Cuba, Puerto Rico, and Venezuela, bringing with them expertise in developing sugar plantations.

1803

LAND. The United States acquires Colorado as part of the Louisiana Purchase.

1804

EXPL. President Thomas Jefferson approves the Lewis and Clark expedition to the Pacific Coast. Spain worries about Jefferson's plans for American expansion.

SETT. Alta California is formed when the Spanish colony of California is divided into two with the north under the administration of Franciscan missions and the south under Dominican missions. The north is also called *California Nueva*, New California, and the south is called *California Vieja*, Old California.

1805

LEGE. While visiting Rome, a young Simón Bolívar, the future liberator of South America, is overwhelmed by stories of heroic deeds in ancient times and also influenced by the liberal ideas of the Enlightenment. On the hill of Monte Sacro, he vows to dedicate his life to the liberation of Venezuela, his homeland, and other South American colonies. It is a pattern that will be repeated throughout political struggles in South America, where Latin American patriots based in other countries, but especially in the United States, will vow to fight for freedom back home, using the United States as a podium.

1806

BIRT. On March 21, Benito Juárez is born. A full-blooded Zapoteca Indian, he will twice be elected president of México and will defeat French forces invading the nation in the 1860s.

LIT. Puerto Rico's first two books, *Poesías* and *Ocios de Juventud,* by the Spanish poet Juan Rodríguez Calderón, are published.

MED. The printing press is introduced in Puerto Rico. The island's first newspaper, *La Gaceta de Puerto Rico*, appears.

1807

EXPL. The American explorer, Zebulon Pike, leads the first non-Spanish expedition into New Mexico. In 1811, he publishes the first description in English of the region: *Exploratory Travels through the Western Territories of North America.*

SETT. Fearing American expansion into the Southwest, the Spanish government in México moves 16 families from Matamoros, in México, to San Marcos, Texas.

TRAD. In July, 18 ships from Puerto Rico arrive in Philadelphia. Since the Revolutionary War, Spanish Caribbean islands have been trading with the United States. For an unspecified number of Puerto Rican sailors, the visit to Philadelphia is probably the first encounter between Puerto Ricans and Americans in the United States.

1808

POLI. Due to political corruption and poor administration in Spain, King Carlos IV (1748–1819) gives up the throne. It is a decision that unintentionally sets up major changes in Spain and in Latin America, leading to the Napoleonic invasion of the peninsula and the wars of independence in Latin America.

REBE. On May 2 the people of Spain rebel against Napoleon Bonaparte, who has established his brother José as ruler of the peninsula. To fight against the French, Spanish citizens create juntas to coordinate the war on the peninsula. The colonists in Latin America sympathize with the Spanish people. Their desire for freedom for Spain from the French will convert within a decade to their own desire for freedom from Spain. This sentiment will be shared by Tejanos, Mexican-Texans of Spanish descent, who live in Texas.

1809

BIRT. William Travis, Alamo defender, is born on August 9 in South Carolina.

POLI. The junta in Cadiz declares Puerto Rico a province, rather than a colony, with full representation before the Spanish *Cortés*, the parliament. The island's representative, Ramón Power y Giralt (1775–1813), helps draft the liberal constitution of 1812. He demands that, should Spain be defeated by the French, Puerto Rico will have the right to declare its independence.

GQ a la Spanish Western Style

"New Mexican men were flashy dressers. A gentleman's outfit was topped by a *sombrero*, a wide-brimmed hat to shade him from the sun. His *chaqueta*, or jacket, had large buttons and was embroidered with elaborate designs. For pants he wore *calzoneras*, with the outer leg of the garment open from the waist to the ankle, the edges trimmed with lace and colored braid. In cold or wet weather, he wore a *serape*, a woolen cape with a hole in the center through which he put his head. When out riding, he put on *chaparerras* . . . leather overalls to protect his legs in high brush. Attached to his boots were a pair of spurs, each with a rowel, a rotating disk with points to nudge the horse along."

Source: Albert Marrin. *Empires Lost and Won: The Spanish Heritage of the Southwest.* New York: Atheneum Books for Young Readers, 1997, p.107.

1809–1820

REBE. Several rebellions are planned in Cuba, often under the leadership of slaves. The rebellions are often betrayed, and the Spanish authorities capture and execute the leaders and imprison the conspirators.

1810

EDUC. A school for underprivileged children opens in San Juan, Puerto Rico.

LEGE. A Spanish friar in Chimayó, New Mexico, spots a light shining from a hill. He uncovers a buried crucifix on the spot from where the light emanates. The crucifix is dubbed the Miraculous Crucifix of Our Lord of Esquipulas. Attempts are made to remove the crucifix from the village but no matter where the crucifix is taken, such as the town of Santa Cruz, it disappears only to appear on the hillside once again. A small chapel is built on the site of the apparition.

REBE. On September 10, Father Miguel Hidalgo calls on Mexicans to rebel against the Spanish government, an event known as *El Grito de Dolores*. Under the banner of the Virgin of Guadalupe, the priest leads an insurrection of 60,000 men, consisting primarily of Mexican Indians and mestizos, the offspring of Spanish and Indian union. It is the beginning of México's war of independence from Spain. In the twentieth century, México will celebrate the occasion with military parades, public fiestas throughout the country, masses, and the tolling of church bells accompanied by massive fireworks, similar to the United States' Fourth of July celebrations. Mexican-American communities in California, New Mexico, and Texas will hold scaled-down celebrations of the El Grito de Dolores. Murals in Mexican-American communities throughout the United States will often depict Father Hidalgo.

1811

OBIT. On July 30, Father Miguel Hidalgo is executed by the Spanish in México for leading a rebellion against the colonial government. A priest, he is first excommunicated by the Church so he can be tried as a civilian. The firing squad shoots him several times before finally killing him; some historians maintain that the soldiers are reluctant to shoot Hidalgo. The corpse is beheaded and the head is placed inside a cage in the town of Guanajato, where it stays for 10 years, to remind would-be rebels of the fate that awaits them. In the twentieth century, murals throughout México and in some Mexican-American communities in the United States will depict the rebellion.

REBE. After the execution by the Spanish of Father Hidalgo, another priest, José María Morelos, continues the struggle, organizing small bands of guerrillas that help him capture the cities of Oaxaca and Acapulco. Morelos advocates for the redistribution of church properties to the poor of México and for equal rights for all Mexicans.

REBE. In the United States, an unspecified number of Tejanos (Mexican-Texans of Spanish ancestry) and Anglo settlers in Texas rebel against the Spanish Empire. The rebellion is quickly put down by Spanish soldiers from México.

1811–1822

REBE. In rapid succession, Latin American colonies proclaim their independence from Spain: Paraguay and Venezuela in 1811; Argentina in 1816; Colombia in 1819; and México, Panamá and Perú in 1821. Guatemala, Nicaragua, Honduras, Costa Rica, and El Salvador establish the United Provinces of Central America in 1821. Ecuador achieves independence in 1822, Bolivia in 1825, and Uruguay in 1828.

1812

POLI. In Spain, the Constitution of 1812 is written, establishing parliamentary rule and limiting the authority of the monarch. The Spanish seek support from the colonies in Latin America, assuring their participation in the war against Napoleon. The colonies realize that Spain is politically and militarily weak and begin to plot their own independence.

REBE. A rebellion by Tejanos, Mexican-Texas, and Anglo settlers, the second in a year's time, is put down once again by Spanish troops.

TRAD. Sugar from Puerto Rico is traded in Boston, New York, and Philadelphia.

1813

MED. *La Gaceta de México* and *El Mexicano* are probably the first Spanish exile newspapers published in the United States. Both newspapers are printed in Louisiana. They are aimed at Mexican readers who live in exile and are critical of the Spanish government in México. These readers support the evolving independence movement in México.

POLI. After expelling the French from Spain, with help from the British, the Spanish monarchy is reestablished and the constitutional government is dismissed. The return to absolute rule prompts many of the Spanish colonies to seek independence.

1815

AGRI. Over 400 Corsicans who settle in Puerto Rico begin planting coffee, sugar cane, and tobacco on the island's southwest. By the 1860s, 7 out of 10 coffee plantations on the island are owned by Corsican families.

OBIT. The leader of México's war of independence and Father Hidalgo's successor, Father José María Morelos, is executed by Spanish forces in the village of San Cristóbal Ecatepec. His lieutenant, Vicente Guerrero, continues the fight for independence.

SETT. To attract white non-Catholic and European immigrants to Puerto Rico, Spain decrees the *Cédula de Gracia*, the Royal Decree of Graces, allowing immigrants to settle in the mountainous countryside of Puerto Rico, in the southwest.

1816

POLI. Cuban-born governor José Coppinger is the last Spanish governor to serve in Florida, five years before the United States acquires the peninsula.

1817

SLAV. In Cuba, there is a population of 239,000 African slaves.

1819

LAND. On February 19, the United States buys Florida from Spain for $5 million. Spain relinquishes Texan territory west of the Sabine. The treaty is known as the Adams-Onís Treaty, because the signers are John Quincy Adams, Secretary of State, and Luis de Onís, Spain's Foreign Minister.

SETT. The Spanish governor of Texas, General Joaquín de Arrendondo, grants prospector Moses Austin the right to settle 300 American families on 200,000 acres. Moses Austin dies shortly after receiving the grant, and his son Stephen Austin continues with the project. The families settle near the Colorado and Brazos Rivers.

SETT. In Brooklyn, New York, a small number of Puerto Rican students, merchant seamen, and tobacco workers settle in and near Columbia Street.

WARS. In South America, Simón Bolívar surprises Spanish troops on the other side of the Andes in Boyacá, Colombia. For nearly 10 years, Bolívar has been fighting against Spanish and loyalist forces, sometimes winning, sometimes losing. The victory at Boyacá assures Bolívar and his troops that final victory is near.

1819–1831

POLI. The Republic of Colombia is established. It consists of present-day Colombia, Venezuela, Ecuador, Perú, and Bolivia. The republic is Simón Bolívar's attempt to create a nation similar in structure to the United States. The republic will crumble as its member nations pursue different political courses and ideology. Despite a common heritage, these nations prefer not to seek unity.

Similar attempts will fail in the United States as diverse leaders, such as Mexican-American Henry Cisneros, will seek political unity within the Latino communities in the 1980s.

1820

REBE. In Texas, James Long leads an independence movement from Spain. He is captured and imprisoned in San Antonio. While pleading for his cause in México City two years later, he is accidentally shot and killed by a guard.

1821

LAND. In an effort to separate the Catholic Church from secular activities, the newly established Mexican government, freed from Spanish rule, passes laws in California to distribute the land owned by the Dominican and Franciscan Orders to Californios, ranchers of Spanish origins. It is the birth of big *ranchos*—ranches of hundred of acres owned by one family or several members of the same family—in California.

SETT. The newly established Mexican government invites Americans from the United States to settle in Texas. Nine years later there are 30,000 American settlers in Texas compared to 4,000 original Tejanos. In Arizona, trappers and traders start to arrive from the United States.

TRAD. The Santa Fe Trail connects Missouri with Santa Fe, New Mexico. The route is a commercial highway. It will also be used by American troops during the Mexican-American War in 1846.

1822

LAWS. On December 2, President James Monroe pronounces the Monroe doctrine, which proclaims that no foreign power will be allowed to invade and maintain a territory in the Americas and that the United States will be responsible for imposing such policy and removing foreign threats from the region. A popular rephrasing of the doctrine emerges as "America for the Americans."

MILI. The United States Navy sends several ships to San Juan, Puerto Rico on March 5. It is the first time the American military appears on the island. Their mission is to search for pirates in the Caribbean Sea but also to explore the island as a potential acquisition for the United States. On April 28, Secretary of State John Quincy Adams reports to the Congress that Cuba and Puerto Rico are natural appendages of the United States.

POLI. General Agustín de Iturbide, representative of conservative forces in México who support a native monarchy rather than a republic, declares himself emperor of the newly established nation.

America for the Americans

"We owe it, therefore, to candor, and to the amicable relations existing between the United States and those [European] powers, to declare, that we should consider any attempt on their part to extend their system to any portion of this hemisphere, as dangerous to our peace and safety. With the existing colonies or dependencies of any European power we have not interfered, and shall not interfere. But with the governments who have declared their independence, and maintained it, and whose independence we have, on great consideration, and on just principles, acknowledged, we could not view any interposition for the purpose of oppressing them, or controlling, in any other manner, their destiny, by any European power in any other light than as the manifestation of an unfriendly disposition towards the United States."

Source: James Monroe. "State of the Union, December 2, 1823." In *The Legacy of the Monroe Doctrine.* By David W. Dent. Westport: Greenwood, CT, 1999.

On July 22, Iturbide is crowned. As Iturbide grows dictatorial, military officers oppose his regime, including a young man named Antonio López de Santa Anna, who within a decade will become a ruthless leader and lead the attack on the Alamo in the United States. Politicians in El Salvador, afraid of political instability, request annexation with the United States.

REBE. Iturbide is forced from office and agrees to go into exile. From England and Italy he plans his return to México.

SETT. On January 3, Stephen Austin receives a grant from México to colonize the Brazos area in Texas. Austin is eager to respect Mexican laws and traditions. In the meantime, Erasmo Seguín, who represents Texas before the Mexican Congress, persuades the United States Congress to pass an act permitting American settlers to move to Texas.

1824

ARTS. The governor of Puerto Rico, General Miguel de la Torre, authorizes a tax for the construction of a municipal theater. Traveling theater companies are popular, staging musicals, called *zarzuelas*, and comedies throughout towns on the island. It is a tradition that will be transplanted to New York City in the 1960s with the creation of the *Puerto Rican Traveling Theater*.

BIRT. On May 16, Mexican folk hero Juan Nepomuceno Cortina is born into a wealthy family in Tamaulipas, México. He will become a bandit, as Texans see him, or a social avenger, as Mexican-Americans interpret it, who will harass racist Texans and will fight against the confederates during the Civil War.

MED. The first Cuban newspaper published in exile appears in Philadelphia under the title of *El Habanero*. The founder is the Cuban philosopher and patriot Father Félix Varela. The newspaper is critical of Spanish rule in Cuba and in Latin America.

OBIT. Agustín de Iturbide, former emperor of México, is executed on July 15 as he returns from Europe with plans for reestablishing his government.

POLI. México combines the districts of Coahuila, in northern México, and Texas into one state. The Tejanos are unhappy with the change. Coahuila is a mining area and not capable of maintaining itself with agriculture, which Texas provides. Tejanos feel that people in Coahuila will take advantage of Texas's land. General Antonio López de Santa Anna helps to write México's Constitution of 1824, which allows for Texas to become a separate state within México. Tejanos and Americans in Texas support the constitution.

REBE. A group of American settlers in Texas rebel against Mexican rule to protest the combination of Coahuila and Texas into one state. They form the Republic of Fredonia, an effort which is put down by Mexican soldiers with the help of such Tejanos and American sympathizers as Stephen Austin, who leads a pro-México voluntary army in the conflict.

WARS. Simón Bolívar defeats once and for all the Spanish forces in South America.

1825

LEGE. On March 29, the Puerto Rican pirate Roberto Cofresí is captured and executed by the Spanish on the island. Cofresí is regarded as a type of Robin Hood, distributing riches to the poor people of the island. He will emerge as a beloved figure in Puerto Rican culture.

1826

EXPL. Captain Jedediah S. Smith is a daring adventurer and self-styled brigade leader. To cross overland to California, he travels the length of Utah. He is the first white settler to cross the Sierra Nevada as well as the Great Basin Desert.

LAND. In California, a non-native can become a Mexican citizen and receive a land grant as long as he or she stays a year and swears loyalty to the Mexican government. The new settler must also convert to Catholicism.

LIT. Father Félix Varela, a Cuban priest, is credited with writing the novel *Jicoténcal*, the first Latin-American novel published in the United States.

The novel is sold in small Spanish bookstores in Philadelphia and New York.

MIGR. The first Euroamerican traders and hunters, under the leadership of Captain Jedediah S. Smith, arrive in California. They are the first non-native and non-Mexican-Spanish to enter the territory.

OBIT. On July 4, 1826, President Thomas Jefferson dies. A legendary figure in North American history, Jefferson desired the continental expansion of the United States and expressed an early interest in acquiring the Caribbean islands of Cuba and Puerto Rico.

1827

SLAV. In Puerto Rico the slave population numbers about 34,240.

1828

MIGR. The first major discovery of gold in the West occurs near Sante Fe, New Mexico. Americans in the East are showing more interest in heading to the Southwest.

1829

BIRT. Joaquín Murieta, the Mexican "Robin Hood," is born either in Alamo, México, or in Chile. During the California Gold Rush he will become a robber and also a protector of Mexican miners abused by racist cowboys. Murieta's legend will inspire several novels and will be confused by the reading public as the inspiration for the fictional character Zorro that appears early in the twentieth century.

EXPL. Spanish and Mexican traders, under the leadership of Antonio Armijo, uncover an oasis in the Nevada desert. They call it Las Vegas.

LANG. American settlers in Texas who are contemplating breaking away from México begin to call themselves Texians to indicate an identity separate from the Mexican-American Tejanos who live in the terrain and are descendants of the early Spanish conquistadores and explorers.

SLAV. The Mexican government abolishes slavery. The question of whether or not to allow slavery in

Texas is a major issue between the Mexicans and the Texians. General Santa Anna believes Texians want Texas as a state of México, with its constitution, to continue the practice of slavery.

TRAN. The Spanish Trail runs from Sante Fe, New Mexico, through Colorado, Utah, Nevada, and Los Angeles, California. It will be used by wagon trails and cattlemen until the 1850s.

WARS. General Antonio López de Santa Anna defeats Spanish troops attempting to invade México to reconquer the country for Spain. Revered by Mexicans as a hero, Santa Anna opposes México's president Anastasio Bustamante, who has overthrown from office and murdered president Vicente Guerrero, a popular leader of the war of independence against Spain.

1830

ARTS. Beginning in this decade, professional companies of actors travel from México and Cuba to California to perform plays in Spanish in cities such as Los Angeles, San Diego, and San Francisco. Performances of Spanish classic drama are the popular genre.

BIRT. July 30 marks the birth of Mexican dictator Porfirio Díaz. His rule of the nation from 1876 to 1911 will send many Mexicans into exile in the United States and will bring about the Mexican Revolution of 1910.

EXPL. On January 8, Antonio Armijo, from Sante Fe, leads a pack train from New Mexico to California, crossing the Las Vegas oasis where they can replenish their water supplies.

POLI. The Mexican government, distrustful of American settlers after the rebellion of Fredonia in 1824, outlaws American immigration into Texas. American Texians want to become a separate state of México.

POLI. In South America, Simón Bolívar attempts to keep the Republic of Colombia from crumbling by enforcing dictatorial powers that are rejected by the people. Bolivar resigns from power and dies on December 17. Popularly known as the "George Washington of South America," he will become one of the few patriots south of the border that most Americans recognize.

1831

BIRT. José Antonio Romualdo Pacheco, Jr., the only Latino to serve as governor of California, is born on October 31 in Santa Barbara, California.

OBIT. Former president James Monroe, the creator of the Monroe doctrine, dies of heart failure and tuberculosis on July 4. He had promoted the belief in Manifest Destiny, meaning the right of the United States to expand its continental territory.

1832

HEAL. A cholera epidemic overwhelms New York City, where over 3,000 afflicted people die. In the slum known as the Five Points, where poor Irish families live and where physicians do not want to visit, Cuban priest Father Félix Varela ministers to the sick and organizes makeshift medical centers. New Yorkers call him the "Vicar of the Irish."

REBE. The relationship between Texas and México is deteriorating. On June 26, Texians clash with Mexican forces over the possession of a cannon located in the town of Velasco. The Texians, under the leadership of John Austin, lose 10 men, with 12 wounded; the Mexican lose 5 with 15 wounded. A truce ends the conflict, but it is a clear indication that the Texians are seeking independence from México and that México is not willing let go of Texas.

1833

POLI. Santa Anna forces Bustamente into exile and is elected president of México. Tejanos approve of Santa Anna's support of the Mexican Constitution. Tejanos and Texians meet in San Felipe, Texas, and draft a document asking for statehood within the Republic of Texas and rebuking immigration restriction into Texas. They believe Santa Anna will oblige them. Stephen Austin travels to México with a pro-statehood document but Santa Anna refuses to grant statehood until Texas has a population of 80,000 rather than 30,000, as mandated by México's laws. In

December, as Austin prepares to return to Texas, Mexican authorities arrest him for inciting political sentiments against Santa Anna, though the authorities do not provide any evidence.

1834

MED. A Mexican officer, Agustín Vicente Zamoranao, establishes the first printing press in California. Twelve years later, American forces will use this printing press to publish the first American newspaper in the state, *The Californian*.

POLI. General Santa Anna dismisses the Mexican Constitution of 1824 and assumes dictatorial powers, claiming México is not ready for democracy. He believes recent American immigrants to Texas are responsible for stirring revolutionary sentiment. One major area of conflict is the issue of

Monument to Father Félix Varela, the "Vicar of the Irish." After leaving New York City, Varela moved to St. Augustine, Florida, where parishioners were impressed by his dedication to the community.

Santa Anna, the Stereotypical Caudillo

The Mexican dictator was not unique in the use of dictatorial power; he belongs to the tradition of strong-willed dictators who practice caudillismo:

"Caudillismo was a logical continuation of colonial practice; local chieftains who were weeks, even months distant from the centers of colonial power assumed positions of great authority in their own regions. Caudillismo, persisting throughout most of Latin America to this day, is the product of three centuries of Spanish colonial institutions and the military means employed to end Spanish rule."

Source: Alberto Prago. *The Revolutions in Spanish America: The Independence Movements of 1808–1825.* New York: MacMillan, 1970, p. 224.

---

slavery: México has abolished slavery, while the American immigrants want to maintain slavery in Texas.

WARS. Tejanos, Mexican-Texans, and American settlers join forces to drive Mexican soldiers out of Texas. The Tejanos and Americans want independence from México.

1835

AGRI. In México, General Santa Anna contemplates the possibility of using the sap from the Sapodilla tree, which grows abundantly in the province of Yucatán, as a kind of chewing gum, the way Mayas used it in ancient times. He will present his idea to American inventor Thomas Adam in 1869.

CRIM. Land speculators in Texas, including future Alamo defender Jim Bowie and the Mexican governor, are illegally selling state land owned by México, in Saltillo, Texas. Santa Anna sends his brother-in-law, a military man named General Martín Perfecto de Cós, to arrest the governor and end the corruption. Rumors assert that General Cós will place all of Texas under martial law.

LAWS. The Mexican Congress passes a law deeming any foreigner who takes up arms against México a traitor or pirate and granting Mexican authorities the right to execute the foreigner. Santa Anna enforces this law in Texas.

REBE. Stephen Austin is released from a Mexican prison after serving two years without a trial.

Austin, who wants to maintain cordial relationships between México and Texas, now believes Santa Anna is a dictator with plans to crush Texians into submission. Austin favors annexation to the United States. On September 19, Austin learns that General Cós is marching with 400 men to San Antonio and assumes the command of the Texas army.

WARS. The war for Texas independence begins. On October 1, Texian and Mexican forces participate in a minor skirmish on a watermelon farm. The Mexicans are in the town of Gonzalez with orders to retrieve an old cannon as part of General Santa Anna's plan to disarm the rebels. The Texians refuse to hand over the cannon. They shoot the cannon at the air and the Mexicans retreat. The Texians move on to San Antonio where General Cós and his army of 1,200 have occupied the old mission; Cós's orders are to wipe out the Texian rebellion. After a seven-week siege and several battles, the Mexicans retreat from San Antonio on December 13 and the Texians take over the Alamo mission. The defeat angers Santa Anna, who wants revenge.

1836

POLI. The Texas Declaration of Independence is signed by Americans and Tejanos on March 2. The declaration is drafted while the Alamo is under siege. One of the signers is José Antonio Navarro, a prominent Tejano who wants independence from México.

How a Santa Anna Supporter Sees the Texas Rebellion

"What is the purpose of this rebellion?. . . . At first the rebels proclaimed that they merely wanted to restore the Constitution of 1824. . . . That was transparent nonsense, of course. The real object is to break away from Mexico and perhaps take two or three Mexican states with them. They will join the United States, or create their own slaveholding republic. Because that is what these sons of Jefferson, these supposed believers in the rights of man, truly desire: an empire for slavery."

Source: Stephen Harrigan. *The Gates of the Alamo.* New York: A. A. Knopf, 2000, p. 303.

Legends of the Alamo

William B. Travis is often shown drawing a line on the sand and asking anyone in the Alamo who wants to stay with him and fight to cross over the line. Although it is often depicted in movies, most historians today do not believe that this incident occurred, since it was never mentioned by some of the Alamo survivors, including Susana Dickenson and Travis' slave, Joe, who was questioned by Sam Houston after the battle.

"Remember the Alamo" becomes a phrase that symbolizes Americans' courage before overwhelming forces. For the United States, the Alamo incident is indicative of the country's ability to recover from defeat and emerge victorious over adversity. For many Latinos, the Alamo suggests America's imperial powers and a sense of superiority over the rest of the world. Latino scholars point out how American history texts tend to ignore the Tejanos' contributions to the independence movement in Texas, emphasizing instead the roles of Bowie, Crockett, and Travis, and neglecting to mention figures like José Antonio Navarro.

WARS. Santa Anna's army of 6,000—some estimates say 4,000—reach San Antonio on February 23. Santa Anna signals his plan not to spare any of the Alamo defenders unless they surrender. The defenders reject the offer. The defenders in the Alamo, 183 men, include Texians and Tejanos. The most famous defenders are Jim Bowie, Davy Crockett, and William Travis. Other defenders include the Texians Juan Seguín, Gregorio Esparza, and Toribio Domingo Losoya. Though of Mexican-Spanish descent, these three men deplore Santa Anna's dictatorial rule. On March 6 at 5:30 A.M., Santa Anna's forces rush the old mission. The Mexican soldiers want revenge for Cós' defeat the previous December. The battle ends 90 minutes later, with the Mexicans victorious and all the defenders dead. Santa Anna piles up the dead defenders and burns the remains with the exception of one defender, Gregorio Esparza, who had fought against his own brother, serving in Santa Anna's army. Esparza is allowed proper burial.

WARS. On March 14, Mexican forces defeat Texian forces in the Battle of Refugio. On March 19, Mexican forces are once again victorious in a battle against Texian commander James Walker Fannin and his forces. The defeated Texians are taken to the town of Goliad, where on March 27 Santa Anna orders the massacre of the 342 captured men. Among those captured is James Walker Fannin who is shot in the head even though he has asked that his face be spared in his execution. Though Santa Anna is acting within Mexican law by executing traitors and pirates, his officers are shocked by the massacre. Enraged by the massacres at the Alamo and Goliad, over

---

The Horror of War: The Mexicans in the Alamo

"As the Mexican gun crews blasted apart the stronghold of the convent, Blas [an officer] and half-a-dozen surviving members of his company were cleaning out the rooms at the south end of the compound where isolated groups of defenders had sought refuge. They were working their way toward the church, from whose doorway and windows the nortes [Texans] were still putting forth a lively and dangerous fire. But the [Mexicans] . . . were in a killing rage now, and they behaved as if this resistance were trivial. Blas saw men fall as they plunged their bayonets again and again into the bodies of defenders who were already dead, or bent down to strip them of their watches and bloody clothes. . . . The four fusiliers who entered the room . . . stabbed [Jim Bowie] with a concerted thrust that knocked him off the cot and then they drove their bayonets into his writhing body again and again."

Source: Stephen Harrigan. *The Gates of the Alamo.* New York: A. A. Knopf, 2000, p. 503.

The Horror of War: Texians Avenging the Alamo

"The lake [near the San Jacinto River] was only a hundred yards across, and it was filled with Mexican soldiers flailing and clawing themselves forward in their attempts to reach the marsh on the other side. The shore of the lake was lined . . . with Texians, who were taking their time loading and firing their accurate long rifles, shooting the Mexicans in the water. The Mexicans called out to God as the balls hit them, they screamed as they drowned in the deep water. The lake turned red with their blood. They thrashed wildly on the surface, some of them caught up in the coils of their own exposed viscera.

'Are you animals?' a Texian officer called out in a hoarse voice to the men shooting the Mexicans. 'Will you not stop shooting those men?' They would not."

Source: Stephen Harrigan. *The Gates of the Alamo.* New York: A. A. Knopf, 2000, p. 556.

---

900 men, under the command of General Sam Houston, attack the Mexican forces on April 21 in the Battle of San Jacinto. Shouting "Remember the Alamo" and "Remember Goliad," the Texians defeat the Mexicans and capture General Santa Anna. The general is taken to Washington, D.C. From there he returns to México with plans to retire from political and military life.

1837

RACE. After the Alamo, Anglos who move into Texas treat Tejanos as enemies. The brother of José Antonio Navarro, a leader of Texas's independence movement from México, is shot down by an Anglo who thinks the victim is plotting against the United States. Many Mexican families, though the number is not known with certainty, leave Texas for México. From now on Tejanos are treated as second-class citizens in Texas.

REBE. In New Mexico, in the town of Chimayo, Mexicans and New Mexicans rebel against the centralized government of México and high taxes. The rebels kill several top officials of the Mexican government.

1838

LIT. The memoir *Relación de meritos* is published by Father Antonio José Martínez in New Mexico.

Father Martínez resists the Anglicization of the Catholic Church and rejects the Americanization of the Southwest, one of the main themes in the narrative. His desire to keep Spanish and Mexican culture alive after the defeat of Santa Anna in Texas and the victory of the Americans during the Mexican-American War will make him the enemy of many Americans. In Willa Cather's 1927 novel *Death Comes to the Archbishop*, Father Martinez is portrayed as an evil man who prevents Mexican worshippers from embracing American culture.

REBE. Dominican Republic patriot Juan Pablo Duarte forms a secret society, called *La Trinitaria* [the Trinity], with the objective of obtaining independence from Haiti. He will become a revered patriot in the Dominican Republic and Dominican communities in the United States in the late twentieth century.

WARS. On April 16, the French Navy blockades and attacks Vera Cruz as a result of the Pastry War, when a baker accuses Mexican officers of ransacking his restaurant and stealing his pastry. The Pastry War is an excuse for France to force México to pay back loans owed by México. The French land 30,000 men, but early in the battle, General Antonio López de Santa Anna, coming back from retirement, pushes back the invaders. During the battle, a cannon ball severs Santa Anna's leg, making him an instant hero and helping him regain the presidency. As president of México, he will fight American forces once again in the Mexican-American War.

1840

POPU. Alta California, consisting of modern-day California, Nevada, Utah, northern Arizona, and southwestern Wyoming, has a population of 15,000 people known as "gente de razón," meaning people born of Spanish descent.

SETT. Afraid of the Texians' expansion into Colorado, México grants land holdings to settlers in Colorado, expecting the recipients to become loyal to the Mexican government.

1841

SETT. Soldiers from Texas move to New Mexico and claim the land east of Rio Grande.

1843

BIRT. William McKinley is born January 29. He will declare war on Spain in 1898 and will take possession of Cuba, the Philippines, and Puerto Rico at the end of the Spanish-Cuban-American War.

LIT. *Aguinaldo puertorriqueño* appears in Puerto Rico, the book credited with the inauguration of Puerto Rican literature. The collection of poetry—romantic and sentimental but celebratory of the island—identifies with a Puerto Rican persona rather than a Spanish persona. The volume is written by several Puerto Rican writers who are university students in Barcelona, Spain, and are homesick. In the twentieth century, many Puerto Rican writers, homesick for the island, will pen great works of art from places like New York City.

1845

LIT. In July, the classic study of Argentine society *Facundo Civilización y barbarie* is published in Chile. Written by Domingo Faustino Sarmiento, the volume explores, among other topics, the evolution and influence of the caudillo in Argentina, in particular, and in Latin America, in general. *Caudillismo*, the rule of the strong man, will become a political characteristic of such rulers as General Antonio López de Santa Anna.

POLI. The Mexican government warns the United States that if Texas becomes an American state, the Mexicans might declare war on the United States. On December 29, when Texas becomes the 28 state in the Union, México breaks off relations with the United States. Even though México sees the United States as committing an act of aggression, it does not declare war.

1846

LANG. The term "gringo" emerges to refer to an American. As American soldiers advance into México, some sing the song "Green Grows the Lilac," but what the Mexicans hear is "Grin gos the lailac." Referring to the soldiers, the Mexican drop the last word and combine "Grin gos" into "gringos." It is used as a derogatory term.

POLI. Americans demand that the U.S. government force México to pay the United States over $3 million in compensation for American property lost during several Mexican revolutions and from theft since the 1820s. President James K. Polk offers México $20 million for California and México, an offer turned down by the Mexicans.

WARS. The Mexican and the American governments dispute over the border between the two nations. For the Mexicans, the dividing line is the Nueces River, near San Antonio. Americans maintain that the Rio Grande, further south in Texas and closer to México, serves as the border. In early April, President James K. Polk orders General Taylor to march up to the Rio Grande with 3,000 soldiers. The Mexicans view the troop movement as an act of aggression, and on April 25 Mexican and American forces clash in the waters of the Rio Grande. The Mexicans defeat the Americans. On May 13, the news of the defeat of the American forces prompts President Polk to declare war on México, claiming that the Mexicans had crossed into American territory and shed American blood. In the twentieth century, Latin American historians will observe that México could have made the same claim. On May 18 General Taylor drives Mexican forces away from the Rio Grande. His forces cross the border and occupy the Mexican town of Matamoros. During June, July, and August, 1,700 American soldiers, led by General Stephen W. Kearny, occupy Sante Fe, New Mexico. On September 23 Taylor occupies the Mexican towns of Saltillo, Victoria, and the city of Monterrey. His swift army responses and victories make him a national hero in the United States.

1847

WARS. On September 13, American forces attack México's military academy, the Chapultepec Castle, which has a commanding view of the valley of México. As the Americans advance and the Mexican soldiers retreat, six young cadets fire at the Americans from the roof of the castle. Ordered to retreat, they remain on their spots until they are killed. It is said that the last two survivors refused to surrender and wrapped their bodies in the Mexican flag as they jumped over the walls to their deaths. In México these young cadets will be remembered as the *Niños Heroes*, the heroic boys.

WARS. In March, President Polk sends troops into México City. Part of General Kearny's troops cross the Rio Grande and take over the Mexican city of Chihuaha. On March 9, 10,000 American soldiers disembark on the east coast of México and capture the city of Veracruz 20 days later. On April 8, American troops advance towards México City, winning major battles at the pass of Cerro Gordo. After a period of resting and ground reconnaissance, American forces defeat the Mexican army on August 19 and 20, under the leadership of the notorious general, and now president, Antonio López de Santa Anna, at the battles of Contreras and Churubusco. On September 15 General Winfield Scott shocks Mexicans by occupying México City.

1848

LIT. Mexican poets in the Southwest begin to write poetry about the American occupation of México and the Spanish Southwest's annexation to the United States after the Mexican-American War.

MUSI. In the Southwest, a Mexican song called "De Las Margaritas" becomes popular. The lyrics make fun of young Mexican women who become Americanized after the United States' victory in the Mexican-American War. Mexican musicians begin to use songs, both humorous and serious, as a way of protesting against the American presence in the Southwest.

OBIT. On February 3, President John Quincy Adams dies of a stroke. He believed in the acquisition of Cuba and was a principal negotiator in the acquisition of Florida by the United States in 1821.

POLI. With the end of the Mexican-American War and the signing of the Treaty of Guadalupe Hidalgo, the 80,000 Mexicans who live in the United States are granted American citizenship. Those who do not want it can return to México and leave their possessions behind. It is the beginning of second-class citizenship for Mexican-Americans across the United States. They are now deemed inferior by Americans moving to the Southwest from the east coast of the United States.

POLI. The United States government, under the presidency of James Polk, offers Spain $100 million for the purchase of Cuba. Spain declines. In 1854, President Franklin Pierce will increase the offer to $310 million, continuing America's ongoing interests in the Caribbean.

POLI. On March 4, General Zachary Taylor assumes the American presidency. He wins the election partly as a result of his participation in the Mexican War.

REBE. Cuban-Venezuelan General Narciso López flees from Cuba to avoid capture by the Spanish authorities, who suspect he is planning a rebellion. He seeks asylum in New Orleans. López supports Cuba's annexation to the United States.

RELI. The end of the Mexican-American War brings changes to the makeup of the Catholic Church in the Southwest. Mexican priests are forced out of the United States and replaced with American clergy, mostly of Irish descent. These priests do not practice the elaborate Mexican religious celebrations, often with music and long processions using hundreds of candles, and they discourage the congregation from such religious manifestations. They also discourage the use of the Spanish language within a church.

RELI. The Protestant church makes its entry into the Southwest with Baptist, Methodist, and Presbyterians pastors recruiting Mexican-Americans.

SETT. Thousands of miners and traders travel to California as part of the gold rush. An unspecified number of miners are brought from Chile because of their experience in copper mining. Mexicans from the state of Sonora also travel to California.

SLAV. The Spanish governor of Puerto Rico decrees the *libreta* system, which mandates that all laborers who live and work in a plantation cannot venture off without the planter's permission. The laborer has to account for his/her movements by indicating on the libreta time off from work, time away from the plantation, and the time of return. Puerto Rican patriots describe the libreta as a form of slavery.

WARS. On February 2 the United States and México formally end the Mexican War by signing the Treaty of Guadalupe Hidalgo in the town of the same name. As part of the treaty, México yields to the United States the territories of Arizona, California, New Mexico, Texas, and parts of Colorado, Nevada, and Utah, over 525,000 square miles. In turn, the United States pays the Mexican government $15 million for these territories. The Mexican War serves as training ground for numerous American officers who will fight on opposite sides during the American Civil War: Jefferson Davis, Ulysses S. Grant, Thomas "Stonewall" Jackson, Robert E. Lee, George B. McClellan, George Gordon Meade, and William T. Sherman, among others. The war also prepares lesser-known officers and soldiers for participation in filibustering excursions into Cuba in the early 1850s.

1849

EXPL. Gold and silver inspires prospectors from the east coast to explore Nevada. It is estimated that about 45,000 settlers cross Nevada on their way to California.

LIT. The essay, "Story of a Woman," by the Dominican Manuela Aybar or Rodríguez, known as La Deana, sketches a life free from male expectations of women, a rare viewpoint during this period in Latin America. La Deana will serve as inspiration to feminist Latinas in New York City, especially women from the Dominican Republic, in the late twentieth century.

LIT. In Puerto Rico, the book of poems *El gíbaro*, by Manuel Alonso, is published. The volume celebrates Puerto Rican customs, traditions, and the countryside, all personified in *el gibaro,* an honest and peace-loving farmer. *El gibaro* represents all that is good in Puerto Rico. The character will become symbolic of the island, and of homesickness for Puerto Ricans living in the United States.

Declarations of War

Less than a year after the end of the Mexican-American War, the conflict is basically forgotten as the United States debates the abolition of slavery and the nation senses an impending civil war. In the twenty-first century, historians will explain that the war is seen as act of aggression rather than an act of defense, which is the explanation the United States provides when entering into conflicts such as the Spanish-Cuban-American War, World War I, and World War II. In these wars, the United States is attacked first, basically without provocation. This is not so with the Mexican-American War.

MILI. Chile dispatches a warship to San Francisco to protect hundreds of Chilean workers who are being attacked by racists in a neighborhood known as Little Chile. In one of the attacks, a Chilean woman is murdered.

OBIT. On June 15, President James K. Polk dies. Twentieth-century historians will portray him as the man who bullied México into a war that the country could not win in order to expand U.S. territories.

POLI. The California state constitution is drafted by Mexican-American and American settlers. Prominent Mexican-Americans politicians assure that voting in California is not restricted just to white male voters but to all males who are American citizens.

RACE. Mexican miners from Sonora, who tend to be dark-skinned, are singled out in California for their participation in the gold rush. Racist gangs attack and abuse them.

REBE. The Cuban flag is designed and created in New York City in June by exiles Narciso López and Miguel Teurbe Tolón. López takes the flag to New Orleans, from where he embarks on an expedition to Cuba to overthrow the Spanish regime.

1850

LAWS. In April, California passes the Foreign Miners Tax, which forces anyone who is not a native American or U.S. citizen to pay $20 a month for the privilege of working in the mines. The legislation affects Chilean, Chinese, French, German, and Mexican laborers.

MUSI. Mexican-American *corridos* begin growing in popularity. Corridos are songs with repetitive stanzas that celebrate the courage of Mexicans who oppose the growing American presence, as well as discrimination, in the West.

MUSI. The *Mariachi* band and music, so characteristic of Mexican culture, evolves into a small orchestra that consists primarily of guitars and violins with the guitarists providing the vocal components as well. The songs are from folkloric traditions, love ballads, as well as corridos.

OBIT. President General Zachary Taylor dies of acute gastroenteritis while in office on July 9, 16 months after taking office. He became famous for his participation in the Mexican-American war.

POLI. Filibustering becomes characteristic of American politics. After the Mexican-American Wars and the popularity of the concept of Manifest Destiny, American adventurers believe that with the support of the American government and the involvement of local politicians it is possible for an individual to take over the government of a nation in Latin America. Often, slavery is a component of a filibustering enterprise as participants want to make sure that the newly acquired nation practices slavery and supports the slave trade. For this reason, many filibusters would tend to be associated with proslavery states in the United States.

POPU. The United States reports a population of 100,000 Latinos, mostly from México or of Mexican descent. There are 60,000 Mexican-Americans in New Mexico, 20,000 in Texas, and

1,000 in Arizona. Alta California, northern California, has a population of 100,000, only 7,500 of which are Californios.

SETT. The United States government purchases the territories in Colorado claimed by Texas. Present-day Colorado is established.

1851

LAND. The United States Congress passes the California Land Act to protect land owned by Californios before the Mexican-American War.

1853

BIRT. Cuban poet and patriot José Martí is born on January 28. His poetry will become popular throughout Latin America. In the twentieth century, American folk singer Pete Seeger will adopt some of Martí's verses for an Americanized rendition of the Cuban song "Guantanamera."

OBIT. On July 25, legendary outlaw Joaquín Murieta is killed and decapitated by Californian Rangers. Murieta first appeared in California during the Gold Rush early in 1850. A victim of racism, Murieta formed a band that committed robberies, stealing more than $100,000 in gold, and stole cattle in Sierra Nevada. The rangers displayed Murieta's head throughout the state, though Murieta' sister claimed that the head was not her brother's. No one knows for sure whether or not the rangers killed Murieta.

POLI. In México, General Santa Anna is elected president once again. He sells the region of Yuma, Arizona, to the United States.

WARS. William Walker, an adventurer and private soldier, sets out to invade northern México on October 15, capturing part of Baja California, which he names the Republic of Lower California.

1854

LAND. Congress ratifies the purchase of Arizona and New Mexico from México. A train route is established between El Paso, Texas, and San Diego, California.

LAWS. Texas passes legislation prohibiting the association of Mexican-Americans and African Americans. Mexican-Americans and slaves are not allowed to talk to each other unless the slave's owner grants permission.

LEGE. Stories begin to circulate about the outlaw Joaquín Murieta and the reasons for his conversion to a life of crime. The most popular story tells how Murieta's wife was raped and killed and his brother hanged for a crime he did not commit. In the story, Murieta swears revenge by killing all the Americans he can find.

SLAV. Mexican-Americans help African slaves escape to México.

1855

BIRT. On January 10, Puerto Rican writer Manuel Zeno Gandía is born. A physician, he would write one of the best naturalist novels of Latin America, *La charca,* The Pond.

HEAL. A cholera epidemic in Puerto Rico kills 30,000 people. Puerto Rican patriot Dr. Ramón Emeterio Betances achieves international recognition for providing his medical services to all the afflicted, especially the poor people. Becoming known as the "doctor of the poor," he writes an account of the epidemic, *El cólera*. For his medical work, he earns a Legion of Honor medal from the French government.

LAWS. In California, legislation prohibits bullfights and cockfights, traditional forms of entertainment practiced by Californios. The legislation is often described as the "greaser laws," since it targets the people of Mexican-Spanish descent.

POLI. General Santa Anna, who has been ruling México on and off for nearly 20 years, is overthrown from office by liberal politicians led by an attorney named Benito Juárez. In México, he is tried in absentia for stealing funds from government and for a corrupt administration. He travels throughout Cuba, St. Thomas, and even the United States, waiting for the Mexican government to pardon him and allow him back.

REBE. Cuban-Venezuelan General Narciso López plans an invasion of Cuba in New Orleans. He sails from that port with 400 men, including American veterans of the Mexican War. The invaders land on the northern side of Cuba. They intend to set up a provisional government and call for the people to rebel against the Spanish. This strategy is imitated throughout Latin American in the 1800s and 1900s, with the United States often serving as headquarters for the conspirators.

WARS. William Walker and a force of nearly 200 men, some from the United States, defeat Nicaragua's army, embroiled in a civil war with conservative rebels, and conquer Granada, the Nicaraguan capital. Walker controls Nicaragua through a puppet president, and his government is recognized on May 20, 1856, by U.S. President Franklin Pierce. After naming himself president of Nicaragua, Walker recruits over 1,000 men to invade the countries of Costa Rica, Guatemala, El Salvador, and Honduras. A coalition is formed to defeat his army and on May 1, 1857, Walker surrenders to American authorities.

1857

CRIM. In July, criminals attack successful Mexican and Mexican-American businessmen and merchants involved in the transportation of goods from the port of Indianola to locations throughout Texas. This so-called "cart war" consists of acts of vandalism and physical violence against Mexicans. While Texans and the press refrain from commenting on the violence, the Mexican minister in Washington protests against the abuses. Texas governor Elisha M. Pease authorizes military protection for the Mexicans. The violence ends by the end of December.

POLI. In México, a liberal constitution is drafted by President Ignacio Comonfort and Vice President Benito Juárez. The constitution separates church from state, creating opposing forces in the process.

SLAV. A slave rebellion is uncovered in Texas. Many Mexicans associated with the slaves are told to return to México. Two hundred slaves are arrested and whipped, two are hanged, and two die as a result of the whipping.

WARS. In December, pro-Church Mexicans and pro-state Mexicans engage in a civil war. The conflict will last until 1861, draining the country of resources.

1858

BIRT. Miguel Antonio Otero, called "Gillie" by his friends, is born on October 17. He will serve as governor of New Mexico Territory from 1897 to 1906. The descendant of Spanish colonists who settled in New Mexico, his father was a politician and banker.

SETT. An unspecified number of Puerto Ricans and Cubans live on 13th Street in New York City, where there is a rich community of Spanish-speaking immigrants from México, South America, and Spain.

1859

REBE. On July 13, the Cortina War takes place in Brownsville, Texas, when Juan Nepomuceno Cortina, from a wealthy Mexican family, defends a Mexican who is being abused by a city marshal. Cortina shoots the marshal and rides out of town. On September 28, Cortina returns with 40 men, and shouting "Viva México," takes over Brownsville. A friend from Matamoros, in México, persuades Cortina to leave, and he retreats to the family ranch. On September 29, he issues a proclamation demanding that the rights of Mexican-Americans be recognized and that anyone abusing a Mexican-American should be punished.

1860

OBIT. On September 12, Honduras soldiers execute adventurer William Walker. Walker, 36, is the embodiment of the Manifest Destiny doctrine, which maintains it is the right of the United States to expand its border. During his lifetime Walker enjoyed popularity as a brave soldier. In the 1850s he served as self-appointed president of Nicaragua. He had attempted to expand the territory of the United States and to set up slavery states in Central America. Southerners called him "General Walker" and the "grey-eyed man of destiny." Northerners thought of him as a pirate.

1861

BIRT. Adina de Zavala is born on November 28. She will become a defender of the Alamo as a historical landmark, preventing the state government and private interests from demolishing the chapel and its surrounding walls. In the early twentieth century in Texas, she will be criticized for attempting to emphasize the role of the Spanish and of the Tejanos in the formation of San Antonio.

MILI. Cuban-born Loreta Janeta Velázquez, a supposed descendant of colonial governor Diego Velázquez, disguises herself as a man and joins the Confederate army. She fights in the first Battle of Bull Run on July 21, Ball's Bluff on October 21, Fort Donelson, February 13–16, 1862, and then becomes a Confederate spy. Though some historians will doubt her claims, Velázquez publishes a book about her exploits, *The Woman in Battle: A Narrative of the Exploits, Adventures and Travels of Madame Loreta Janeta Velázquez, Otherwise Known as Lieutenant Harry T. Buford, Confederate States Army*, published in 1876.

POLI. As a result of the Mexican civil war, México is essentially bankrupt. On July 17, Mexican President Benito Juárez stops making loan payments to Great Britain, France, and Spain. The three European nations agree to send troops to México to retrieve some of their money.

WARS. The American Civil War begins. On April 12, forces from the Confederacy attack Fort Sumter, held by Union Troops. During the war, over 10,000 Latinos will join the ranks of either the Union or the Confederate army. In May, Mexican folk hero Juan Nepomuceno Cortina, fighting on the side of the Union, attacks the city of Carrizo, in Texas, to drive confederate forces away. He is defeated and retreats into México.

1862

LAND. The Homestead Act is passed in Congress, allowing squatters, Americans living on Mexican land without paying for it, in the West to take ownership of land. Often, the lots are within ranches and farms owned by Mexican-Americans, who suddenly find themselves losing land and not being reimbursed for the acquisition.

1863

BIRT. On March 9, Puerto Rican poet and patriot Francisco Gonzalo Marín, known as Pachín Marín, is born. He will become one of the most romantic figures of the Spanish Caribbean, celebrated during the 1890s for his love of freedom and his dedication to the Cuban and Puerto Rican cause.

OBIT. On July 26, General Sam Houston dies of pneumonia in Huntsville, Texas. He was the first elected president of the Republic of Texas and is remembered for his defeat and capture of General Santa Anna during the battle of San Jacinto in 1836.

SLAV. In Spain, Puerto Rican patriot and intellectual Julio L. Vizcarrondo founds the Abolitionist Society to fight slavery. A branch is soon established in Puerto Rico.

WARS. On May 31, Benito Juárez and his cabinet retreat from México City and the French enter México. A provisional government is established and México is declared a Catholic Empire.

1864

MED. *La Voz de Puerto Rico* is the first Puerto Rican newspaper published in New York City.

POLI. Maximilian of Habsburg is crowned emperor of México by the provisional government.

1865

POLI. The American government protests the French occupation of México. The American navy blockades México to prevent any more arrival of French troops.

WARS. The American Civil War ends in April, freeing the United States to supply arms to the Mexicans in their war against French invaders.

1867

LIT. Alejandro Tapia y Rivera, one of Puerto Rico's greatest writers, writes a play entitled *La cuarterona*, a criticism of slavery and racial relations on the island.

OBIT. On June 19, Emperor Maximilian of México is executed by a firing squad.

POLI. Puerto Rican patriot Ramón Emeterio Betances arrives in New York City to meet with exiles from Latin American countries and promote Puerto Rico's independence from Spain.

SLAV. Segundo Ruíz Belviz writes an antislavery manifesto, *Proyecto para la abolición de la esclavitud en Puerto Rico*, Project for the Abolition of Slavery in Puerto Rico.

1868

LAWS. On July 9, the 14th Amendment is ratified, granting American citenzhip to Latinos born in the United States.

POLI. In Spain, a revolution overthrows Queen Isabella II and a new king, Amadeo of Savoy, is placed on the throne. The new Spanish government, confronting its own political uncertainties and battling dissent, responds to the requests from Cuba and Puerto Rico for autonomy and liberal reforms with harsh measures, which include increasing the power of the military, shutting down the press, outlawing political meetings, and increasing taxes and tariffs.

REBE. On September 23, Puerto Rican revolutionaries take over the town of Lares and raise a banner, the island's first flag. A provisional government is established, slavery is abolished, and a pile of the hated *libretas* are torched. As the rebels move on to another town, a Spanish militia surprises them. After a battle, the rebels are dispersed. Though the insurrection lasts one day, it indicates Puerto Rico's desire to break away from Spain. *El grito de Lares*, (the cry of Lares), as the rebellion is known, will become a national holiday in Puerto Rico and will be celebrated by Puerto Ricans in the United States into the twenty-first century. In Cuba, plantation owners in the province of Oriente begin their own rebellion on October 10 with an army of 12,000 men. The Cuban rebellion results in the writing of a constitution and the establishment of a House of Representatives.

1870

AGRI. The first bananas from Central America reach the United States.

MED. *La Azucena,* one of the first journals published in Latin America for women, appears in Puerto Rico. It is published and edited by Alejandro Tapia y Rivera.

1871

OBIT. José Antonio Navarro, one of Texas's earliest proponents of independence from México, dies on January 13. He was a state senator and in the 1830s had defied Santa Anna's rule over Texas, signing the state's Declaration of Independence. Navarro County, Texas, was named in his honor in 1846.

TRAN. Minor Keith, from Brooklyn, builds a railroad connecting the coast of the Caribbean with Costa Rica.

1872

OBIT. On July 18, Mexican President Benito Juárez dies while working at his desk at the presidential office. A Zapateca India, the only full Native America in México elected to the presidency, he defeated Emperor Maximilian and the French forces that invaded México in the 1860s. His progressive reforms helped to modernize México.

1874

BIRT. Arthur Schomburg is born on January 24 in San Juan, Puerto Rico, the son of a German father and St. Croix mother. The self-trained librarian and scholar will create the first archives to document African American history. His initial collection of 10,000 documents will grow to 5 million in the mid-twentieth century.

1875

BIRT. Gregorio Cortes is born on June 22 in Matamoros, México. He will become a Mexican folk hero when he is unjustly accused of killing a sheriff and is able to outrun hundreds of rangers chasing him across Texas.

LAWS. The U.S. Supreme Court rules that only the federal government has the right to regulate immigration.

POLI. On February 27, Romualdo Pacheco, a prominent Californian and state representative, is elected governor of California, the only Latino to serve that state in that capacity.

1876

CULT. The Ateneo Puertorriqueno is founded in San Juan to raise educational levels on the island, enrich cultural awareness, and affirm a Puerto Rican identity. Throughout the century, the majority of the island's major writers will become members of the Ateneo.

OBIT. General Antonio López de Santa Anna dies forgotten in México City. During his lifetime he was elected president on seven occasions. In the United States, he will be remembered as the villain who massacred the Alamo defenders.

POLI. Mexican war hero and congressman Porfirio Díaz appoints himself president of México on November 29.

SLAV. Slavery is abolished in Puerto Rico.

1877

CRIM. On October 10, disputes over the use of salt deposits in San Elizario, Texas, lead to the killing of attorney Luis Cardis by judge Charles Howard. The latter favored private use of the salt deposit; the former advocated public and free use of the salt. Angry Mexicans kill Howard on December 17 and attack his supporters. After a few days of looting by the Mexicans, the U.S. Ninth Cavalry, the black riders known as Buffalo Soldiers, restore peace.

1878

TREA. The Pact of El Zajón ends the 10 Years War between Cuba and Spain. The treaty grants freedom to all slaves who fought in the conflict and amnesty to the insurgents who fought at home or conspired from abroad. Many Cuban exiles in New York City use the amnesty to return to the island.

1880

AGRI. Puerto Rico produces 12 million pounds of tobacco leaves a year.

LIT. Cuban poet and patriot José Martí settles in New York City where he writes for the *New York Sun* and several Latin American newspapers. In his articles and essays, he tries to develop a political and cultural consciousness that reflects Latin America's needs and that is not influenced by U.S. politics. In these writings, Martí cautions Latin America against succumbing to the economic, cultural, and political influence of the United States.

POLI. Mexican President Porfirio Díaz leaves office on November 20 and promises not to run again, an empty claim he will make several times during his dictatorship.

1880–1890

LIT. Self-trained historian Hubert Howe Bancroft, with a team of supporters and friends, conducts extensive interviews of residents of Arizona, California, New Mexico, Texas, and Utah, among others, to write a history of the Southwest that includes Mexican-Americans. His volumes help to recapture the lives of Californios, Tejanos, and Mejicanos before the transfer of the territory to the United States. Some of his books are *History of Arizona and New Mexico* (1889), *History of California* (1884–1890), and *History of Nevada, Colorado, and Wyoming* (1890).

1882

LIT. *Cecilia Valdés o La Loma del Ángel: novela de costumbres cubanas* is published in New York City. The author, Cirilo Villaverde, has essentially dedicated his life to the writing of this book. Within the frame of an illicit love affair, *Cecilia Valdés* exposes the evil of slavery in Cuba. Villaverde first began the novel as a short story in 1839.

LIT. In Argentina *Recuerdos de viaje* (1882), by Eduarda Mansilla de García, is published. The travelogue describes America for Latin American readers. Based on the author's visit to the United States in the early 1860s, the volume describes racial conditions in the United States and the tension that led to the Civil War in 1861.

MEDI. Cuban doctor Carlos J. Finlay concludes that the dreaded yellow fever disease is transmitted from one person to another via a mosquito. He presents his findings in a study entitled *El mosquito hipotéticamente considerado como agente de transmisión de la fiebre amarilla* (The mosquito hypothetically considered the agent for transmission of yellow fever).

1884

POLI. On December 1, Porfirio Díaz is reelected president of México. He will rule as president until 1911.

1885

LIT. The publication of the novel *The Squatter and the Don*, by Maria Amparo Ruiz de Burton, is a landmark in the development of Mexican-American literature. The novel is the first published narrative to depict how Mexican-Americans become second-class citizens after the Alamo and the Mexican-American War of 1846.

1886

SETT. Ybor City is founded in Tampa by Cuban-Spanish tycoon Martínez Ybor, who creates it as a factory town for cigar makers. Other manufacturers of hand-rolled cigars follow Martínez Ybor and the area becomes the world's largest manufacturer of hand-rolled cigars.

SLAV. Slavery is abolished in Cuba.

1887

POLI. In Puerto Rico, the Autonomous Party is founded to negotiate autonomy from Spain.

1888

TRAD. As a result of the War of the Pacific, a bankrupt Perú signs a contract with W. R. Grace to administer shipping, develop jungle land, and export guano.

1889

LIT. The children's magazine, *La Edad de Oro*, published by José Martí, comes out in New York City. It is the first children's magazine published in the Spanish-speaking world.

1890

AGRI. Large cotton scale planting begins to replace cattle ranching in Texas, robbing many Mexican-Americans of a livelihood.

ARTS. In Ybor City-Tampa, Florida, Cuban and Spanish cigar makers invite traveling theater companies to perform plays in Spanish while also encouraging local talent to write and produce their own plays. Comedies and *zarzuelas*, Spanish operettas, are the preferred genres.

Birth of Ybor City, Florida

"The immigrant cigar workers settled onto a ninety-acre tract situated to the east of Tampa's small commercial center. This subdivision was owned by the Ybor City Land and Improvement Company, of which [Vincente Martínez] Ybor was president. Ybor City, as it was named, was annexed into the city limits in 1887. . . . Lying between Ybor City and the commercial center of Tampa was the African American settlement known as the Scrub, which increased greatly in size and density during the 1880s.

Well buffered from the heart of the host community, Ybor City developed into a relatively insular geographic enclave. Separatism was enhanced by the fact that the factory owners, as well as the workers, were foreigners. There were few pressures or incentives to 'Americanize.' Doctors, shopkeepers, and virtually everyone who had contact with each other in Ybor City spoke Spanish. Rarely was it necessary to go outside of the neighborhood."

Source: Susan D. Greenbaum. *More Than Black: Afro-Cubans in Tampa.* Gainesville: University Press of Florida, 2002, p. 61.

OBIT. On August 27, Tejano politician and Alamo defender Juan Nepomuceno Seguín dies in Nuevo Laredo, México. Seguín opposed Santa Anna's dictatorial rule and joined Texians in the revolt against the Mexican president. Sent as a courier to Gonzalez, Texas, he survived the attack on the Alamo and was the only Tejano to participate in the battle of San Jacinto, where Santa Anna was defeated by General Sam Houston. He served as mayor of San Antonio and was elected state senator of the Republic of Texas. Tensions between Texians and Tejanos forced him to México, where he joined the Mexican Army during the Mexican-American War. After the war, he returned to the United States but often traveled back and forth between México and the United States. He is the author of *Personal Memoirs of John N. Seguín* (1842).

MUSI. During the 1890s, French salon music known as "contre dance," a blend of African and Caribbean rhythms, Cuban ballroom dance, and Spanish zarzuelas, results in an early version of a dance that becomes known as tango. The sad and lilting tango music with its energetic and provocative acrobatic dance steps becomes popular with Italian and other immigrants in Argentina. In the 1920s, tango will become vogue in the United States as movie star Rudolph Valentino, an expert tango dancer, tours the country.

TRAN. On November 22 and December 10, leisure ships sail for Puerto Rico, where wealthy passengers can vacation during the holidays and the early winter. It is the beginning of the Caribbean region as a tourist destination for Americans.

1891

LAND. The Court of Private Land Claims is established to settle claims by Mexican-Americans whose lands have been taken by Americans after the Mexican War.

LIT. *Nuestra América*, Our America, by José Martí, is published in New York City. The collection of essays reveals the author's fascination with

life in the United States but also his preoccupation with America's growing imperial power. One of the essays contains the legendary line, "I have lived inside the monster and know its entrails," which radical Latinos in the United States and Latin American revolutionaries will often repeat in the 1960s and 1970s to criticize America's military involvement overseas.

REBE. José Martí travels to Tampa, where Cuban cigar workers embrace him as a leader and applaud his call to all Cubans, regardless of race, to fight as one against the Spanish. Money collected by the cigar workers helps fund the invasion of Cuba by Cuban forces in exile and on the island.

WARS. In Chile, civil war erupts on September 19.

Monument to José Martí in Ybor City, Tampa, Florida. The Cuban poet and patriot, who worked as a journalist in New York City, united black and white Cubans in the war against Spain.

The White Rose

Written in New York, José Martí's "La Rosa Blanca/The White Rose" is one of Cubans' favorite poems:

> Cultivo una rosa blanca,
> En julio como en enero,
> Para el amigo sincero
> Que me da su mano franca.
> Y para el cruel que me arranca
> El corazón con que vivo,
> Cardo ni ortiga cultivo:
> Cultivo la rosa blanca.
> A white rose I grow
> I grow it in January, grow it in June
> I grow it for a friend I know,
> Grow it for a friendship in bloom.
> And for my enemy, so cruel, so mean,
> So bent on tearing my heart,
> I do not grow thistles, sharp and lean,
> Instead, for him I grow a white rose.

Source: Luis Martínez Fernández, et al. *Encyclopedia of Cuba: People, History, Culture.* Westport, CT: Greenwood Press, 2003, p. 632. Poem translated by Danilo Figueredo.

1892

LIT. The novels *Hijo de la tempestad* and *Tras la tormenta la calma*, both by Eusebio Chacón, are published in Sante Fe in the newspaper *El Boletín Popular*. The works depict the lives of Mexican-Americans in the West.

POLI. Two hundred Puerto Ricans found the Borinquen Club in New York City. They seek autonomy from Spain.

REBE. In New York City, the poet and orator José Martí founds the *Partido Revolucionario Cubano*, Cuban Revolutionary Party, with the objectives of fighting for Cuban independence and establishing a republic on the island, as well as liberating Puerto Rico from Spanish rule.

1894

LIT. Puerto Rican writer Manuel Zeno Gandía publishes the internationally recognized novel, *La charca* (The Pond), to great acclaim. The novel depicts the oppression and poverty experienced by Puerto Ricans who work in the coffee plantations on the island.

SOCI. The Alianza Hispano-Americana is founded on January 14, 1894, in Tucson, Arizona, to offer life insurance at low rates and provide social and cultural activities to Mexican-Americans. This fraternal society, which spreads to Texas, also helps Mexican-Americans deal with discrimination and provides protection against racist activities of Americans in Arizona.

1895

POLI. On December 22, a group of Puerto Ricans meet in New York City to form the Puerto Rican section of the Cuban Revolutionary Party. Puerto Rican patriots promote independence from Spain and oppose annexation to the United States.

WARS. Cuba begins to wage a war of independence from Spain.

1895–1898

OBIT. José Martí, Cuba's beloved poet and patriot, is killed in action in Cuba while entering into combat for the first time. He is a symbol of patriotism, love of freedom, and equality for all.

POLI. On December 22, the Puerto Rican flag is first hoisted. The occasion is a meeting in New York City where 60 Puerto Ricans gather to advocate independence for their island and support of Cuba's war against Spain. For this reason, the Cuban and Puerto Rican flags bear similar designs; it is an indication of solidarity with the cause of freedom.

1897

OBIT. In November, Pachín Marín, Puerto Rican journalist, poet, and patriot, dies in the Cuban jungle where he has joined Cuban insurgents in the war against Spain. Too sick to travel and continue fighting, he asks to be left behind so as not to slow down his colleagues' retreat from Spanish forces. When the colleagues return to rescue him, they find him dead, holding on to his rifle. Numerous schools in Puerto Rico will be named after him in the twentieth century.

POLI. Puerto Ricans gain autonomy from Spain.

POLI. Miguel Antonio Otero becomes the governor of New Mexico. His father is a prominent politician. Governor Otero will also write several accounts of life in the American West.

TRAN. The American railroad man and financier Archer Harmar builds the railroad system that connects Guayaquil and Quito in Ecuador.

1898

CULT. In Puerto Rico, the Puerto Rican flag is used as a symbol to reaffirm Puerto Rican culture and to protest American presence on the island. In the United States, Americans, as reflected in such newspapers as the *Boston Globe,* prefer to call the island Porto Rico rather than Puerto Rico.

LIT. Methodist preacher José Policarpo Rodríguez publishes an autobiography titled *"The Old Guide": Surveyor, Scout, Hunter, Indian Fighter, Ranchman, Preacher: His Life in His Own Words.* The autobiography depicts frontier life as well as religious activities on the West Coast.

RACE. White Puerto Ricans notice that white American soldiers on the island do not salute black American soldiers. Black Puerto Ricans, who are not so overtly discriminated against by the Spanish, wonder if it would be better to remain under Spanish tutelage.

RELI. Spanish editions of the Protestant Bible, which has fewer Old Testament books than the Catholic Bible, are distributed throughout San Juan.

WARS. On February 15 the battleship USS Maine, anchored in Cuba to protect American lives and property during the island's war of independence, explodes, killing 266 of its crew. The United States accuses Spain of sabotage. The Americans rally to the Cuban cause, calling for revenge against Spain. In the mean time, the Spanish government claims its innocence. On April 25 President McKinley declares war against Spain. Over 125,000 young men volunteer for service. On July 25 American Marines land in southern Puerto Rico with plans to march to San Juan and occupy the island. On October 16, the Spanish leave the island and American forces officially take over the government.

1899

AGRI. Agriculture professor Fabian García experiments with planting methods that could lead to a standardized variety of chile and a faster way of growing the spice. The primary interest is achieving consistency in the growth of the pod by applying a uniform heat level. As a result of his work, New Mexico is capable of growing varieties of chile not available before, including greens, reds, jalapeños, and paprikas chile. His work will convert the chile industry, the predominant source of income for New Mexico.

OBIT. On January 23, José Antonio Romualdo Pacheco, Jr., the only Latino governor ever to

---

United Fruit Company's Occupation

"[T]he town had . . . become transformed into an encampment of wooden houses with zinc roofs inhabited by foreigners who arrived on the train from halfway around the world, riding not only on the seats and platforms but even on the roof of the coaches. The gringos, who later on brought their languid wives in muslin dresses and large veiled hats, built a separate town across the railroad tracks with streets lined with palm trees, houses with screened windows, small white tables on the terraces, and fans mounted on the ceilings, and extensive blue lawns with peacocks and quails. The section was surrounded by a metal fence topped with a band of electrified chicken wire which during the cool summer mornings would be black with roasted swallows."

Source: Gabriel García Márquez. *One Hundred Years of Solitude.* New York: Harper Perennial, 1970, p. 233.

---

serve California, dies in Oakland, California. Pacheco was also the first Latino representative to serve in Washington, D.C.

POLI. Luis Muñoz Rivera founds the Federalist Party in Puerto Rico while his compatriot José Celso Barbosa establishes the Republican Party.

POPU. Puerto Rico now has a population of 933,000.

SOCI. Sociedad La Unión Martí-Maceo, a mutual aid society, is founded by white and black Cubans in Tampa. Its primary purpose is to offer a place where Cuban men can socialize and play dominoes.

TRAD. On January 20, President William McKinley orders that Puerto Rico can only trade with the United States. The island is not allowed to trade with either Cuba or Spain, old trading partners.

TRAD. The merging of the Boston Fruit Company and the United Fruit Company (UFCO) forms the largest banana company in the world with plantations in Colombia, Costa Rica, Cuba, Jamaica, Nicaragua, Panama, and Santo Domingo. The company will have political influence on local affairs. In the twentieth century it will work with the United States to overthrow an elected government in Guatemala.

WARS. In July, liberals and conservatives in Colombia fight each other in a bloody civil war that will claim the lives of 60,000 to 130,000 men and women. The War of a Thousand Days, as it is known, will end in 1903 and will be depicted in the novel *One Hundred Years of Solitude*, written by Gabriel García Márquez in 1967.

TWENTIETH CENTURY

1900

LANG. In Tampa, a new expression evolves to describe Cubans who live in Tampa: *Tampeños*. The Tampeños will remain interested in developments on the island during the next century but prefer to stay in the United States. They attempt to speak Spanish and over the generations develop a stylized Spanish that has American inflection and uses of words in English.

LAWS. The Foraker Act establishes a civilian government in Puerto Rico. Puerto Ricans can now elect members of Puerto Rico's House of Parliament. The island's governor, however, is to be appointed by the U.S. president.

MUSI. Tejano music is slowly becoming popular and identifiable with Mexican-Americans from the Southwest. *Musica tejana* is the marriage of Mexican folk songs and Texas music that was influenced in the 1830s and 1840s by French, Irish, and German music, especially polkas and waltzes. It is a fast-paced dance that combines a two-step movement with the sideways swinging of bodies while holding hands. The musicians use accordions, 12-string guitars, and a drum.

RACE. Relationships between Puerto Ricans and Americans are strained. The former feels the latter are imposing American culture and the English language on them, evidenced by the transformation of the name of the island to "Porto Rico" and the promotion of an educational system based on the American model. Americans, on the other hand, feel superior to Puerto Ricans to the extent that an American senator tells a journalist that he just does not like Puerto Ricans. A distraught Luis Muñoz Rivera writes: "Within half a century, it will be a disgrace to bear a Spanish name."

SOCI. In Tampa, segregation laws force the black and white Cuban members of the mutual society Sociedad La Unión Martí-Maceo to separate and form two organizations, one for white and the other for black Cubans. La Union Marti-Maceo is for Afro-Cubans. The society offers medical aid and insurance at a time in Florida when such are not available to blacks.

1901

EDUC. On August 6, millionaire Andrew Carnegie funds the construction of the San Juan Public Library.

MED. Luis Muñoz Rivera publishes the first issue of the *Puerto Rican Herald* on July 13. Written in Spanish and in English, it is one of the first attempts at introducing bilingual news to Spanish and American readers. The newspaper will appear 152 times, ceasing publication in July 1904.

MIGR. An unspecified number of Puerto Ricans travel to Cuba, Hawaii, and the Dominican Republic: some to seek employment, some to escape what they see as an American invasion of the island.

MILI. The First Battalion of the U.S. Infantry in Porto Rico is formed on the island. Over 200 Puerto Ricans join.

A Tampeño cigar maker in Ybor City, Tampa, Florida. Tampeños—Cubans who live in Tampa—have developed a stylized form of Spanish that uses both Spanish and English expressions.

OBIT. On September 6, President William McKinley is shot by an assassin. He dies eight days later. The president was responsible for leading the Spanish-Cuban-American War, which brought the end of Spanish rule in the Americas.

POLI. Cubans approve a constitution. The United States inserts an amendment allowing for American intervention when deemed necessary by the United States. Known as the Platt Amendment, after its sponsor Senator Orville Platt, the legislation defines Cuba's relationship with the United States for the next three decades and influences how Cubans will view the United States for the rest of the twentieth century. Throughout Latin America, the Platt Amendment is seen as a symbol of American imperialism.

POLI. Puerto Rican politician Federico Degeteau is the first from the island to serve in the U.S. House of Representative as the Resident Commissioner of Puerto Rico, a non-voting office responsible for promoting and protecting Puerto Rican interests in Washington, D.C.

RACE. On June 12, a sheriff in Texas approaches Mexican vaqueros Gregorio and Ronaldo Cortez. The sheriff, who does not speak Spanish, uses a translator to question the Cortez brothers about recent horse robberies in the area. The translator is not well versed in Spanish and the ensuing miscommunication results in a fracas in which the sheriff wounds Ronaldo. Gregorio, in self-defense, kills the sheriff. Word spreads that Gregorio has murdered the sheriff in cold blood and a posse is formed. Cortez runs away and avoids capture for 10 days. In the meantime, American cowboys target Mexican-Americans in several small towns in Texas, and Texas newspapers demand the lynching of Cortez. When he is eventually arrested, Cortez is prosecuted in several towns. He serves in prison from 1904 until 1913, when the Texas governor pardons him. Cortez leaves the United States and joins the Mexican Revolution, where he dies of pneumonia on February 28, 1916.

WORK. The *Federación Libre de los Trabajadores*, representing Puerto Rican laborers, is affiliated with the American Federation of Labor, which for the first time accepts as members individuals not considered white. The labor negotiator responsible for the affiliation is Santiago Iglesias Pantín, who will become the island's Commissioner of Puerto Rico in Washington, D.C. in the 1930s.

1902

HEAL. Puerto Rican scientist Agustín Stahl works with American military officer Bailey K. Ashford on the discovery of a local tapeworm that causes anemia in thousands of Puerto Ricans.

LAND. As a result of the Treaty of Paris, which ended the Spanish-Cuban-American War, the public lands that belonged to Spain in Puerto Rico are now transferred to the United States.

MUSI. On April 22, Puerto Rican tenor Antonio Paoli holds a recital in New York City's Mendelssohn Hall where thousands, including many Puerto Ricans, give him a standing ovation. He is the first Puerto Rican singer to achieve international fame.

POLI. On May 20, Cuba's first president, Tomás Estrada Palma, takes office. U.S. military governor Leonard Wood announces the end of the occupation; his departure signals the inauguration of Cuba as a republic.

1903

EDUC. In March, 150 Puerto Rican students enroll at the newly founded University of Puerto Rico.

LAND. The United States sets up a naval base in Guantanamo, Cuba. The base will be an issue of conflict between dictator Fidel Castro and the Americans throughout much of the later twentieth century.

LIT. In Puerto Rico, the novel *Luz y sombra* is published. Written by feminist Ana Roque Duprey, the novel explores marriage and adultery. In the novel, Sara, the protagonist, is seduced by her best friend's husband. There are no consequences for the seducer, but Sara is shunned by Puerto Rican society. This is an early attempt to protest sexual discrimination on the island and, later on, in the United States, especially the treatment that Puerto Rican women will receive in the workplace in cities like New York.

MIGR. An unspecified number of Dominicans, mostly young, live on West 15th Street in New York City, some taking residences in boarding houses. Among those young people are three future scholars and sons of Dominican Republic President Dr. Francisco Henríquez y Carvajal—Fran, Max and Pedro Henríquez Ureña.

OBIT. On August 11, the Puerto Rican patriot and philosopher Eugenio María Hostos dies in the Dominican Republic, where he lived after the United States occupied Puerto Rico in 1898. Hostos had visited Washington to ask the president and the congress to grant independence to his island but had retired to the Dominican Republic upon the rejection of his request. Hostos fought alongside José Martí for the independence of Cuba and Puerto Rico during Cuba's war against Spain in the mid-1890s.

POLI. In Oxnard, California, 2,000 Mexican and Japanese beet workers go on strike and form a farm worker's union, which the American Federation of Labor refuses to recognize since the membership is non-European.

POLI. The Puerto Rican Republican Party joins the National Republic Party in January. The members of this party support statehood for Puerto Rico. It is the beginning of political tensions between those supporting statehood and those seeking independence.

REBE. Panama breaks away from Colombia with assistance from the United States. An American warship sails into port to lend support to the rebels, who call Panama a republic. The United States recognizes the new republic, much to Colombia's surprise, offering money to purchase the canal.

1904

EDUC. Five hundred Puerto Rican teachers travel to Cornell University and Harvard University to enroll in summer courses on American history, culture, and pedagogy.

LAWS. On January 5 the U.S. Supreme Court rules that Puerto Ricans are not aliens and can therefore travel to the United States without restrictions.

LIT. The short story, "The Caballero's Way," by O. Henry, appears in the anthology *Hearts of the West*. The short story introduces the Cisco Kid, modeled on Billy the Kid and Mexican vaqueros. The Cisco Kid is essentially portrayed as a trickster.

POLI. Luis Muñoz Rivera and José de Diego, both Puerto Rican poets, philosophers, and patriots, found the Partido Unionista de Puerto Rico to fight against the establishment of a colonial government on the island by the United States.

1905

TRAD. A Puerto Rican commerce department is set up in New York City to promote trade and capital investment on the island.

Where Do Puerto Ricans Belong?

"The American newspapers contain tales about persons who have forgotten who they are, their names, and where they live. The Puerto Ricans find themselves in the same predicament as those absent minded people. To what nationality do they belong? What is the character of their citizenship? . . . [Mrs. González], native born Puerto Rican, came from San Juan to New York. She was forbidden to land, the reason allegedly being that she was an 'alien' and that she was liable to become a public charge. . . . The U.S. Circuit Court . . . declared that Mrs. González was a 'foreigner.' . . . The U.S. Supreme Court . . . decided that [she] could land but that the Puerto Ricans were neither Americans nor foreigners. . . . It left the nationality of Puerto Ricans in suspense, and it continues to be in suspense."

Source: Cardona, Luis Antonio. *A History of the Puerto Ricans in the United States of America.* Bethesda, MD: Carreta Press, 1995, p. 146.

1906

BIRT. Lucille Ball is born on August 6. With her Cuban husband Desi Arnaz she will pioneer innovative ways of filming and producing television programs in the 1950s. She and her husband will become the first multicultural couple on American television.

POLI. President Teddy Roosevelt embarks on a tour of Panama and Puerto Rico. He is the first American president to travel outside the United States in such capacity. In Puerto Rico, Roosevelt delivers a speech advocating American citizenship for Puerto Ricans.

1907

BIRT. On February 15, Cesar Romero is born in New York City, the son of a concert pianist, and the grandson of Cuban patriot and poet José Martí. In the 1930s, Romero will become a Hollywood icon as the tall, dark, and handsome Latin Lover. As an older man, he will enchant a generation of television watchers as the villainous Joker in the popular *Batman* series of the mid-1960s.

TRAN. The New York Porto Rico Steamship Company runs five ships between New York and San Juan. Four ships bear the names of Puerto Rican cities: Camoa, Carolina, Ponce, and San Juan.

1908

CULT. The image of the banana republic is being formed in Central America, where nations are known for the production of one crop whose cultivation and exportation is administered by the United Fruit Company. Part of the image includes constant political turmoil as one dictator overthrows another, usually with support of the United Fruit Company. The company itself builds towns for its American workers, fostering separation from the local laborers and encouraging Americans to feel superior to them.

SPOR. José Méndez, who plays for the New York Giants, shuts out the Cincinnati Reds over a period of two weeks and several games. When he walks into a restaurant, fans stand up to applaud him. Known as "Cuba's Black Diamond," José Méndez is the first Latino baseball legend.

1909

WARS. In Nicaragua, dictator José Santos Zelaya negotiates with Germany and Japan for the construction of a canal, an action in direct competition with the construction of the Panama Canal. Unhappy with Zelaya, the United States supports a conservative rebellion against the dictator and sends 400 Marines to help in the effort.

1910

MED. On December 8 the first issue of the newspaper *Porto Rico Progress* is published in San Juan, aimed at American readers.

MIGR. With the onset of the Mexican Revolution, middle-class Mexicans near the border flee to the American Southwest, an area they call "México de afuera," akin to "México in exile." Other Mexican exiles of less economic means follow, finding employment in industry, mines, and agriculture.

POPU. There are 30,000 Mexicans in Arizona, 32,500 in California, 11,000 in New Mexico, and 125,000 in Texas. Some are new arrivals and others are long-term residents.

WARS. On November 10, the Mexican Revolution begins when Francisco Madero, a well-to-do teacher, calls for Mexicans to rise against the dictatorship of Porfirio Díaz. Guerrilla warfare rages across the nation. One of the rebel leaders is Pancho Villa, a former bandit turned revolutionary.

1911

CULT. The exploits of the daring Pancho Villa capture the American imagination. In the process a stereotype is created: the *bandido*. This individual wears a *sombrero*, has a drooping mustache, laughs easily, and is treacherous by nature. The bandido is always dark-skinned. In the next few decades, there will be variations of the type, but generally the Mexican bandido will be portrayed as either a villain or a useless fool.

RACE. When two Cuban baseball players, Armando Marsans and Rafael Almeida, join the Cincinnati Reds in April, fans complain of the presence of the dark-skinned players on the team.

WARS. Francisco Madero returns to México and joins Pancho Villa's forces in February. In southern México, the revolution is conducted by rebel leader Emiliano Zapata. U.S. President William Taft puts American warships on standby in the Gulf of México. Porfirio Díaz signs a truce with the rebels on May 21 and Francisco Madero assumes the presidency.

1912

POLI. Ladislas Lázaro is elected to the U.S. House of Representatives, representing Louisiana. He is the first Latino from that state to serve in Congress.

POPU. It is believed that anywhere from 1,500 to 3,000 Puerto Ricans live in New York City. They are students, merchant mariners, and dock workers, among other trades.

RELI. The New York City Mission Society establishes a Spanish branch in Manhattan to reach Puerto Ricans and Spanish-speakers. The Mission provides educational programs in Spanish and English.

RELI. *La Primera Iglesia Evangélica Española* opens its doors to serve Puerto Rican parishioners in New York City.

1913

MED. In February, the daily *La Prensa* is founded in Texas by Ignacio Lozano to service the Mexican-American community of San Antonio. The daily publishes news about the Mexican Revolution as well as developments in the United States. Lozano sets up his own newsstands to deliver the paper, and within a couple of years he is shipping the daily to major cities in the United States. Lozano also sets up a bookstore to sell books in Spanish, popular novels, and self-help volumes.

WARS. The Mexican Revolution becomes a civil war. President Francisco Madero is opposed by Former Díaz's supporters and other factions who consider the new president too liberal and inefficient. After 10 days of fighting the president is arrested and executed. General Victoriano Huerta assumes the presidency. In the north of México, a Constitutional Army forms to oppose Huerta. The United States joins the fray by landing Marines in Veracruz.

1914

ARTS. A silent film adaptation of O. Henry's short story, "The Caballero's Way," introduces the Cisco Kid to American audiences. The role is played by an actor from New York, Herbert Stanley Dunn, who has a short career in Hollywood. The film will prove popular and inspire a television series.

ARTS. Essanay studios, a movie company owned by western star Bronco Billy Anderson, releases the film *Bronco Billy and the Greaser*, the latter term referring to the Mexican villain. *The Greaser*, another western with a Mexican as the villain, is also released. Hundreds of films will follow with the Mexican bandido character as the villain.

BIRT. Julia de Burgos is born on February 17 in Santa Cruz, Puerto Rico. Raised in a poor but literate family, she will be introduced to the Spanish classics by her father and will demonstrate an early talent for writing. In 1938, she will write one of the most moving poems in Puerto Rican literature, "Río Grande de Loíza," a tribute to the countryside colored with the awareness that one day she will be torn away from it. Her sentiment will be shared by her compatriots in places like New York City.

BIRT. On April 8, Mexican actress María Felix is born in Alamos, México. She will become México's most famous actress, and her physical beauty will be celebrated by composers and artists. A favorite of Latinos in the United States, she will not be known by Anglo audiences since she works in the French, Italian, and Mexican film industries.

MED. The Spanish daily *La Prensa* begins publishing in New York City.

TRAN. On January 7, the Panama Canal is completed. The Canal opens for service on August 14. Ships can now cross from the Atlantic to the Pacific, and vice versa, without having to sail around the furthermost tip of South America.

WARS. World War I erupts on January 28 after the assassination of Archduke Franz Ferdinand, heir to the Austria-Hungarian Empire. The assassin is from Serbia. Austria-Hungary declares war on Serbia. Eventually Belgium, France, Great Britain, Italy, Japan, Montenegro, Portugal, Romania, Russia, Serbia, and the United States will join forces against Austria-Hungary, Bulgaria, Germany, and the Ottoman Empire.

WARS. On July 20, Mexican President Huerta, no longer able to finance the war against his opposition, leaves México. On August 15, the Constitutional Army marches into México City.

1915

ARTS. W. Griffith films *The Martyrs of the Alamo*, the first feature about the Alamo. The Mexicans are depicted stereotypically. It is the first of more than a dozen films on the subject, with Mexicans often portrayed as treacherous and cowardly.

LIT. The publisher of the Texas newspaper *El paso del norte* serializes a novel about the Mexican Revolution, *Los de abajo*. Written by a physician, Mariano Azuela, this is the first novel about the conflict and one of the best studies of the revolutionary process in world literature. The novel creates a new genre in literature: the novel of the Mexican Revolution.

LIT. Newspaper publisher Ignacio Lozano establishes a publishing house, *La Casa Editorial Lozana*, to publish history tomes, popular novels, and biographies of Mexican figures.

MIGR. About 82,000 Mexicans flee the violence and chaos of the Mexican Revolution, crossing the border into the United States.

WARS. Mexican rebel Venustiano Carranza assumes the nation's presidency on May 1.

1916

OBIT. Luis Muñoz Rivera dies of cancer on November 15. He is the father of future governor of Puerto Rico Luis Muñoz Marín. Muñoz Rivera had successfully convinced Spain to grant Puerto Rico autonomy just before the outbreak of the Spanish-Cuban-American War. In 1910, he was elected Resident Commissioner of Puerto Rico. Muñoz Rivera was also a poet.

POLI. President Woodrow Wilson prohibits elections in Puerto Rico, preventing the Unión de Puerto Rico party from voting against the granting of American citizenship to Puerto Ricans, which is being discussed in the U.S. Congress. President Wilson himself favors American citizenship for Puerto Ricans.

POLI. Ezequiel Cabeza de Baca, a descendant of a prominent Spanish-Mexican family with commercial and political influence in New Mexico, is elected governor but dies shortly after taking office. His replacement is Octaviano A. Larrazolo, a Mexican native.

WARS. In México, President Venustiano Carranza, representative of the middle class, faces rebellions lead by Pancho Villa and Emiliano Zapata, supporters of land distribution and economic opportunities for peasants and Indians. Upset with the support the United States is offering Carranza, Pancho Villa conducts a raid against Americans in the border town of Columbus, New Mexico, killing several citizens. General John J. Pershing, with permission from Carranza, crosses the border with his troops in a futile search for the Mexican rebel. In the state of Morelos, Zapatas organizes his own government, supported by an army of farmers, peasants, and Indians that is 20,000 strong.

1917

BIRT. On March 22 Desiderio Alberto Arnaz y de Acha III is born into a wealthy family in Santiago de Cuba, Cuba. He will become famous as Desi Arnaz in Hollywood, where with his wife, the actress Lucille Ball, he will pioneer a filming and producing style that will lead to the creation of the television situation comedy, or "sitcom."

LAWS. In February, the Immigration Act of 1917 is approved by Congress. The act requires literacy for all immigrants.

OBIT. Puerto Rican scientist Dr. Agustín Stahl dies on July 12. He wrote numerous treatises on the island's zoology and diseases affecting the sugar cane. He was the first to treat leukemia on the island and was co-discoverer, with Bailey K. Ashford, of an endemic tapeworm that caused anemia in Puerto Ricans.

POLI. On March 2 President Woodrow Wilson signs into law the Jones Act, which grants American citizenship to Puerto Ricans on the island. The new law gives the island more power over local matters and creates a Puerto Rican Senate and House of Representatives. The Jones Act permits Puerto Ricans to travel back and forth between the United States and Puerto Rico without documents and makes Puerto Ricans subject to the military draft. The Puerto Rican Félix Córdova Dávila serves as the Resident Commissioner of Puerto Rico in Washington, D.C. His task is to assure that the same benefits and protection that apply to Americans on the mainland are applied to Puerto Ricans on the island.

POLI. In México, the constitution of 1917 is approved by President Venustiano Carranza. The constitution bans foreign ownership of land near the border and reserves mineral mine rights for Mexicans only, fostering conflicts and disagreements between the United States and México in the area of international commerce.

SOCI. *La Liga Femenina Puertorriqueña* is founded in Puerto Rico by Ana Roque de Duprey to obtain voting rights for literate women on the island.

WARS. In February, the tsarist regime of Russian is overthrown and replaced with a provisional government, consisting of liberals and progressives. On November 7, Vladimir Lenin leads Bolsheviks into a rebellion that succeeds in overthrowing the provisional government. Lenin advocates the end of capitalism and a world revolution led by workers. His agenda for social change will influence dozens of leaders and intellectuals in Latin America, including Fidel Castro of Cuba, and Daniel Ortega, from Nicaragua. The muralist Diego Rivera will render tribute to Lenin in his paintings.

WARS. Eighteen thousand Puerto Ricans are serving in the American armed forces.

1918

BIRT. On June 4, Puerto Rican composer Noel Estrada is born. He will write one of Latin America's most famous boleros, "En Mi Viejo San Juan."

POLI. José de Diego, member of the Puerto Rican House of Representatives, asks President Wilson to allow the island the right to self-rule.

WARS. The Porto Rico ship Carolina is torpedoed by a German U-boat on June 15. Most of the passengers survive but the ship's cargo, consisting of sugar and tropical fruits, is lost.

WARS. On November 11, World War I ends.

WORK. More than 10,000 Puerto Ricans travel to the United States to work during the labor shortage of World War I. It is the beginning of a pattern that will persist until the twenty-first century: Puerto Ricans traveling to the mainland to seek better economic opportunities. The U.S. Department of Labor draws up plans to transport up to 50,000 Puerto Ricans to work in agriculture and maintenance in the South and Southwest.

1919

BIRT. On October 19, Puerto Rico's best known playwright, René Marqués, is born in Arecibo, Puerto Rico. A poet and short-story writer, his drama *La carreta* will characterize the hard life Puerto Ricans encounter when they leave the island for New York City. The play will become a classic of the genre known as immigrant literature.

LIT. The popular character Zorro is introduced in the short story, "The Curse of Capistrano," published in the magazine *All Story* and written by Johnston McCulley. The character is inspired by the hero of the novel, *Scarlet Pimpernel* (1909). He is a fumbling aristocrat who is in reality a daring swashbuckler who rescues noblemen and women from the guillotine in Paris during the French Revolution. Many readers and movie watchers through the century will incorrectly assume that Zorro is based on an actual Mexican or Californio personage. The story is set in the California of the Spanish empire of the 1820s.

MILI. Luis Esteves, the first Puerto Rican to graduate from West Point, founds Puerto Rico's National Guard. After three years guarding the Panama Canal, the Porto Rican Regiment of Infantry, formed in 1899, returns to the island. Over 600 Puerto Ricans serve in the regiment.

POLI. On February 11, the Puerto Rican Commissioner in Washington D.C., Félix Córdova Dávila, pushes Congress to decide whether Puerto Rico should be granted statehood or independence.

POLI. At Harvard University, law student Pedro Albizu Campos, from Puerto Rico, becomes interested in the independence movement in India as well as Irish independence from England. A polyglot, he is offered a position within the U.S. State Department and the U.S. Supreme Court but prefers to return to Puerto Rico.

POLI. A monumental statute of Simón Bolívar is unveiled in Central Park.

RELI. In Cuba, the murder of a young girl panics parents who are told the crime is part of a *Santería* religious ceremony. A congressman suggests legislation to outlaw the practice of Santería.

SOCI. On June 20, the charter for the League of Nations is signed. It is hoped that the international body will help countries negotiate conflicts rather than get into the type of confrontation that brought about World War I. Eventually, the league will reshape itself into the United Nations.

SPOR. Cuban Adolfo Luque is the first Latino player to appear in a World Series game. He pitches one inning of relief for the Cincinnati Reds.

Discrimination in Baseball

"In the majors Luque endured being the butt of many racial epithets, including being called a "Cuban nigger," to which he responded with murderous beanballs. Once, while pitching for Cincinnati, Luque charged the Giants' bench and punched Casey Stengel on the jaw because he had heard invectives coming from this direction."

Source: Roberto González Echevarria. *The Pride of Havana: A History of Cuban Baseball.* New York: Oxford University Press, 1999, p. 145.

WARS. To end the fighting in México, President Carranza coaxes Pancho Villa into retirement with monetary rewards, but orders the execution of Emiliano Zapata, who refuses to stop fighting. Eighty years later, Indians from the region will rise against the Mexican government, calling themselves Zapatistas. On campuses across the United States in the 1960s and 1970s, Zapata's portrait will adorn dorms and student centers as a symbol of protest against capitalism and racism and a romantic icon of revolutionary movements.

WORK. Nearly 100 Puerto Rican laborers on an Arkansas farm die as result of malnutrition, cold weather, and poor living conditions in the migrant's camp.

1920

ARTS. The silent film *The Mark of Zorro* is released. It becomes an international sensation that spawns dozens of versions and sequels. Douglas Fairbanks portrays the aristocratic Don Diego de la Vega, a Californio, whose alter ego is the dashing Zorro, a Robin Hood type who aids peasants and laborers oppressed by a dictatorial *alcalde*, or mayor.

LIT. La Casa Editorial Lozano, in Texas, publishes a series of novels about the Mexican Revolution, helping to popularize in the United States the emerging genre of *Novela de la Revolución Mexicana*, novels of the Mexican Revolution. The novels depict realistic battle scenes, explore the numerous political views expressed by opposing forces in the war, and draw complex characters who are neither heroic nor villainous but simply soldiers caught in the passion of war.

MIGR. By the beginning of the 1920s, over 173,000 Mexicans have crossed the U.S.–México border into the Southwest.

POLI. In Puerto Rico, Antonio R. Barceló, president of the Puerto Rican Senate, urges the American government to grant self-rule to Puerto Rico. Politician Santiago Iglesias Pantín, from the *Partido Socialista Puertorriqueño*, is elected to the Puerto Rican Senate, the first socialist to hold such post.

POPU. It is estimated that over 11,000 Puerto Ricans are living in the United States, especially in East Harlem, New York City, though there is no exact count.

SPOR. During the decade of the 1920s the New York and Porto Rico Line travels weekly from New York to San Juan and back, bringing tourists to the island for winter vacations. The company serves white middle-class Puerto Ricans. The steamship company tries not to mix passengers of diverse ethnicities during lunch and dinner. First-class fare is about $50.

WARS. In México City, President Carranza is assassinated on May 21. On December 21, General Alvaro Obregón assumes the presidency of México.

1920–1930

ARTS. Spanish theaters proliferate in California, New York, and Texas with about 40 sites staging productions in Spanish. Traveling companies from Latin America and Spain tour such cities as Los Angeles, New York, and San Antonio. However, local productions are just as popular. Mexican-American playwright Adalberto Elías González achieves celebrity status with the numerous dramas he writes. His most popular work, *Los amores de Ramona*, is a staging of the novel *Ramona,* by Helen Hunt Jackson, about a *misteza* in love with an Indian chief. Staged in 1927, the drama attracts an audience of 15,000. The playwright will later move to Hollywood to work as a scriptwriter.

ARTS. In New York City, comedies and variety shows prove popular. Based on a Cuban art form known as *teatro bufo*, a combination of blackface farce and vaudeville, Spanish-speaking audiences in Manhattan enjoy works that feature Afro-Cuban music and slapstick comedy with a hint of sexuality. In Ybor City, the productions tend to address such social issues as poverty and racism.

1920–1950

LANG. The term "Latin" goes into popular usage, to identify Latinos. The word alludes to the linguistic roots of Spanish and all romance languages. "Latin" also is short for "Latin American." The term does not connote dark-skinned Puerto Ricans or mestizos from México; rather, it suggests a European connection. It also brings to mind the Hollywood Latin lover that is in vogue: tall, dark, and handsome. Latin is connected to a type and not a particular country. Latinos who want to avoid discrimination use the term "Latin" to identify themselves in public. The expression "Hispanic" is also being used in some areas of the country. Unlike Latin, Hispanic refers to ancient Hispania, Spain, and the Spanish language. It is an English word created for English-speakers. "Hispano," used in the Spanish-speaking world, refers to a person from Latin America. In the United States, "Hispano" is used in the Southwest by people of Spanish descent whose ancestors participated in the conquest of the territory during the 1500s.

1921

ARTS. Hollywood releases the film *The Four Horsemen of the Apocalypse*, based on the popular novel by Spanish author Vicente Blasco Ibáñez. The role of the Argentine protagonist is played by Rudolph Valentino, thus introducing the dashing image of the Latin lover: tall, dark, handsome, ready to rescue a damsel in distress. The creation of this type would soon allow several Latino performers to play such roles. As a result of the film, the tango, in its dance form, becomes popular in the United States. In the film, Valentino performs a tango. Afterwards, the actor tours the country, performing as a tango dancer.

CULT. In México, writer and philosopher José Vasconcelo recruits artists to develop a type of art that is evocative of México's mixed ethnic compositions. Some of the artists he hires include muralist José Clemente Orozco, Diego Rivera, and David Alfaro Siqueiras. Vasconcelo is also a promoter of a racial concept in which he sees all people from Latin America united by the brilliancy of ancient civilizations and a spirituality based on native traditions and the mixing of African, Latin American, Native American, and Spanish blood.

His idea of *la raza* will foster political and cultural bonding for Mexican Americans in the United States in the 1960s and 1970s.

EDUC. The American governor of Puerto Rico, E. Mont Reily, proposes the elimination of Spanish in school curricula on the island, advocating for English as the language of instruction.

POLI. On February 27, the chairperson of the Committee on Insular Affairs, Horace M. Tower, informs Puerto Rican senator Antonio R. Barceló that promotion of independence for Puerto Rico can damage relationships between the United States and the island. On July 30, the American governor of Puerto Rico, E. Mont Reily, urges statehood for the island. Furthermore, he states that he will not appoint to political or official positions any Puerto Rican who promotes independence.

SOCI. *The Orden Hijos de América* is founded in Corpus Christie, Texas, to ensure that the rights of Mexican Americans are not violated and to help Mexican Americans seek better economic and educational opportunities.

1922

MED. A Puerto Rican weekly called *El Caribe* begins publication. The periodical is funded by the Porto Rican Democratic Club.

POLI. The U.S. Supreme Court declares that Puerto Rico is an American territory and that the U.S. Constitution does not apply to Puerto Rico.

POLI. On January 19, the U.S. House of Representative introduces a bill promoting autonomy for Puerto Rico and allowing Puerto Ricans to elect their own governor. A second bill introduces the creation of a Free Associated State.

POLI. In Puerto Rico, the Partido Nacionalista is founded with the objective of seeking independence from the United States.

SOCI. The first Puerto Rican society created to aid Puerto Ricans is founded in a barbershop in New York City on June 4. It is called the Porto Rican Democratic Club.

1923

OBIT. On July 23, Pancho Villa is assassinated while riding in his car in Chihuahua. To Mexican-Americans, Villa will become a folk hero, a symbol of the struggle against oppression.

1924

IMMI. The Immigration Act of 1924 favors immigration from Europe. People coming from Latin America and Spain are grouped together under the quotas assigned to Spain.

MEDI. *The Daily Worker*, the official organ of the Communist Party, appears. The publication carries a column by Puerto Rican social observer Jesús Colón who writes about Puerto Ricans in New York, racial discrimination, and social oppression. His columns address a general reader; written with wit and humor, the pieces are critical of the United States. In the 1960s, Colón, a self-taught intellectual, will be considered the father of the Nuyorican movement, referring to Puerto Ricans who live or have spent most of their lives in New York and who tend to identify more with social issues in the United States than on the island.

SOCI. The Puerto Rican Brotherhood of America is founded in Manhattan. It is a self-help organization that advocates the union of all Puerto Rican organizations in New York City in order to address discrimination, labor disputes, and educational opportunities.

1925

IMMI. The Border Patrol is created by Congress. It is given the right to search and detain Mexican immigrants crossing the border.

LIT. The book, *La raza cósmica*, by the Mexican intellectual Jose Vasconcelos is published. Vasconcelos maintains that the people from the New World have in their veins the blood of all the world's races.

POLI. Gerardo Machado is elected president of Cuba. He will soon turn into a dictator and will remain in power until 1933.

POLI. In New York City, Puerto Ricans favor mayoral candidate Jimmy Walker, a Democrat. This is a pattern that will become characteristic of the political profile of Puerto Ricans in the United States, who favor the Democratic Party.

1926

ARTS. The film *Ben Hur*, a biblical epic, is released to great acclaim. The leading star is Ramon Navarro, a native of Durango, México, whose family has escaped the Mexican Revolution. Navarro will play the Latin lover in numerous films and will become one of the first Latino superstars of the twentieth century. As Navarro ages in the late 1940s and early 1950s, producers look for substitutes, hiring such young performers as Ricardo Montalban, from México, and Fernando Lamas, from Argentina.

BIRT. On August 13, Fidel Castro is born into a well-to-do family. He leads a life of privilege and attends some of Cuba's best private schools. Three decades later, he will change Cuba by establishing a Communist regime and the longest-lasting dictatorship in Latin America.

MED. Ignacio Lozano founds the Spanish daily, *La Opinión*, in Los Angeles to address the

---

The Other: The Latin Lover

"There was a bit of the sinister to the Latin lover, suggestive of something darker and mysterious. As sexually desirable as the Latin lover was, he was still the other, the outsider, as far as Americans knew. It was no accident that in Latin America the type didn't exist."

Source: D. H. Figueredo. *The Complete Idiot's Guide to Latino History and Culture.* New York: Alpha Books, 2002, p. 213.

Cuban Chess Genius

"One of the legendary grandmasters of chess was José Raúl Capablanca . . . who won some of his greatest triumphs while he lived in New York City. A graduate of Columbia University, he made his first mark in chess circles in 1909, when at the age of twenty he defeated U.S. champion Frank Marshall at the Manhattan Chess Club, in New York. Over the next few years he lived in Cuba and New York, where he won several tournaments between 1913 and 1919. Beginning in 1916, he went eight straight years without losing a game. He won the World Championship in Havana in 1921, when he defeated Emmanuel Lasker of Germany. . . . Chess players today continue to study the games of the Cuban master, who has been called the greatest natural chess genius of all time."

Source: Alex Anton and Roger E. Hernández. *Cubans in America: A Vibrant History of a People in Exile.* New York: Kensington Books, 2002, pp. 111–12.

information and cultural needs of the growing Mexican population in that city.

POPU. The Puerto Rican Brotherhood of America estimates that 100,000 Puerto Ricans make New York City their home. It is estimated that Puerto Ricans own about 200 *bodegas*, grocery stores, and 125 small restaurants.

RACE. In Harlem, Puerto Ricans and white and other ethnic groups fight against each other as opposition grows to the Puerto Rican presence in the neighborhoods.

RELI. The first Catholic church for Puerto Ricans is opened in New York City; it is called the Milagrosa.

SOCI. On August 8, the Latin League is founded in New York City with the objective of seeking cooperation and cordiality with Puerto Ricans and other ethnic groups in the city. A particular concern is the rivalry between Spanish grocery store owners and Jewish merchants, each accusing the other of not supporting their businesses based on ethnic and national preferences.

SPOR. Cuban chess champion José Raul Capablanca, who has not lost a game since 1916, participates in a sextangular tournament in New York City, beating all six opponents. In 1942, he

will die of a brain hemorrhage at the Manhattan Chess Club while watching a chess match.

1927

OBIT. On March 30, Louisiana representative Ladisla Lázaro dies in office in the U.S. House of Representatives, where he first served in 1912. Lazaro was reelected seven times. In 1919 he wanted to amend the law on national prohibition before it went into effect, allowing for the medical use of alcohol. He was prophetic in his contention that the proposed prohibition amendment was too difficult to enforce.

POLI. Luis Muñoz Marín, the president of the Puerto Rican Senate, arrives in New York City to promote capital investment on the island. He promises tax-free business opportunities and land grants to companies interested in relocating or setting branches on the island.

WORK. A union for Mexican-American agricultural workers is formed under the name of *Confederación de Uniones Obreras Mexicanas*. It has 3,000 members and 20 local branches.

1928

ARTS. Dolores del Rio, born in Durango, México, plays the lead in the film version of the popular novel *Ramona*, written by Helen Hunt

Jackson, a story of forbidden love between a mestiza and an Indian chief. Del Rio brings beauty, elegance, and dignity to the role, but she remains the "other," an exotic object of desire for clean-cut American protagonists.

BIRT. Cultural icon Ernesto "Che" Guevara is born in Argentina on June 14. He will become symbolic of the Latin American rebel who sacrifices everything for his ideals.

BIRT. Mexican-American tennis legend Pancho González is born on May 8 as Ricardo Alonso González.

MUSI. RCA Victor releases three recordings of Merengue music, the popular dance from the Dominican Republic. Merengue will become a favorite dance in New York City in the 1930s and 1940s. Again, in the 1960s, the dance will be regularly played in Latino clubs and parties and by the 1970s it will be considered the musical rival of *salsa*. The merengue dance emerged on slave plantations in the 1800s, where slaves imitated the way white planters performed ballroom dancing.

OBIT. On July 12, Mexican pioneer aviator Emilio Carranza dies in a plane crash in the Pine Barrens of New Jersey. A friend of Charles Lindbergh, Carranza is attempting a non-stop flight from New York City to México City. He was an early promoter of the plane as a tool for transatlantic and transnational commerce and tourism. In 1933, thousands of children in México collect money so that a monument can be erected on the spot where Carranza died in a desolate area in New Jersey.

WARS. Mexican President Alvaro Obregón is assassinated on July 17 by a seminary student who opposes the president's anticlerical positions. Emilio Portes Gil, Minister of the Interior, assumes the office of interim president for the next two years.

WORK. The *Confederación de Uniones Obreras Mexicanas* goes on strike in California's Imperial Valley. The strike ends when many of the 3,000 union members are arrested and deported to México.

1929

ECON. On October 27, the U.S. economy crashes. The Great Depression is a global economic recession that will last until 1941. It causes bank failures and high unemployment, as well as drops in industrial production and in the value of shares in the stock market. In Cuba, the Great Depression ushers in a period of social unrest as sugar-cane workers find themselves employed only two months out of the year, as a result of a 60 percent drop in sugar production; one million workers are unemployed, out of a population of 3.9 million; and the majority of Cubans live on a salary of $300 a year. In Puerto Rico, most banks close their doors and farmers claim bankruptcy. In Central America, banana exports drops to near zero, causing political instability.

LIT. The novel *Las aventuras de Don Chipotes o cuando los pericos mamen,* by Daniel Venegas, is published and sold in Los Angeles. It is the story of a picaresque Mexican who travels throughout the United States, looking for work and adventure. The novel is first serialized in small newspapers in Los Angeles. The novel, written in the vernacular of working-class Mexicans living in the United States who do not adhere to Spanish grammatical rules and vocabulary, is also the beginning of Chicano literature, a genre that early on is meant for Mexican-Americans who live in the United States and who defy American influence and values. Chicano literature emphasizes the lot of poor Mexican-Americans.

MUSI. Puerto Rican composer Rafael Hernández finishes the song *Lamento Borincano*, which tells the story of a poor Puerto Rican peasant who has a difficult time making a living and providing for his family. The song celebrates the beauty of Puerto Rico but also laments economic and political conditions on the island. Performed the world over, *Lamento* is considered the island's second anthem.

Puerto Rico's Beautiful Lament

His lament is heard everywhere;
As the sad Puerto Rican farmer walks,
Crying out on the road:
What would become of Borinquen
My Dear God!
What would become of my children
And my home!

POLI. Teddy Roosevelt, Jr. is the new governor of Puerto Rico. He speaks in Spanish to an audience in San Juan, the first American governor to do so. He promotes education, good health, and prosperity for all Puerto Ricans.

SOCI. On May 18 in Corpus Christi, Texas, the first General Convention of the League of United Latin American Citizens, LULAC, is called to order, signaling the beginning of an organization that will champion the rights of Latinos throughout the twentieth century. LULAC will establish chapters in Puerto Rico, México, and South America.

SOCI. In San Antonio, Texas, the Hispanic Chamber of Commerce is established to protect interests of Latino merchants and to emphasize the Spanish culture in the Latino experience. Because many Americans are using the expression Hispanic, it is easier for this organization to work within the non-Latino community while also suggesting a desire for conformity with the English language.

TRAN. On January 9, Pan American Airline establishes flights from Puerto Rico to New York.

In the 1940s, this route will become the path of entry into the United States for thousands of Puerto Ricans.

WORK. The Communist Party in California forms the Trade Union Unity League to help Mexican laborers who are not aided by the American Federation of Labor.

1930

LIT. A group of Puerto Rican writers on the island fight against the obligatory teaching of English in Puerto Rico, advocating a need to maintain the island's Spanish heritage in schools and cultural institutions. These writers are known as Generación del 30. Two of the most famous members of the generation include Enrique A. Laguerre and Emilio S. Belaval, both preoccupied with the potential that the Puerto Rican identity might vanish before the growing American presence on the island.

MUSI. Cuban singer and actress Rita Montaner introduces the song "EL Manicero," "The Peanut Vendor," to Broadway audiences while performing in a variety show with Al Jolson. Montaner then tours the United States. The song will become popular and will be used in several Hollywood films during the decade.

MUSI. The Cuban Rumba is the rage in New York City and Los Angeles. The dance, of Afro-Cuban origins, is a back-and-forth style with hip motion.

POLI. Rafael Leónidas Trujillo, chief of the Dominican Republic's armed forces, is elected president. He will rule the nation for 31 years.

The Birth of LULAC

"As pioneers searching for a Mexican-American place in the American sun, LULAC leaders attempted to define what Americanization meant to them. This involved both the evolution of a set of principles, what one historian has termed the "Mexican-American mind," as well as a praxis through particular struggles. Mexican Americans in LULAC desired integration and acceptance as U.S. citizens but at the same time wanted to negotiate maintaining their Mexican heritage. . . . Could such a pluralistic assimilation be accomplished? This was one of the questions faced by the initial LULAC generation."

Source: Mario T. García. *Mexican Americans: Leadership, Ideology and Identity, 1930–1960.* New Haven, CT: Yale University Press, 1989, p. 33.

POLI. In Puerto Rico, the Partido Popular is founded in the town of Ponce in June. The party endorses a socialist agenda and is critical of the United States. Pedro Albizu Campos is elected president of the Nationalist Party. His political ideals will be a major component of political thought throughout the twentieth century. In New York, he will become a political icon for Puerto Ricans living in the city.

POLI. At the University of Puerto Rico, Albizu Campos affirms that the island is not a nation but a spoil of war. He believes that 60 percent of Puerto Ricans want independence from the United States.

POLI. In México, Interim President Emilio Portes Gil hands over the government to the newly elected president Pascual Ortíz Rubio. The peaceful transfer of power signals the end of the Mexican Revolution and the beginning of modern México.

POPU. About 30,000 Puerto Ricans live in New York City. One million Mexicans migrate to the United States.

RACE. An ad for cruise ships owned by the Porto Rico Line depicts two tango dancers next to the heading of "Cruises of Enchantment to the West Indies." The emphasis is on European-looking Latinos rather than Latinos of Spanish or Caribbean appearance, emphasizing Americans' dislike of appearances that are not reflective of Anglo-Saxon physiognomy.

RELI. On January 6, Epiphany Day becomes an official holiday in Puerto Rico. It celebrates the day the three kings, or magi, visited the young Christ. Throughout Latin America, families exchange gifts and children receive toys at dawn. The holiday emphasizes the Spanish heritage of the people of Puerto Rico. Later, in the United States, Puerto Rican families will celebrate both December 25 and January 6.

1930–1933

ARTS. Mexican muralist Diego Rivera travels to the United States to paint a series of murals in museums across the nation. The most controversial work is a mural to be placed at the RCA building within the Rockefeller Center complex in New York City. The mural includes a drawing of communist leader and dictator Vladimir Lenin as representative of hope and a better future for the masses. Rivera is removed from the project and after he is paid in full, the mural is destroyed. Since Rivera can't protest because he accepted full payment, he returns to México.

CULT. In the Southwest, young Mexican-Americans begin to develop a subculture of rebellion against American culture and values, which they see as tending to belittle Mexican culture. They wear a stylized suit known as a Zoot Suit, also fashionable with some African-American youths, and speak a dialect called Caló, which combines Mexican street vernacular with English slang. These youths are known as Pachucos and are stereotyped as criminals.

The Birth of Modern México

"The most devastating civil war in Mexican history produced contemporary Mexican society. In the 10 years of its military phase, between 1910 and 1920, as many as 2 million people may have been killed. . . . Trains were blown up, haciendas were burned, and corruption prevailed. Yet the Mexican Revolution created new political structures and produced the Constitution of 1917. It destroyed the privilege of the Creole and gave birth to the mestizo nation. It ended feudalism and peonage and created labor unions and redistributed land. . . . The revolution gave Mexicans a sense of national pride and a deeply held appreciation of their culture, called *mexicanidad*."

Source: Lynn V. Foster. *A Brief History of Mexico.* Rev. ed. New York: Checkmark Books/Facts on File, 2004, p. 161.

1931

ARTS. Universal Studios films two *Dracula* movies simultaneously, one in English and one in Spanish. Both films are identical; the performers even stand on the same X marks, which indicate location on the set, and use similar gestures. In the Spanish-language version, the female lead wears clothes that reveal more than in the English version. The Spanish version is distributed throughout Latin America; the English version is released years later with subtitles or dubbed. For most Latin American fans, their first encounter with Dracula is not Bela Lugosi but Spanish actor Carlos Villaría, who resembles Lugosi.

EDUC. President Hebert Hoover deems it necessary for Spanish to be the language of instruction in Puerto Rico for the first eight grades; afterwards, classes should be taught in English.

IMMI. More than 300,000 Mexicans are detained by the Border Patrol and deported to México.

SPOR. Cuban boxer Kid Chocolate, whose real name is Eligio Sardinias Montalbo, wins the championship in the Junior Lightweight category in Philadelphia, defeating boxer Benny "The Fish" Bass. For the next eight years he fights in Havana, New York, Madrid, and Paris, winning 135 fights and losing 9.

1932

ARTS. Mexican artist David Siqueiros paints on an exterior wall in a Los Angeles arts center the mural *America Tropical,* which depicts the crucifixion of Christ, with Christ portrayed as a person from Latin America and with an American eagle representing Roman executioners and American imperialism. The mural is the first ever painted in an open space in the United States, encouraging a trend that will bloom throughout the country in the 1960s and 1970s.

ARTS. Mexican artist José Clemente Orozco begins painting a mural at Dartmouth College, New Hampshire, about the history of the Americas from the Aztec Empire to the modern age. Orozco will finish the mural, consisting of 24 large panels, in 1934.

LIT. *Perez and Martina: A Portorican Folk Tale* is one of the first children's books published in the United States aimed at Puerto Rican children. The picture book is written by librarian Pura Belpre, who, while working in the New York Public Library system, notices an absence of books written in English about Puerto Rican culture and heritage. The book is the product of a successful program she conducts at the library, telling young children of all races stories from Puerto Rico, using hand puppets and homemade props. Belpre will become famous in the library field for developing innovative programs to reach Latino children who do not use local libraries.

POLI. On May 17, the U.S. Congress passes a law that changes the name of Porto Rico to Puerto Rico.

POLI. María Luisa Arcelay is the first woman elected to serve in the Puerto Rican legislature.

RELI. Fifty-five Spanish-speaking Protestant churches serve Latinos in New York City.

1933

LAWS. President Roosevelt ends the policy of using English as the official governmental language in Puerto Rico.

POLI. President Franklin D. Roosevelt transfers jurisdiction over Puerto Rico from the War Department to the Interior Department. The Puerto Rico Emergency Relief Administration is created to help alleviate poverty on the island.

REBE. In August, a general strike takes place in Cuba. The military turns against dictator Machado, demanding his departure from the island. Many prominent Cuban families and politicians connected with the regime must flee the country. The new president, Carlos Manuel de Céspedes y Quesada, takes office and forms a new cabinet on August 14, but a month later army sergeants under the command of Sergeant Fulgencio Batista lead a revolution that forces the new president from office.

SPOR. Cuban baseball player Adolfo Luque, playing for the New York Giants, is the first person from Latin America to post a World Series pitching victory.

WARS. In Nicaragua, the United States ends its occupation by recalling the 5,000 Marines stationed there. Nicaragua's National Guard assumes control of the nation and continues the war against the guerrillas who had opposed American intervention. A year later, General Anastasio Somoza, in charge of the guard, convinces rebel leader Augusto Sandino to surrender. Somoza tricks Sandino to a meeting where he is assassinated. Though the United States is not implicated, people throughout Latin American assign guilt to the Americans. Sandino will become a symbol of rebellion and his political ideology will lend strength to the Sandinista government in Nicaragua half a century later. In the meantime, Somoza and his sons will run the country, provoking a civil war in the 1970s that will send thousands of refugees to the United States, settling primarily in the Miami area.

1934

MUSI. Tango singer and composer Carlos Gardel writes one of the most beloved songs in Latin America, "Mi Buenos Aires Querido." The tango laments the fact that the singer has had to leave his native city of Buenos Aires. He believes that once he returns to Buenos Aires, he will no longer feel sorrow and sadness. Argentines in New York City, nostalgic for their country, treasure the song. The theme of exile will be repeated in others songs, such as "En Mi Viejo San Juan," written by Latino artists.

POLI. President Franklin D. Roosevelt develops the "Good Neighbor Policy" of maintaining cordial relationships with Latin American nations and backing away from direct participation in the internal affairs of other countries.

SOCI. Casita Maria is established in New York City to assist Puerto Ricans who live in the city with educational and cultural programs.

SPOR. In Montreal, Canada, Puerto Rican boxer Sixto Escobar knocks out opponent Baby Casanova, becoming the island's first world boxing champion. Escobar is a bantamweight fighter, a boxer who weighs between 112 and 118 pounds.

1935

OBIT. Famous tango singer Carlos Gardel dies in a plane crash in Medillin, Colombia at the age of 45.

POLI. Antonio R. Barceló, the president of Puerto Rico's Liberal Party, writes to President Franklin D. Roosevelt that Americans do not understand Puerto Ricans and that the island should be an independent republic.

POLI. Voting rights are granted to all Puerto Ricans on the island and the literacy requirement is removed.

REBE. During a confrontation between university students and police in Puerto Rico, on the campus of the University of Puerto Rico in Río Piedras, four nationalists and a policeman are killed. The nationalists want independence from the United States.

1936

BUSI. Goya, the best known Puerto Rican business in the United States, is founded by Spanish immigrant Prudencio Unanue Ortíz. The businessman had moved to Puerto Rico from Spain in the early 1910s. In 1915, he relocated to Manhattan, where he noticed a growing Puerto Rican population and an absence of Puerto Rican products in stores. Nostalgic for Puerto Rican food, Unanue started to import beans, desserts, and vegetables from the island. He canned those products under the label of Goya, which was a popular brand of Spanish olives in his native Spain.

POLI. Dennis Chavez, from New Mexico, is elected on November 3 to the United States Senate. He will serve until 1960, supporting President Roosevelt's New Deal, irrigation and flood control projects for New Mexico, and civil rights for all Americans.

REBE. Two Puerto Rican nationalists kill an American colonel, Francis E. Riggs, who is serving in Puerto Rico's police force, to avenge four comrades killed by police in Río Piedras the year before. The assassins, Elias Beauchamp and Hiram Rosado, are arrested and killed in the fracas. The Puerto Rican and American governments agree to

Goya products in a bodega in the northeast. Goya is the most recognizable Latino brand in the United States, sold not only in bodegas but in major supermarkets.

replace American officers in the police with Puerto Ricans officers.

REBE. Independence leader Pedro Albizu Campos is arrested for plotting to overthrow the American government. He is found guilty and sentenced to a federal prison in Georgia. On March 21, nationalists organize a rally to protest Albizu Campos's arrest and to demand independence for Puerto Rico. When the march begins, the police fire on the demonstrators, killing 19 and wounding over 100 protestors. The nationalists call the incident the Ponce Massacre.

WARS. The Spanish Civil War begins on July 17 when General Francisco Franco leads a military uprising to unseat the government of the Popular Front, a coalition that includes Communists and Socialists. The war will end on April 1, 1939, with Franco's victory and over 500,000 deaths. Spanish republicans, usually liberals, communists, and socialists, flee to Cuba, the Dominican Republic, France, and México. Numerous Spanish actors leave as well, settling in Cuba, México, Puerto Rico, and the United States, where they work in Latino theaters, especially in New York City. Mexican students join the Abraham Lincoln Brigade, consisting of volunteers who want to fight against Franco.

WORK. Puerto Rican government workers on the island must take an oath of loyalty to the United States in order to maintain their jobs.

1937

ARTS. The Museum of Modern Art in New York City exhibits for the first time the painting *Fulang Chang and I* by Mexican artist Frida Kahlo. The painting is a self-portrait of the artist with a monkey in her arm. Though not famous during her lifetime, Kahlo will become one of the most recognizable artists of the late twentieth century. She will also become a favorite of American feminist art critics and scholars for the use of bold images that bitterly denounce how Diego Rivera abused her during their marriage.

POLI. Oscar García Rivera is elected to the New York Assembly, the first Puerto Rican elected to public office in the continental United States. He will be reelected in 1938 and will serve in the state Assembly until 1940.

1938

POLI. At a protest in East Harlem, New York City, over 2,000 Puerto Ricans demand independence for Puerto Rico. It is the beginning of a political trend with Puerto Ricans on the mainland favoring independence over statehood.

POLI. In Puerto Rico, tension builds between government officials and university students in favor of independence.

SOCI. The Federation of Puerto Rican Societies holds its first meeting in New York on November 12. The society represents 29 Puerto Rican organizations.

1939

ARTS. The film *Mexican Spitfire*, produced by RKO studios, capitalizes on the stereotypical image of Latinas as being explosive and impulsive. The lead role is played by Lupe Velez, who will star in six additional films of the series known as the Mexican Spitfire movies.

LAWS. On January 30, the American Civil Liberty Union requests the release of Puerto Rico's independence leader Pedro Albizu Campos, claiming jurors in his trial had planned to persecute him and the other nationalists, regardless of evidence.

OBIT. On December 5, Resident Commissioner of Puerto Rico Santiago Iglesias Pantín dies. The father of the Puerto Rican labor movement, he pressured the United States to provide for the poor of Puerto Rico and to improve wages.

POLI. In May, the Puerto Rican Senate considers a resolution for the statehood of Puerto Rico, but aware that the island seems equally divided between statehood and independence, no action is taken.

WARS. World War II begins on September 1, when Germany attacks and invades Poland. In Puerto Rico, a U.S. military air base is constructed on Punta Borinquén on a northwest corner of the island.

1940

ARTS. On October 8, the musical *Too Many Girls*, an RKO adaptation of a Broadway show written by Richard Rodgers and Lorenz Hart, introduces to American audiences a young actor named Desi Arnaz. On the set, Arnaz falls in love with leading lady Lucille Ball.

ARTS. The film *Down Argentine Way*, starring Don Ameche as a wealthy Argentine horse breeder, insults Argentine audiences in Buenos Aires who complain the ambiance is too tropical for Argentina and the tango music in the background is closer to Cuban rumba. For many Latin Americans, the film demonstrates the United States's insensibility towards Latin American culture and diversity.

ECON. In Puerto Rico, the Puerto Rican Industrial Development Corporation is created to furnish credit and tax exemptions for companies on the island.

EDUC. From 1940 to 1941 Dominican scholar Pedro Henríquez Ureña occupies the prestigious Charles Eliot Norton chair at Harvard University, where he delivers eight lectures that will be collected in the book *Literary Currents in Hispanic America* four years later. The lectures and the volume promote the study of Latin American literature in the United States at a time when most American scholars prefer the literature from Spain.

LAND. In anticipation of potential involvement in the war in Europe, the United States purchases

---

Santería: The Way of the Saints

"Santería is comprised of an Iberian Christianity shaped by the Counterreformation and Spanish folk Catholicism, blended together with African orisha worship as it was practiced by the Yoruba of Nigeria and later modified by nineteenth-century Kardecan spiritualism, which originated in France and became popular in the Caribbean. But while the roots of Santería can be found in Africa's earth-centered religion, in Roman Catholic Spain, and in European spiritism, it is neither African nor European . . . it formed and developed along its own trajectory.

Santería is not exotic, but rather common . . . it is a cultural fusion more than a religious one . . . a Latino/a form of popular religiosity."

Source: Miguel de la Torre. *Santería: The Beliefs and Rituals of a Growing Religion in America*. Grand Rapids, MI: Wm. B. Eermands Publishing Co., 2004, pp. xiii, xvii.

old sugar plantations, farms, and abandoned lots, totaling 26,000 acres, on the island of Vieques, off the coast of Puerto Rico. The U.S. Navy develops the land as a site for military games and target practices. The acquisition will remain controversial for the next 60 years, with many Puerto Ricans opposing the American presence on the tiny island.

MILI. In Los Angeles, a U.S. Naval Armory is constructed on a field, the Chavez Ravine, near Mexican-American neighborhoods. The military presence creates tension in the Mexican-American community.

MUSI. Latin American music sweeps through the United States, with big bands playing tunes from the Caribbean and south of the border. Some of the most popular tunes are "Green Eyes," a translation of "Aquellos ojos verdes" by the Cuban Nilo Menéndez; "Always in my Heart," a translation of "Estas en mi corazón;" "Siboney" by Ernesto Lecuona, of Cuba; and "Besame mucho," by the Mexican Consuelo Velázquez.

POLI. In Cuba, Fulgencio Batista wins the presidency.

POLI. In Puerto Rico, the Resident Commissioner Bolívar Pagán promotes statehood and the ability of Puerto Ricans to elect their own governor. On July 22, Luis Muñoz Marín becomes the president of the Partido Popular de Puerto Rico; in the next few years, he will change the political makeup of the island by supporting commonwealth status for the island, thus creating a third alternative to statehood or independence.

POPU. Los Angeles has a Mexican population of 250,000. There is conflict between whites and Mexican-Americans, with the former regarding themselves as racially and culturally superior to the latter.

POPU. The U.S. Census estimates that 70,000 Puerto Ricans live in the United States and 1.8 million live in Puerto Rico.

SPOR. The Third Annual Amateur Baseball Championship tournament takes place in Cuba. The United States, Hawaii (not a state yet), Cuba,

México, Nicaragua, Puerto Rico, and Venezuela are the participants.

WORK. In Puerto Rico, the Confederación de Trabajadores Generales replaces the Federación Libre de los Trabajadores as the island's major labor union.

1941

LAWS. On June 25, the Fair Employment Practices Act is signed by President Roosevelt, banning racial discrimination in the defense industry and ordering the investigation of any complaints of employment discrimination.

MUSI. Margarita Lecuona composes the song "Babalu," a tribute to an Afro-Cuban god. The song is recorded by Miguelito Valdés, considered Cuba's best singer, who performs it on the island and in the United States. Later on, Desi Arnaz will appropriate the song. Some music historians claim that Valdes did not become successful in the United States because he was darker-skinned and less Americanized than Arnaz.

POLI. In Puerto Rico, the last non-Puerto Rican governor, Rexford Guy Tugwell, is appointed to that position.

WARS. On December 7, the Japanese air force attacks Pearl Harbor. The following day, the United States and Britain declare war on Japan. On December 11, Germany declares war on the United States. Latinos in the United States support the war effort; a reported half-million will serve in the armed forces.

1942

ARTS. The war effort affects film production in Hollywood, presenting an opportunity for the Mexican film industry to expand its commercial horizon north of the border. In Los Angeles and New York, movie houses show Mexican and Argentine films produced for Latin American and Latino audiences. Such important Mexican-American actors as Pedro Armendariz travel back and forth between the two countries, working in American and Mexican films. Mexican director Emilio Fernández "El Indio" and cinematographer Gabriel Figueroa gain international recognition. The film *María Candelaria* will win the 1943 Cannes Film Festival Award.

ARTS. Films from Argentina are equally important, where 29 studios produce musicals, comedies, and epics that are distributed throughout Latin America and in New York City. One of the most popular films is a war epic entitled *La Guerra Gaucha,* which recounts Argentina's war of independence. Two performers, leading man and tango singer Hugo del Carril and leading lady Libertad Lamarque, achieve superstardom status in Latin America and travel regularly to New York City.

ARTS. In the United States, American audiences are wowed by a seductive beauty from the Dominican Republic named Maria Montez in the film *Arabian Nights.* Montez will star in numerous epics, filmed in a Technicolor at a time when using color in movies was uncommon, and will earn the appellation of the "Queen of Technicolor Epics." Her most enduring film will prove to be *Cobra Woman,* achieving status cult with film aficionados and college students.

MUSI. The song "Always in my Heart," by Cuban composer Ernesto Lecuona, is nominated for an Oscar (it is the soundtrack to the film of the same name).

MUSI. While waiting to be shipped overseas to fight in the South Pacific, Puerto Rican singer and composer Daniel Santo writes the song "Despedidad," about a young Puerto Rican going off to war. The song is a hit on the island and throughout Latin America. Santo performs with the Xavier Cugat band, the same orchestra in which Desi Arnaz first achieved popularity, and after his return from the Pacific, he will travel back and forth between Havana and New York City, performing in night clubs. His stylish musical phrasing, consisting of separating syllables and then holding on to the last word to the beat of the music, afford him a soulful quality that makes Daniel Santos popular with women fans. Before his death in 1992, he will become one of the best-known Puerto Rican performers in Latin America.

RACE. On June 3, more than 50 sailors from the Naval Armory on Chavez Revine, in Los Angeles, attack Mexicans who are wearing "zoot suits," a stylized suit favored by young Mexican-Americans and African Americans. The sailors are avenging a fight that broke out four days before between sailors and Mexican-Americans; in that fracas, a sailor was seriously wounded. The incident is the beginning of a week of rioting, with sailors targeting Mexican-American and African-American youths. About 5,000 people are involved in the riots, with sailors and soldiers arriving from San Diego as reinforcement. On June 8 military officials ban military personnel from Los Angeles and the city council bans the wearing of zoot suits in public. On June 17, first lady Eleanor Roosevelt calls the incident a race riot.

SPOR. On April 15, Hiram Bithorn is the first Puerto Rican to pitch in the major leagues, playing for the Chicago Cubs.

The Subtle Ways of Discrimination

Chicano author Manuel Ramos explains in his novel *The Ballad of Rocky Ruiz:*

"Funny about that guy. I've known him for years . . . . Had cases with and against him. He's always treated me like a lady . . . never a word out of line, never anything concrete. But it was there. That brittleness these people have. That invisible line they draw around themselves and that nobody can cross without the right credentials. They squirm when they have to interact with that they think are the lower classes. The guy cannot stand to deal with women or minorities."

Source: "The Stuff Dreams Are Made Of: The Latino Detective Novel," by Danilo H. Figueredo. *Multicultural Review* 8, no. 3 (September 1999): 24.

WARS. Puerto Rico is surrounded by German submarines, making it difficult for American ships to bring supplies to the island. German submarines patrol the northern coast of Cuba; American novelist Ernest Hemingway, who spends most of his time in a farm near Havana, patrols Cuban water, searching for German submarines while working undercover for the American government.

WORK. On August 4, 1942, the U.S. and Mexican governments create the Bracero program to replace loss of labor in farms and industries due to World War II. Thousands of impoverished Mexicans take up the opportunity to find employment in the United States. According to the contract, the Mexican laborer will receive the minimum legal wages and housing, usually in a migrant's camp, and will return home once the contract expires. The Bracero program will last until 1964. The term refers to *brazo*, meaning arm.

1943

ARTS. In New York City, audiences are fascinated by a production of Shakespeare's *Othello* with African-American actor Paul Robeson in the lead and Puerto Rican thespian José Ferrer portraying Iago. It is a pioneer attempt at diversity on the Broadway stage.

ARTS. Cuban artist Wilfredo Lam finishes his masterpiece *La Jungla*, the jungle, to be placed on permanent display at the Museum of Modern Art in New York City. Lam uses African themes in his cubist depiction of a jungle. By emphasizing his African roots, the artist is rebelling against a trend in Cuba in which the leading figures of the day boast about their Spanish heritage, negating the African presence on the island.

MUSI. On August 2, Puerto Rican composer Noel Estrada writes the bolero "En Mi Viejo San Juan," one of the most famous songs in Latin America and a favorite of Puerto Ricans serving in the army. The song expresses the regret of a Puerto Rican who must leave the island to seek better opportunities elsewhere. It is a song of lament and homesickness, which captures the sentiments of any one who is away from the homeland.

POLI. Antonio Manuel Fernández is elected New Mexico's representative to the U.S. Congress.

SOCI. The Spanish American Youth Bureau is founded on December 18 to prevent juvenile delinquency in Harlem and the Bronx.

WARS. The Sixty-Fifth Infantry Regiment of Puerto Rico's Third Battalion, with nearly 3,000 men and more than 100 officers, all Puerto Ricans, sees action in France in December.

1944

ARTS. Hoping to turn Mexican actor Arturo De Cordova into a Latin lover type, Paramount Studios casts him in the role of a French pirate in the movie version of the Daphne Du Murier's novel *Frenchmen's Creek*. The romantic film, which emphasizes the love story more than the swashbuckling, is not the anticipated hit. De Cordova, of medium height and slight built, does not meet the stereotype American audiences expect of a Latin Lover: tall, dark, and handsome. De Cordova returns to México and becomes a superstar in the Spanish-speaking world, working, later on, for such geniuses as film director Luis Buñuel.

MIGR. In November, schoolteacher Antonia Pantoja arrives in New York City, where she finds employment as a welder in factory. She notices how her co-workers are poorly treated by employers and how fragmented their lives are outside the factory. An activist, Pantoja sees the need to create an organization that would help young Puerto Ricans attend college and pursue professions.

OBIT. On December 13, Mexican-American film star Lupe Velez, whose real name is Guadalupe Villalobos Velez, commits suicide in Hollywood. She had begun her film career in silents and was able to transition to sound, playing the comic role of a temperamental Latina in the Mexican Spitfire film series. Movie studios describe her as the "Mexican Wildcat" or "Hot Tamale," belittling her humanity. Engaged once to actor Cary Cooper, the latter was persuaded by his family not to marry her because she was Mexican.

RACE. To protect Mexicans against racism, Mexican nationals form the Comite Mexicano Central Contra el Racismo.

SPOR. A dark-skinned Cuban baseball player, Tommy de la Cruz, is harassed out of his team, the Cincinnati Reds, because of his skin color.

1945

LAWS. The California LULAC Council successfully sues the Orange County School System to integrate Mexican children into the school system. The county-wide system has maintained that Mexican children are inferior to white children and could therefore not attend the same schools.

LIT. In Puerto Rico, the writers who make up the Generación del 45, or the Desperate Generation, pen stories and novels that take place in urban settings, either on the island or in New York City, and lament American influence on Puerto Rican culture. Two of the most famous writers in the group are the playwright René Marqués, who regrets the loss of land in Puerto Rico to American companies, and José Luis González, who is critical of American imperialism.

POLI. The Puerto Rican legislature submits the Tydings-Piñero, which proposes three pathways for the island: independence, statehood, or dominion status. Due to military concerns during the war, the bill is tabled for future discussions.

SOCI. The charter of the United Nations is signed on October 24. The purpose for this international organization is to seek cooperation in international law, international security, economic development, and social equity. The ultimate objective of the U.N. is to avoid global wars such as World War II.

WARS. On May 7, Germany surrenders to Allied forces. On September 2, Japanese forces surrender. World War II ends. Over 65,000 Puerto Ricans in the armed forces have participated in the European and Pacific Theaters.

1946

ARTS. The epic western *Duel in the Sun* is released. It has the unique distinction of presenting as its heroine a complex and well-drawn Latina, Pearl Chavez, who is independent and free-spirited. The movie is originally intended for Mexican superstar María Félix, but her limited knowledge of English prevents her from accepting the role; it is given instead to Jennifer Jones. The film does not receive good reviews, but it grosses $17 million in the United States. As for María Félix, she becomes an international star, working in Italy and France while dominating the Mexican film industry for the next three decades.

EDUC. Spanish is made the primary language of instruction in Puerto Rico; English is the secondary language.

MILI. In Panama, the United States founds the Army School of the Americas, where officers from Latin American countries friendly toward the United States are invited to attend. Since many of these officers, like Somoza, assume power over their countries and violently repress dissent, people in Latin America and Latino scholars in the United States call it the School of the Dictator and the School of Assassins.

OBIT. Puerto Rico's first international star, opera singer Antonio Paoli, dies in San Juan. A rival of Enrico Caruso, in 1907 Paoli performed the first opera ever recorded, *Pagliacci*. Losing his fortune of $2 million after World War I, Paoli, who was no longer singing, began a short-lived career as a boxer. In 1993, the Paoli award will be created to honor the accomplishments of Latino singers.

POLI. President Harry S. Truman appoints the first Puerto Rican governor, Jesús T. Piñero. In November, Felisa de Rincón de Gautier is elected mayor of San Juan, the first woman voted to the position in the Americas. The Puerto Rican Independent Party is formed.

POLI. On February 24, Juan Domingo Perón is elected president of Argentina. His second wife, Eva Perón, a former actress, becomes intensely popular in Argentina. Perón supports a political position that he dubs the "third position," meaning economical and political plans that fall between communism and capitalism. Evita, as she is called throughout the nation, espouses the cause of the poor people, the *descamisados,* the shirtless ones. Evita will gain enough political acumen and support to present herself as vice-presidential candidate during her husband's reelection campaign. Perón will remain in office until 1955 and will be reelected in 1973. In time, Evita will become a cultural icon in Latin America and the United States, due to several books, films, and a Broadway musical about her life.

RELI. A Cuban Santería priest, a Babalao, named Francisco "Pancho" Mora establishes a divination center in New York City. He is the first *Santero,* as practitioners of the religion are also called, in the United States ordained to practice divination and Santería in New York City.

1947

POLI. On January 24, the Republican National Committee in the United States promises to help Puerto Rico become a state. The Democrats support self-rule for the island. On August 6, Puerto Ricans are allowed to vote for their own governor.

POLI. On December 15, independence leader Pedro Albizu Campos is released from prison; he returns to Puerto Rico where he continues to plan the overthrow of the American government. He urges Puerto Ricans not to support Muñoz Marín's candidacy for the governorship of the island.

POLI. The Community Service Organization is created to encourage political activism and voter registration within the Mexican-American community in California. Cesar Chavez is one of its organizers.

POPU. The New York City Welfare Council reports that there are an estimated 350,000 Puerto Ricans living in New York.

TRAN. Regular flights begin between San Juan and Miami and San Juan and New York, facilitating traveling to the mainland for Puerto Ricans looking for work.

1948

LAWS. In Puerto Rico, the governor signs a law on June 11 making it illegal to promote independence in public gatherings.

POLI. Luis Muñoz Marín is elected the first Puerto Rican governor of Puerto Rico on November 2.

REBE. When the chancellor of the University of Puerto Rico refuses permission for Pedro Albizu Campos to visit the campus on April 16, students storm into his office to protest.

SOCI. On March 26, 700 Mexican-American veterans, under the leadership of physician Hector P. García, organize the American G.I. Forum, with the objective of assuring equal rights for Latinos. The organization lobbies the Veterans Administration to deliver to Latino veterans earned benefits through the G.I. Bill of Rights of 1944.

SPOR. Twenty-year-old tennis player Pancho González wins the U.S. Championship at Forest Hills, New York. Gonzalez is a Mexican-American from Los Angeles whose full name is Ricardo Alonso González. A year later, after another victory at the same competition, he turns professional. In a 12-year period, he wins the U.S. Professional Championship eight times and the Wembley title, in London, four times. He is known as the most aggressive tennis player ever in the sport. González began playing tennis at the age of 12 when his mother refused to give him a bike for his birthday, opting for a tennis racket instead.

WORK. Operation Bootstrap begins in Puerto Rico. With the assumption that the island can no longer support agricultural production, the emphasis is placed on developing industries and inviting foreign companies to establish factories and plants on the island. The plan is spearheaded by Luis Muñoz Marín. The Puerto Rican Department of Labor sets up a Division of Migration in New York City.

1949

MILI. The Rice Funeral Home, in Three Rivers, Texas, refuses to bury Private Félix Longoria. The American G.I. Forum, led by Hector P. García, organizes protests that gain national attention. Through the intervention of Senator Lyndon B. Johnson, the Mexican-American veteran is buried in Arlington National Cemetery.

SOCI. New York's Committee for Puerto Rican affairs is established to help Puerto Ricans adjust to life in New York City.

1949–1950

REBE. Puerto Rican leader Pedro Albizu Campos calls the proposed creation of the commonwealth of Puerto Rico a colonial farce and proposes an armed rebellion against the United States.

SPOR. Luis Olmo, the first Puerto Rican to play in a World Series, hits a home run and gets three hits in a Series game. He plays for the Brooklyn Dodgers.

1950

ARTS. The Latin lover in Hollywood films continues to gain popularity with Fernando Lamas, from Argentina, and Ricardo Montalban, from México, dominating the roles. The two actors portray the role in more than 20 films. Veteran actor Gilbert Roland, whose real name is Luis Antonio Damaso de Alonso, from México, portrays a more matured, and cynical, Latin lover in a dozen films during the early 1950s. Roland has been in films since the 1920s.

ARTS. In April, Puerto Rican actor José Ferrer wins the Oscar for his role in the film *Cyrano de Bergerac*. The first Latino actor to win the award, Ferrer donates the statue to the University of Puerto Rico.

LEGE. The romantic exploits of a real Latin lover dominate Hollywood and the New York jet set. His name is Porfirio Rubirosa, a diplomat from the Dominican Republic. He woos, marries, and has dozens of affairs with international beauties, including millionaires Doris Duke and Barbara Hutton, and actresses Eva Gabor and Zsa Zsa Gabor. Rubirosa will serve as the inspiration for the protagonist of the Harold Robbins novel and 1970 film, *The Adventurers*.

MIGR. There about 15,000 Cubans living in New York City, with a little fewer than 200 settling in Union City and West New York, in New Jersey. They are in the United States to seek economic opportunities and to escape political instability in Cuba. In the early 1960s, the Union City and West New York Cuban residents invite relatives to stay with them rather than live in New York City, since the Jersey side of the Hudson is more economical but still near Manhattan.

POLI. Vito Marcantonio, a Congressman from Harlem, introduces on March 16 legislation demanding the removal of Americans from Puerto Rico. Congressman Marcantonio had advocated for the island's independence since taking office in 1936.

POLI. President Truman signs into law the Puerto Rican Federal Relations Act, which allows Puerto Ricans to draft their own constitution.

POPU. The U.S. Census reports 300,000 Puerto Ricans live in the United States; 2.2 million live on the island.

SOCI. The Hispanic Young Adult Association, created by Puerto Rican college students, begins training sessions in leadership and community work for young Puerto Rican professionals.

REBE. On April 3, someone climbs unto Puerto Rico's capital dome in San Juan and lowers the America flag, replacing it with the Nationalist banner.

REBE. On October 30, uprisings occur in several towns in Puerto Rico. In the town of Jayuya, nationalists attack the police station, kill one officer, and wound several others, and then take over the facility. After cutting telephone lines and burning the post office, the nationalists declare Puerto Rico a free republic. They hold the town for three days. The United States declares martial law as Puerto Rico's National Guard surrounds the town. There is air bombardment and artillery fire. The National Guard defeats the rebels and arrests the leaders. An assassination attempt is made on Governor Muñoz Marín.

Hearing news of the defeat, nationalists Oscar Collazo and Griselio Torresola plan to assassinate President Harry S. Truman to bring the world's attention to the political situation in Puerto Rico. On November 1, the two men break into Blair's residence in Washington, D.C., the temporary home for President Truman and his family while reconstructive work is going on in the White

House. During the attack, a police officer is killed and several are wounded; Torresola is killed and Collazo is wounded and arrested. Sentenced to death, Collazo's sentence is commuted to life in prison by Truman.

SETT. Over five million Americans move into new homes across state lines. Many leave urban centers like New York City, vacating apartments that are now occupied by Latinos and African Americans.

TRAD. Puerto Rico buys over $300,000,000 of American products annually. The island is the major per capita consumer of American goods.

WARS. The Korean War begins on June 25. North Korea and the People's Republic of China, with support from the Soviet Union, fight against the United States, the United Kingdom, Canada, and Philippines. Nearly 20,000 Latinos participate in the war. The Puerto Rico's 65th Infantry Regiment arrives in Korea in September.

WORK. About 10,000 Puerto Rican farmers work in agriculture in the United States, especially in the south.

1951

ARTS. On October 15, the television comedy *I Love Lucy* debuts to popular acclaim. The comedy stars Desi Arnaz and Lucille Ball as the first multicultural couple on television. It is the first television show in which the performers own the show and the first to introduce live filming of a television production. It also pioneers the concept of the 25-minute show to allow for commercial time, and the first to perfect the three-camera filming technique for sitcoms. *I Love Lucy* introduces the concept of reruns and presents the subject of pregnancy on TV for the first time. To produce and film the show, the couple creates their own production company, Desilu, which will become a major television studio during the next two decades.

ECON. Through an arrangement made between the U.S. Labor Department and Puerto Rico, 50,000 to 100,000 Puerto Rican farmers are available for work on American farms from July to December, supplementing the work these farmer do in the sugar industry on the island from January to June.

EDUC. New York Mayor Vincent R. Impellitteri's Committee on Puerto Rican Affairs reports that schools in the city need 1,000 teachers who are fluent in Spanish. There are schools in the city with Puerto Ricans making up more than two-thirds of the student body.

REBE. On January 4, Albizu Campos, Nationalist Party leader, is arraigned on charges of trying

---

Latinos Fighting for the United States

"By the beginning of the Korean War there were about 20,000 Puerto Ricans serving in the U.S. military, the majority in the Army and Marines. With over 4,000 U.S. soldiers, Puerto Rico's 65th Infantry Regiment arrived in Korea in September 1950 well led and well trained. The largest U.S. Infantry regiment on the American side, it fought in every major campaign of the war thereafter. Composed of Puerto Rican soldiers and sergeants and mostly continental officers, the 65th Infantry (Borinqueneers) won nine Distinguished Service Crosses, some 250 Silver Stars and more than 500 Bronze Stars for valor in three years of fighting, killing almost 6,000 communist soldiers and capturing another 2,000. Over the next three years, the 65th Infantry was awarded a Presidential Unit Citation, a Meritorious Unit Commendation, two Republic of Korea Presidential Unit Citations and the Gold Bravery Medal of Greece. The all-Puerto Rican unit was finally integrated in March 1953 and remained in Korea until November 1954."

Source: Col. Gilberto Villahermosa. "America's Hispanics in American Wars; September 2002." *Army Magazine.* www.valerosos.com/HispanicsMilitary.html. Accessed October 24, 2005.

to overthrow the American government by force. On March 17, he is sentenced to serve 7 to 15 years of imprisonment.

RELI. The Presbyterian Labor Temple begins offering services in Spanish to the Puerto Rican community of New York.

TRAD. On August 2, the Economic Development Administration of Puerto Rico opens an office in New York City with the objective of attracting business to the island.

TRAN. The first direct air flight from New York to Puerto Rico occurs on March 23. It takes five hours.

WORK. The Bracero Program, which allows Mexican workers into the United States, is renewed. It is now known as the Mexican Farm Labor Supply Program and the Mexican Labor Agreement. The Bracero Program aims to recruit 350,000 laborers a year.

1952

ARTS. In April, Anthony Quinn becomes the first Mexican-American actor to win an Oscar. He receives the Academy Award for Best Supporting Actor for his portrayal of Eufemio Zapata, Emilio Zapata's brother, in the film *Viva Zapata*, released in the same year. Quinn will receive a second Oscar for his role as Paul Gauguin in the film *Lust for Life*, released in 1956. A versatile actor, Quinn plays dozens of ethnic characters, from an Eskimo

to an Italian don. In 1964, he will portray a free-spirited Greek in his most popular film, *Zorba the Greek*. As a young performer in the 1930s, Quinn had not emphasized his Mexican background to avoid being typecast. But in the mid 1950s, he begins to reminisce in interviews about his Mexican-Irish parents. In the 1970s, Quinn will describe himself as a Hispanic and in 1971 he will play the Mexican-American mayor of a California town in the television series *The Man and the City.*

MIGR. The Immigration and Nationality Act of 1952 assigns quotas to countries recognized by the United Nations. The act excludes Asia from those regions that are allowed to send immigrants to the United States.

OBIT. In Buenos Aires, Argentina, Evita Perón succumbs to cancer on July 26.

POLI. In July, the island of Puerto Rico becomes a commonwealth of the United States with a free associated status, known in Puerto Rico as *Estado Libre Asociado*. Though over 80 percent of registered voters voted in favor of commonwealth, Puerto Rican nationalists reject the results, maintaining that the island is nothing else but an American colony.

POLI. In November, Luis Muñoz Marín, a strong advocate and supporter of the commonwealth status, is reelected as governor of Puerto Rico.

POLI. In Cuba, when Fulgencio Batista cannot win his second bid for the presidency, he moves

---

Afro-Cuban from Tampa Remembers Young Castro

"[Castro] was looking for a place to talk against [Cuban dictator] Batista. By the by-laws of the [Afro-Cuban club] we recognized the government of Cuba, whatever government it was. That was the legal government, so we had to recognize it. . . . So we couldn't let him use the club to talk against the government. . . . So [Castro] said 'Do you mean to tell me that a government like that'—and this and that—'and you're not going to let me talk?' And we told him no . . . and he called us stupid. . . . So he got mad. He got hot about it. . . . He called [us] all kinds of names and everything."

Source: Susan D. Greenbaum. *More Than Black: Afro-Cubans in Tampa.* Gainesville: University Press of Florida, 2002, pp. 272–73.

against the democratically elected president, Carlos Prío Socarrás, and ousts him from office on March 10th.

1953

LIT. Puerto Rican playwright René Marqués writes *La carreta*, one of the most famous dramas in Puerto Rican theater. The play, which takes place in Puerto Rico and New York City, depicts the tragic lives of a Puerto Rican family that seeks a better life in New York but only finds death and tragedy. The play affirms Marques's vision that it is better to stay in Puerto Rico than to live in New York, a position maintained by many of the island's intellectuals.

MED. The *Diario Las Americas* is founded in Miami, the city's first Spanish-language newspaper. The founders, the brothers Francisco and Horacio Aguirre, originally from Nicaragua, are looking for a city with a small Latino population and physical proximity to the Caribbean and Latin America. The paper publishes extensive reports on local Latino societies as well as events in Latin America.

MIGR. Between 1953 and 1956, more than 2 million Mexicans and Mexican-Americans are deported, mostly from the Southwest. Some of those deported are actually legal residents or American citizens.

OBIT. On July 5, the Puerto Rican poet Julia de Burgos dies on the streets of Harlem. Though she is one of Latin America's greatest poets, she has no identification papers on her and is placed in the morgue, where she is identified by friends. Her poetry, melodic and emotional, has touched the hearts of readers across the Spanish-speaking world. She was one of the first Puerto Rican poets to internationalize the literature from the island.

"History Will Absolve Me"

In 1953 Fidel Castro was arrested for his attack on the Moncada garrison in Santiago de Cuba. During the trial, he delivered a speech now considered a classic of political rhetoric. In the speech, Castro listed the objectives of his revolutionary government and claimed that history would recognize his role as a leader and Cuba's liberator:

"The first revolutionary law would return power to the people and proclaim the 1940 Constitution the Supreme Law of the State until such time as the people should decide to modify or change it. . . .

The second revolutionary law would give non-mortgageable and non-transferable ownership of the land to all tenant and subtenant farmers, share croppers and squatters. . . .

The third revolutionary law would assure workers and employees the right to share 30% of the profits of all the large industrial, mercantile and mining enterprises, including the sugar mills. . . .

The fourth revolutionary law would grant all sugar planters the right to share 55% of sugar production and a minimum quota of 1,000 pounds for all small tenant farmers who have been established for three years or more. . . .

The fifth revolutionary law would confiscate all the properties and ill-gotten gains of those who had committed frauds during previous regimes . . .

I know that imprisonment will be harder for me than it has ever been for anyone else, filled with cowardly threats and hideous cruelty. But I do not fear prison, as I do not fear the fury of the miserable tyrant who took the lives of 70 of my comrades. Condemn me. It does not matter. History will absolve me."

Source: Fidel Castro. *La historia me absolverá.* Translated by D. H. Figueredo. Habana, Cuba: [s.n.], 1959, p. 30.

POLI. On November 1, the mayor of New York City, Vicent Impellitteri, proclaims for the first time the first week in November as Puerto Rican Week.

REBE. Fidel Castro plots to overthrow the Batista regime. The attack is a complete fiasco, resulting in the death of 70 of the 120 plotters and Castro's arrest.

WARS. More than 61,000 Puerto Ricans have fought in the Korean War. Over 700 are killed in the conflict and more than 3,000 are wounded.

1954

ARTS. The film *Salt of the Earth* receives little notice due to its limited release. Nevertheless, the movie is a serious attempt at documenting the true events of a strike of Mexican miners in New Mexico. The film, which addresses racism in the Southwest, is a pioneer work in the areas of feminism and civil rights.

LAW. The Hernández v. Texas case acknowledges that Latinos are not being treated as "whites" in the United States. The Supreme Court recognizes that Latinos are suffering from racial discrimination.

LAW. LULAC ends the segregation of Mexican-American prisoners at the Texas State Prison in Huntsville

MIGR. From Puerto Rico, 21,531 migrate to the United States. An average of 40,000 Puerto Ricans a year migrate from 1950 to 1954. However, in 1953 over 25,000 Puerto Ricans had returned to the island. The back-and-forth moves indicates a trend that will be characteristic of the Puerto Rican population in the second half of the century, evolving into a cultural sense of duality as the travelers attempt to live in two places: the mainland and Puerto Rico.

REBE. Four Puerto Rican nationalists interrupt a session of the U.S. House of Representatives with gunfire. Five Congressmen are wounded.

WARS. The United States organizes a coup d'etat in Guatemala. A period of political unsettlement begins that will last four decades, forcing thousands of Guatemalans to seek asylum in the United States.

WORK. On February 8, Chicago authorities send 30 unemployed Puerto Ricans back to Puerto Rico. Complaining about job shortages, the authorities discourage migration from the island.

1955

LAWS. Mexican-Americans are guaranteed the right to serve as jurors.

POLI. The Mayor of New York City, Robin Wagner, replaces the Mayor's Committee on Puerto Rican Affairs with a Civil Rights Commission. Juan Avilés, president of the Institute of Puerto Rico, is appointed to the commission. Some Puerto Rican leaders object to the termination of the Committee on Puerto Rican Affairs, fearing that the larger commission will not look carefully at matters pertaining only to the Puerto Rican community.

POLI. In New York City, the mayor of San Juan, Felisa Rincón de Gautier, one of the few woman politicians in Latin America, is awarded on April 17 the Woman of the Americas award by United Women of the Americas, a volunteer society that honors the accomplishments of American women in the arts, medicine, and politics.

REBE. Ernesto "Che" Guevara and Fidel Castro meet in México City. They become fast friends and "Che" joins Castro's revolutionary movement against the dictatorship of Fulgencio Batista. "Che" will guide Castro's growth as a communist and will draft guidelines and policies for revolutionary changes in Cuba once they rule the island. He will also become a romanticized image of the Latin American revolutionary for his willingness to give up the comfort of an administrative post in Cuba to fight and die in a South American jungle because of ideology.

SOCI. On June 25, the Instituto de Cultura Puertorriqueña, the Puerto Rican Institute of Culture, is founded in Puerto Rico to study, preserve, and foster Puerto Rican culture and heritage. It is a cultural attempt at resisting growing American influence on the island.

1956

ARTS. The film *Around the World in Eighty Days* wins five Oscars. The popular feature introduces to American audiences the genius of Mexican comic actor Mario Moreno, known as Cantinflas. In the film, Cantinflas displays his clownish and acrobatic abilities. His forte, though, is not translatable: Cantinflas has the ability to juggle

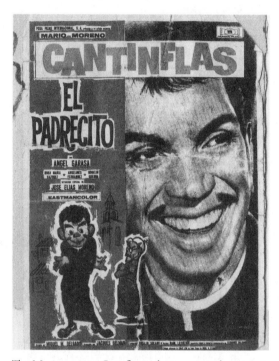

The Mexican actor Catinflas is the most popular actor in the Spanish-speaking world. He is admired for his word games with the Spanish language.

Spanish words into long sentences that often have no meaning, as well as clever games with Spanish vocabulary. In the mold of Charlie Chaplin, Cantinflas usually plays a tramp placed in embarrassing situations that he handles in a courtly manner. Cantinflas is the most popular actor in the Spanish-speaking world.

ARTS. The blockbuster *Giant*, starring Rock Hudson, Elizabeth Taylor, and James Dean, about a cattle dynasty that trades the big ranch for the oil field, is the first large studio film to present the discrimination experienced in the Southwest by Mexican-Americans. In one scene, a young Dennis Hopper is not allowed into his father's banquet because his wife is Mexican. In another scene, Mexicans are not served at a restaurant, provoking Hudson's character into a fight with the owner. Hudson loses the fight but gains respect for his entry into what could be seen as an early version of the civil rights movement.

CRIM. After teaching a class at Columbia University on March 12, scholar Jesús de Galíndez is kidnapped by Rafael Trujillo's secret service and murdered in the Dominican Republic. The scholar had written a thesis, entitled *The Era of Trujillo*, documenting how the dictator had illegally amassed his wealth and committed criminal acts against the people of the Dominican Republic.

ECON. In New York City, Puerto Ricans own about 3,500 bodegas.

IMMI. Under the Bracero Program, 432,000 Mexican workers are admitted into the United

---

American Audiences Get a Taste of Discrimination

"The importance of *Giant* . . . is that it was the first major film to expose the racism that Mexican Americans suffered in the Southwest and at the same time highlighted the problem of racism in general in the United States to audiences on the national and international levels. The problem was presented in a sympathetic liberal light in which the Mexicans were not the main players. The ending of the film, with its fusing of the Anglo and Mexican through intermarriage and the birth of their baby, signaled hope for a better future through integration and understanding."

Source: Luis Reyes and Peter Rubie. *Hispanics in Hollywood: An Encyclopedia of Film and Television.* New York: Garland Publishing, 1994, p. 116.

States to work in agriculture, industry, and service jobs. The implementation of the Bracero Program versus the implementation of the Immigration Act of 1952 confuses many Mexican-Americans, because there are times when Immigration target Mexicans to detain and then deport them.

MUSI. The choir of the University of Puerto Rico performs in Carnegie Hall on March 3.

POPU. Twenty thousand Puerto Ricans live in Chicago. The New York Times reports on July 18 that 800,000 Spanish speakers live in New York City. There are 7,300 Puerto Ricans living in the city of Philadelphia.

RACE. A superior judge in New Jersey publicly insults Puerto Ricans by stating that the island is filthy and that people there live in squalor. He suggests that Puerto Ricans live in slums in the United States because they are accustomed to such living conditions. On January 18, the governor of New Jersey, Robert B. Meyner, removes the judge from the post.

REBE. On March 2, four Puerto Rican nationalists shoot at the House of Representatives on the floor of Congress. The nationalists, Andres Cordero, Irving Flores, Lolita Lebrón, and Rafael C. Martínez, are wrestled down by the police and congressional aids. In her possession Lebrón has a letter stating that the United States is subjugating the Puerto Rican people. On May 27, 17 leaders of the Nationalist Party in Puerto Rico are arrested for conspiring against the United States. The FBI arrests nationalists in New York City and in Chicago as well.

RELI. The Catholic Church in Chicago organizes the Bishop's Committee for the Spanish Speaking to address the religious and cultural needs of Latinos in the Windy City.

REVO. In December Castro returns to Cuba, intending to launch a war of liberation against

---

New York in Puerto Rico

Nuyorican Poet Miguel Algarin recalls how the term Nuyorican became a literary expression:

"I came to Puerto Rico once with Miguel Piñero and when we came out of the plane we were talking away. We had had some drinks and kept talking, and then I heard the word newyorican but I did not know they were talking about Piñero and me. I did not understand. Finally, when we were waiting for our bags I paid attention: new-yo-rican, that is, New York and Puerto Rican. They were looking down on us, as if we were nothing. We were Puerto Ricans talking in English and that to them was contemptuous.

I thought, 'Well, here they are on this island, under a master who speaks English. We come speaking perfect English.' Not only did we speak good English, but we were presenting a play on Broadway, we were writing for TV, and we were famous in Europe, but for them, we were just newyoricans. They were passing judgment on us, looking down on us.

Then, when we got back to New York, I found that William Morrow had sent me a contract for an anthology that was published in 1975 and that they wanted to call *Puerto Rican Poets in English*. And I said to Piñero: 'Why don't we give the title of newyorican to this anthology?' Piñero said: 'But I am not new anything, I am not *neo*, that is intellectualism.' So I asked him, 'What are we then?' And we both said, 'We are nuyoricans.'"

Source: Carmen Dolores Hernández. *Puerto Rican Voices in English*. Westport, CT: Praeger Publishers, 1997, pp. 39–40.

Batista. The landing energizes the urban resistance groups on the island.

WORK. Nearly 7,000 Puerto Rican migrant workers arrive in Glassboro, New Jersey, on April 9 to work in agriculture.

WORK. George Meany, president of the AFL-CIO unions, investigate allegations that Puerto Rican workers are not being represented by their union leaders, who are not Puerto Ricans and who collect their dues but do not advocate for their cause. Many union leaders who have pocketed the dues paid by the Puerto Ricans are expelled by Meany.

1958

CULT. The first New York Puerto Rican Day Parade takes place on Sunday, April 12, in Manhattan. The first president of the parade is Victor López and the Grand Marshall is Oscar González Suárez, a prominent attorney. Governor Don Luis Muñoz Marín attends the event.

IMMI. Over 3 million Mexicans are deported without hearings.

POLI. On July 28, delegates from the Puerto Rican legislature visit the United Nations and Latin American embassies in Washington, D.C., to promote independence for the island. President Dwight Eisenhower offers support for independence if requested by Puerto Rico's legislature.

1959

ARTS. There are more than 650 theater houses in the country that specialize in showing films from México and Argentina as well as American films, either with subtitles or dubbed. Some times, after the showing of the films, some of the theaters present variety shows or one-act plays written in Spanish.

CRIM. On September 4, over 150 representatives from Puerto Rican organizations, labor unions, and churches meet at the Migration Division office in New York to address the issue of juvenile delinquency within the Puerto Rican community. Since the late 1940s and early 1950s, Puerto Rican gangs have been battling each other, and other white and African American gangs, on the streets of Manhattan.

POLI. In Puerto Rico, Governor Muñoz Marín maintains that commonwealth status is the best political condition for the island. In Washington, D.C., the Fernos-Murray Bill, which allows Puerto Rico the possibility of assuming federal responsibilities and emphasizes that the island is neither a colony nor a territory of the United States, is rejected by Congress. The intent of the bill is to give the island more autonomy.

POLI. In Cuba, Batista and his family flee in the early hours of the morning of January 1. Within hours of his departure, the first wave of migration from Cuba to the United States begins as his

---

Barrios Gang Life in the Early 1950s

"Some times we used to stab guys, sometimes we used to get stabbed. We wasn't thinkin' about the other guys being Puerto Ricans . . . if he was your enemy, you kill him . . . a brother named King Kong got shot at 117th Street. When he got killed I was hurt—that was my main man, you see, one of my brothers. A week after that, the Dragons came down to 112th Street in a car and they started shooting at us. We had a gun on us, so when they started shooting, one of the brothers was gonna run over to the car to . . . shoot the Dragons. But the Dragons, they shot him in the arm with a .38 and he fell. So this guy named Chico grabbed the gun . . . and shot the Dragon in the head. . . . [The Dragon gang member] fell against the horn dead, and the car went out of control and went into that store on the corner of 112th."

Source: Michael Abramson. "Palante: Young Lords Party." In *The Puerto Ricans: A Documentary History.* Ed. Kal Wagenheim and Olga Jimenez Wagenheim. Princeton, NJ: Markus Weiner, 2002, pp. 304–5.

closest supporters and military personnel flee Castro's advancing army. It is the beginning of an exile that will last more than four decades. Castro forms his first cabinet, composed of a cross-section of all economic classes. There is no obvious hint of Marxism in the first months of the revolution. Castro describes himself as "humanist." On November 1959 the revolutionary government passes the Fundamental Law, which charges individuals as counter-revolutionaries if engaged in any activities threatening to the revolution. Counter-revolutionary activities are defined in the broadest terms, and as a result thousands of political dissidents are imprisoned.

1960

BUSI. The Riverside neighborhood in Miami, near the port of Miami, is occupied by Cuban exiles who promptly set up restaurants and shops along Fourth Avenue, dubbing the area "Little Havana." By the late 1960s, the area includes professional buildings including doctor's offices, banks, lawyer's offices, and so on.

CRIM. In California, several Mexican-American gangs emerge, often having formed in prisons. *Nuestra Familia*, one of the best known, is involved in bank robberies but also in the killings of members from other gangs or former members that betray gangs' secrets.

CULT. In Puerto Rican neighborhoods in New York City, *bodegas*, grocery stores that sell Caribbean and Spanish products, form vivid parts of the urban landscape. In Miami and in Union City and West New York, New Jersey, Cuban-owned bodegas begin to appear. The bodega engenders a certain type of culture where the owner is friendly with the customers and customers meet to discuss events in the homeland. In poverty-stricken neighborhoods, the bodega owner keeps tabs, which customers pay when they have money. In some bodegas, the illegal game of bolita goes on: a person selects a number connected to a horse race, or even legal lottery games in another country, and plays that number. The winner gets half the purse and the bodega owner takes the other half, which he then shares with the men who run the bolita in town. Games of bolita had been played in the Cuban community in Tampa at the end of the nineteenth century.

LANG. The U.S. Census begins to use the term "Hispanic" to indicate a person of Latin American descent. The term emphasizes the connection with the Spanish language. Newspapers also begin to use the term, though it carries the wrong connotation of race, because "Hispanic" is a cultural designation and not a racial category. Activists in the barrios question the term and suggest the use of Latino to indicate a direct connection with the Spanish-speaking people of Latin America.

LANG. Spanglish grows in use in the Mexican-American, or Chicano, and Puerto Rican communities. It is the combination of English and Spanish, both in written and oral forms.

LANG. Mexican-American activists begin to use the term "Chicano" to indicate identification with a Mexican past freed from American influence, and to affirm solidarity with the humble origins of Mexican migrant workers.

The Latino community created economic enclaves across the United States where bodegas are common sights. These Latino shops are in Union City, New Jersey.

"Chicano" is also a political stance against racism and discrimination. It rejects assimilation with American culture. The term "Chicano" suggests a leftist ideology, while the Mexican-American designation is more conservative.

LIT. A genre emerges in Latin American Literature: anti-Castro literature. Hundreds of poems and dozens of plays and novels have been written since 1959 criticizing Cuban leader Fidel Castro. The works chronicle Castro's transformation from liberator to dictator, recount major historical events, such as the Bay of Pigs invasion, explore life in exile, and express a longing for a return to pre-1959 Cuba.

LIT. *Nuyorican* becomes a literary term, referring to Puerto Rican writers who identify themselves with New York while still acknowledging their Puerto Rican roots. This literary movement reaffirms a move away from the American mainstream by examining different uses of language, as the authors play with both English and Spanish and employ code switching, meaning to speak in one language but export words and sentences from another. The Nuyorican Movement becomes a unique literary activity of writers who live in New York but whose origins are based in Puerto Rico, either through birth or heritage.

MED. The bodegas and businesses owned by Latinos serve as a place where free newspapers are distributed. The publications, which come out once a week, contain information about Latin America, Latino organizations, and political events. The periodicals are handed out free to the customers and are supported by ads from local businesses. These newspapers are sometimes called *periodiquitos*. They offer vivid portrayals of diverse Latino communities.

MIGR. Operation Pedro Pan begins in Cuba on December 26, the largest exodus of unaccompanied minors in the history of the Americas. Over 14,000 children between the ages of 6 and 18 are sent alone to the United States by their parents, who fear communist indoctrination and rumored plans that the government will usurp parental custody. The operation is conducted in secret with cooperation from the U.S. Catholic Church. Reasons given to the Cuban government for sending the children abroad are educational and medical. Suspicion by the revolutionary government that the children are leaving for political reasons could lead to the parents' arrest.

MUSI. *Salsa* music evolves in New York City. Its origins are the Cuban mambo, rumba and son, and Puerto Rican music, including the *plena*. It also incorporates the fast pace of jazz with touches of the big band sound. Musicians and producers like the Dominican Johnny Pacheco, the Cuban singer Celia Cruz, and Puerto Rican timbales player Tito Puentes will be responsible for promoting salsa throughout the United States.

POLI. In November, John F. Kennedy is elected president of the United States. He is one of the first national figures to court the Puerto Rican vote.

POPU. The U.S. Census reports that 892,000 Puerto Ricans live in the United States. There 2.36 million on the island.

POPU. It is estimated that 5 million Mexican-Americans make the United States their home, mostly in the Southwest.

SOCI. The Mexican American Political Association, MAPA, is created to elect Mexican-Americans to political positions. The first president of the group is Edward Ross Roybal, who will be elected to Congress in 1963, the first Latino Congressman from California since the nineteenth century. MAPA lobbies, unsuccessfully, to incorporate East Los Angeles as a city, claiming the large Mexican presence in the area gives it unique cultural and political characteristics.

1961

ARTS. The film version of the play *West Side Story* wins 10 Oscars and is one of the most popular films of the era. A Romeo and Juliet story, with

Puerto Rican gangs battling a mixture of teenagers of Irish, Italian, and Polish descent, the film features Rita Moreno in the role of Anita, for which she wins a Best Supporting Actress award. Latino film historians regret that the tragedy of the racism encountered by Puerto Ricans in New York is featured a film that hardly touches the subject, emphasizing the love story component.

ARTS. Hundreds of Cuban actors, artists, and writers who dissent from Castro's ideology seek exile in Spain and in the United States. Castro encapsulates the revolution's approach towards artistic and political dissent with the phrase "Within the revolution everything; outside the revolution nothing." Cuban writers and artists are forced to walk an intellectual tightrope between creative independence and the need to stay on the correct side of ongoing ideological debates. The revolution views art as a vehicle by which to strengthen loyalty in the citizenry with Castro clarifying that the role of art is to make "men happier, better."

MED. Using Miami as a center base to reach Latinos in the United States, the Telesistema Mexicano, a Mexican network, launches the Spanish International Network, broadcasting soap operas from México and variety shows from Puerto Rico and México as well as American films dubbed in Spanish, though the preference is for films from Argentina and México.

MED. *The San Juan Star* wins the Pulitzer Prize in journalism for its coverage of clerical influence in Puerto Rican politics and elections.

POLI. In Texas, Democrat Henry B. González is the first Mexican-American from that state to be elected to the U.S. House of Representatives. In March, President John F. Kennedy appoints the first Puerto Rican ambassador, José Teodoro Moscoco Mota Rodríguez. He will be the U.S. ambassador to Venezuela.

POLI. On April 15, Castro proclaims that the Cuban revolution is a socialist enterprise. He announces that he is a communist.

POPU. One million Spanish-speakers make New York City their home.

REBE. After bombing Cuban airfields on April 15, Cuban exiles from Miami land on April 17 and occupy Girón beach, in southern Cuba, for a day. The invaders are soon defeated by Castro's forces as the promised air support from the United States is turned down by President John F. Kennedy. Thirteen hundred Cuban exiles participate in the landing. The Cuban exiles' invasion of the island embarrasses the United States, where the operation was planned by the CIA with U.S. governmental support. Photos of Castro leading the defense from a tank on the beachhead romanticizes his image as a brave revolutionary and defender of Cuban and Latin American sovereignty. The Cuban government describes itself as the first country ever to defeat the Americas. Throughout Latin American, John F. Kennedy is portrayed as an aggressor.

REBE. Dictator Rafael L. Trujillo is assassinated on May 30. His absence from power leads to chaos in the Dominican Republic.

REBE. In Nicaragua, the Sandinista Movement, *Frente Sandinista de Liberación Nacional,* is founded to fight against the dictatorship of the Somoza dynasty, in power since 1937.

RELI. La Hermosa Christian Church serves the Protestant Puerto Rican community in the neighborhood of 110th Street, in New York. The church has a congregation of 1,000.

SOCI. Dr. Antonia Pantoja, a prominent educator and activist, founds Aspira in New York City. The bilingual agency provides Puerto Rican high school students with career and life counseling.

SOCI. In December, 66 professionals from Cuba—accountants, bankers, and teachers—form a military organization that with support from the CIA plans commando raids against Castro's forces and military installations on the island. Under the name of Alpha 66, the group, first organized in Puerto Rico, holds military training in Miami.

WARS. In May, President John F. Kennedy sends 400 Green Beret advisors to South Viet Nam. It is the beginning of a war that will last 16 years. Over 80,000 Latinos will serve as soldiers during the conflict.

1962

EDUC. Cuba reports a 96 percent literacy rate. More than 600 rural and more than 300 urban schools are built and 4.5 million primary texts are published. Such progress attracts the support of the Latinos in the United States, who tend to criticize Cuban exiles as right-wingers, thus creating a split between Cubans and Mexican-Americans and Puerto Ricans, which in turn creates a lack of support for each other's political agendas in the United States.

IMMI. The United States ends the Bracero Program. However, Mexican laborers continue to cross the border, this time now as illegal workers. In the Southwest, Mexican-Americans, influenced by the civil rights movements and political activities on campuses, increase their own political awareness and activism.

MIGR. With the death of dictator Rafael Trujillo in the Dominican Republic, a wave of immigration begins with over 4,000 Dominicans traveling to the United States. The pattern will reach an average of over 20,000 a year in the 1980s.

POLI. The Dominican Republic holds its first democratic presidential election in 30 years. The winner is poet and writer Juan Bosch.

POLI. Fearing political instability in the Dominican Republic, the United States dispatches Ambassador John Bartlow Martin to look for ways of reducing tension on the island. Believing that by increasing the exodus of Dominicans to the United States there will be more jobs on the island and therefore less political and economic friction, Martin encourages facilitating the process of granting visas to Dominicans. A year later, over 10,000 Dominicans are granted visas.

SOCI. On December 14, the first mutual help association for Dominicans is founded in New York City, Centro Cívico Cultural Dominicano. In the 1950s, there had been Dominican organizations in the city but they tended to be politically oriented, either in favor of or against Trujillo's dictatorship.

SOCI. In New York City, the Puerto Rican Family Institute is created to help recent arrivals deal with the cultural and economic pressures of being in New York and away from Puerto Rico.

WARS. On October 14, 1962, an American U2 spy plane photographs nuclear missile installations in Cuba. For next the 13 days, a strategic duel takes place between Kennedy and Soviet Union Prime Minister Nikita Sergeyevich Khrushchev. On October 22, Kennedy announces to the world that the presence of the missiles is aggressive conduct that can not be tolerated. On October 26, Castro tells Khrushchev that an invasion of Cuba by the Americans should lead to a global war. The next day, the Cubans shoot down an American U2 flying over the island. It seems that the three nations, Cuba, the Soviet Union, and the United States, are ready for war. But on October 27, the United States agrees not to invade the island and to remove warheads—Jupiter missiles—from Turkey, if the Soviet Union disarms and withdraws the Cuban missiles. On October 28, Khrushchev agrees. War is averted. The peaceful resolution of the crisis assures Castro that while the United States will continue a covert war against his regime there will be no military invasion of the island. The crisis signals for Cuban exiles the long-term survival of Castro's rule and the reality of a permanent settlement in the United States—up to now, Cubans have thought they would be returning to the island. In Cuba, the resolution angers Castro because the Soviets did not consult with him, reaching an agreement with the United States without Cuban input.

WORK. Cesar Chavez organizes the National Farm Workers Association, later called the United Farm Workers, to help Mexican migrant workers in California.

1963

BUSI. Oscar de la Renta, the son of a Dominican mother and a Puerto Rican father, arrives in New York City to design a high-fashion clothing line for Elizabeth Arden, the owner of a cosmetics empire. Two years later de la Renta will establish his own ready-to-wear line, becoming a household name in the fashion world.

MIGR. From the Dominican Republic, 10,683 leave for the United States. They come from the middle class and tend to be cosmopolitan. This directly contradicts an early stereotypical concept that the Dominicans moving to the United States are poor and from the countryside.

MUSI. Dominican Republic musician Johnny Pacheco founds the record label and company, Fania Records, which promotes an early version of salsa music, launching the career of many salsa performers.

OBIT. On November 22, President John F. Kennedy is assassinated. Though most findings point towards a lone assassin, Lee Harvey Oswald, it is rumored that the president was assassinated by Cubans. Some theorize that Castro had planned the assassination to avenge himself over the Cuban Missile Crisis; others believe that Cuban exiles were behind the plot to avenge the Bay of Pigs fiasco two years earlier.

POLI. Seven months after taking office, Juan Bosch is ousted from the presidency in the Dominican Republic by the military and conservative forces.

POLI. Joseph P. Montoya, New Mexico, is elected a senator and Eligio "Kika" de la Garza, from Texas, is elected a congressman.

SOCI. There are 52 Aspira clubs in the United States. Aspira works with Puerto Rican high school students.

1964

ECON. On January 8, President Lyndon B. Johnson announces the War on Poverty during his state of the union address. Congress establishes the Office of Economic Opportunity to administer local grants to fight poverty. Job Corps, the Community Action Program (CAP), and Volunteers in Service to America (Vista) are established.

EDUC. In Brooklyn, a new public school is named after Carlos Tapia, a Puerto Rican bodega owner who gave away his money to help the needy. His bodega went out of business because Tapia provided free food to many Puerto Ricans in the area.

LAWS. Congress passes the Civil Rights Act of 1964. Affirmative action programs are established.

The act prohibits discrimination based on gender, race, creed, or ethnic background.

POLI. On February 25, President Lyndon B. Johnson signs legislation authorizing a commission to study the political status of Puerto Rico. The commission is composed of Puerto Ricans and non-Puerto Ricans.

POLI. In November, Luis Muñoz Marín completes his final term as governor of Puerto Rico. In office since 1952, the governor is controversial because of his support for commonwealth status. However, even his opponents applaud his efforts to bring businesses to the island and improve the lot of the working and rural poor of Puerto Rico.

WORK. Puerto Rican Alberto E. Sánchez is named vice president of the International Ladies Garment Workers Union (ILGWU), the first Puerto Rican to hold the position.

1965

ARTS. Off Broadway, the play *La carreta,* by the Puerto Rican author René Marqués, is staged to great acclaim. The protagonists are Miriam Colón and Raul Julia, who will become a major Hollywood figure in the 1980s. The success of the play prompts Colón to envision a theater where poor Spanish-speaking families can see quality productions for free. Her vision will lead to the Puerto Rico Traveling Theater, one of the major drama ensembles of Manhattan, founded two years later.

ARTS. In the Southwest, director and playwright Luis Valdez creates the *Teatro Campesino* to promote Cesar Chavez's work as a labor organizer and to offer migrant workers a venue to address injustices through the use of drama. The Teatro travels from one migrant camp to another, often performing the plays atop a flatbed.

CULT. On June 5, the seal of the island of Puerto Rico is placed on a street light on West 41st Street and the Avenue of the Americas in New York City. The seal was originally designed in 1511.

LAWS. The Civil Rights Act of 1965 abolishes literary tests in English as requisite to vote.

Legendary actress and promoter of Latino culture Miriam Colón was the founder of the Puerto Rican Traveling Theater.

LAWS. The Immigration and Nationality Act of 1965 ends the national origin quotas, opening the doors of immigration to people from Asia and Latin America. Though quotas no longer exist, they are replaced with requirements for worldwide limitations, assigning limits to the number of entry visas granted. Through this system, 366,000 family-sponsored immigrants a year are allowed entry and 123,291 immigrants may obtain visas with evidence of a job offer. Nations have a limit of 7 percent immigrants a year per national population.

MIGR. Through the Freedom Airlift, an agreement between the United States and Cuba to provide transportation for Cubans fleeing the country, 4,000 political refugees a month reach American shores. The airlifts begin in December and continue until April of 1973.

OBIT. Pedro Albizu Campos dies on April 21. During his lifetime, he was the heart and soul of the independence movement in Puerto Rico. In

Latin America, he was seen as a Puerto Rican David battling the giant Goliath north of the island. Albizu Campos was trained as an attorney. A stint in the U.S. army, where he served as an officer in a black battalion, turned him against the United States, as he and his comrades experienced discrimination.

OBIT. In Viet Nam, Specialist Fourth Class, U.S. Army, Daniel Fernández throws himself over a grenade to protect his comrades on February 18. He is 22 years old. Fernández is the first Mexican-American to receive the Congressional Medal of Honor.

POLI. Herman Badillo becomes the first Puerto Rican president of the borough of the Bronx in New York City.

POLI. The United States-Puerto Rico Status Commission is formed on December 1 to study the island's status in relationship to the United States. In 1966, the findings report that the matter of commonwealth, independence, or statehood should be settled by a vote of the Puerto Rican people.

POPU. By now, two hundred thousand Cubans have settled in the United States, mostly in Miami.

REBE. "Che" Guevara disappears from Cuba. There are speculations about the end of the friendship between Che and Castro. But in actuality, Che leaves Cuba to participate in revolutionary movements in Africa and in Bolivia.

WARS. A civil war begins in the Dominican Republic, as supporters of exiled president Juan Bosch occupy the Presidential Palace and begin to plan Bosch's return from exile in Puerto Rico.

WARS. There are 48,000 Puerto Ricans in the armed forces, 60 percent of which are volunteers. During the next 10 years, 270 will die in combat and 3,000 will be wounded in Vietnam.

WORK. Maquiladoras are established on the Mexican border to provide employment to local workers as well as former Bracero laborers who return to México or are deported from the United

States. The maquiladora is a factory that assembles parts of a product that originate somewhere else. These factories are usually owned by American companies.

1966

CRIM. The shooting of a Puerto Rican youth in Chicago ignites riots in the Puerto Rican community with hundreds of young people burning cars and breaking into shops and small stores.

LAW. President Lyndon B. Johnson signs into law the Cuban Adjustment Act on November 2. The law forbids the deportation of any Cuban who reaches American soil and grants permanent residency to the arrivals a year after entering the United States. The law irritates Castro. Would-be refugees from Latin America consider the law discriminatory because it singles out Cubans for special treatment.

POLI. Joaquin Balaguer wins the presidential election in the Dominican Republic. His repressive policies, alongside economic difficulties on the island, encourage thousands of Dominicans to flee to the United States.

SOCI. In Denver, Colorado, the *Crusada Para la Justicia* is founded to encourage Mexican-Americans to get involved in politics. The founder is Rodolfo "Corky" Gonzales, an activist and a former boxer.

SOCI. In New York, the Puerto Rican Community Development Project (PRCDF) receives a grant of nearly half a million dollars to contract Puerto Rican civic organizations, religious groups, and business to develop self-help initiatives in Puerto Rican neighborhoods. The services include job finding, consumer education, school guidance, and legal services.

SPOR. Puerto Rican baseball player Roberto Clemente, with the Pittsburgh Pirates, is elected the league's Most Valuable Player.

WORK. The United Farm Workers, under the leadership of Cesar Chavez, begin a five year boycott of grapes cultivated in California to demand higher wages and benefits for farm laborers. In his protests, Chavez employs the methods of nonviolence advocated by Mahatma Gandi.

1967

HEAL. The mayor of New York City, John Lindsey, asks Puerto Rican activist Efrem Rodríguez to set up a drug rehabilitation program in the city, aimed specifically at Puerto Ricans. Rodríguez had established a similar program in Puerto Rico.

LIT. The autobiography *Down These Mean Streets*, by Piri Thomas, is published, becoming a classic of the literature of crime. The work describes the Puerto Rican experience in New York during and after the Depression as well as the depravities experienced by Puerto Ricans who enter a life of crime. The novel regenerates interest in the genre of immigrant literature and it establishes Piri Thomas as a major Puerto Rican American writer.

OBIT. Che Guevara is captured by local Bolivian troops advised by the CIA and under the guidance of a Cuban-American operative. Che is executed on October 9. His hands are chopped off and are reportedly sent to Castro as evidence. His body is buried in an unmarked grave.

POLI. In Puerto Rico, the New Progressive Party is founded to promote statehood. On April 16, a march of 5,000 demonstrators is organized to demand independence for the island. On July 23, a plebiscite over commonwealth status takes place with 60 percent of the voters favoring its maintenance.

REBE. On June 5, Mexican-American activist Reies López Tijerina raids the courthouse in the town of Tierra Amarilla with the objective of making a citizen arrest of the district attorney. Tijerina is a member of Alianza, a group that believes the land in the Southwest should be returned to the descendants of the original Mexican settlers. The attorney is not present, and after a fight with the court guards, López Tijerina heads for the countryside. A massive manhunt occurs and López Tijerina turns himself in. He is eventually found innocent of all charges against him. The incident is celebrated in the corrido *The Ballad of Rio*

Arriba. Composed by Roberto Martínez, the ballad becomes a popular song on local radio stations.

1968

EDUC. The first bilingual college in the country is established in the Bronx, New York City. It is named Eugenio María Hostos Community College, to render tribute to the great Puerto Rican patriot, philosopher, and writer.

LAWS. On September 17, President Lyndon B. Johnson signs Public Law 90-498, approving a proclamation for the establishment of Hispanic Heritage Week. In 1988, the law will be amended to extend the celebration to a month.

MED. The publishing house Quinto Sol is founded to promote works by Chicano authors, reach bilingual readers, and challenge stereotypical perspectives often printed by American mainstream publishers. Quinto Sol is responsible for introducing Rudolfo Anaya, whose novel *Bless Me, Ultima* will be a classic of both Chicano and American literature, and Tomás Rivera, whose *Y no se lo trago la tierra* will be considered one of the best Chicano novels ever written.

POLI. Rodolfo "Corky" Gonzalez convenes the first-ever Chicano youth conference, attended by many future Chicano activists and artists. The conference also promotes the *Plan Espiritual de Aztlan*, Aztlan's Spiritual Plan, a manifesto advocating Chicano nationalism and self-determination for Chicanos/Mexican-Americans.

POLI. In Puerto Rico, the candidate for the New Progressive Party, Luis A. Ferré, is elected governor of the island. Ferré is pro-statehood.

POLI. In New York, four Puerto Ricans are elected to the state senate and assembly: Roberto García, Armando Montano, Luis Nine, and Manuel Ramos. It is a clear demonstration of how Puerto Ricans are gaining influence in New York City and how young Puerto Ricans are mastering the political process in Manhattan.

POLI. In November, Richard M. Nixon wins the U.S. Presidency.

SCIE. A Californian of Spanish descent, Dr. Luis Álvarez wins the Nobel Prize in Physics for his discovery of subatomic particles that exist for a fraction of a second.

SOC. The Mexican American Legal Defense and Education Fund (MALDEF) is established to provide legal assistance to Latinos.

SPOR. In June, Lee Trevino, the first Mexican-American professional golf player, wins the U.S. Open in New York. Trevino will go on to win 20 Professional Golf Association Tours. During the 1970s he will be golfer Jack Nicklaus's principal rival.

1969

ARTS. *El Museo del Barrio* is founded in New York City to exhibit Puerto Rican and other Latino artworks.

EDUC. A department of Puerto Rican studies is established in the City University of New York.

MUSI. On March 16, Puerto Rican singer and composer José Feliciano wins a Grammy.

POLI. A special drive is conducted in New York City to register Puerto Rican voters.

POLI. Cuban-American John Joseph Jova is appointed U.S. ambassador to the Organization of American States.

SOCI. The Young Lords, a Chicago-based activist organization of Puerto Rican members of a gang, sets up a chapter in New York City. Influenced by the Black Party, the organization supports people's control of all public institutions in the community. The organization provides free breakfast to children in Harlem as well as preventive health care. The Young Lords present a new approach in the politics and culture of Puerto Ricans living in New York. The group identifies with social conditions in Manhattan rather than in Puerto Rico.

SOCI. Latino actors, led by Ricardo Montalban, form the organization *Nosotros* to improve the image of Latinos on television and in films and to provide training and educational opportunities for Latinos in the film industry. Montalban confronts

No Need for Visas

In 1917, Puerto Ricans were granted American citizenship. Birth in Puerto Rico equals birth in the United States. Since Puerto Ricans are Americans, they can enter and exit the United States without immigration papers. Prior to the September 11 attacks, Puerto Ricans could enter and leave the United States without the use of passports. In 2005, security changes in flying mandated the need for passport as a form of identification. However, Puerto Ricans do not need a visa to visit, stay, or work in the United States. Other immigrants need immigration papers but as Americans, Puerto Ricans can travel from the island to the mainland as if they were driving from one U.S. state to another.

studio heads, producers, and writers, demanding reevaluation of stereotypical images of Latinos in contemporary films.

1970

LANG. The expression "reverse discrimination" is used by whites who feel they are not receiving the same benefits, or have been denied an employment or educational opportunity, as a result of new laws aiding minorities.

LIT. The Nuyorican Poets Café becomes a space where Nuyorican writers, as well as experimental writers, meet to read and discuss their works. It is in the spirit of the Beat Generation cafes that flourished in California in the 1950s, and Allen Ginsberg, the renowned poet of that generation, is a visitor to the Nuyorican Café.

OBIT. On August 29, Mexican-American journalist Rubén Salazar is shot and killed after attending a protest against the Viet Nam War led by Chicanos. The protest, called the National Chicano Moratorium March, ended in a rally that was broken up by the police. Salazar is covering the event for the Spanish television station KMEX. Some believe that the murder is premeditated, but the investigation does not lead to a prosecution.

POLI. Herman Badillo is elected to Congress, representing his congressional district, the South Bronx. The New Yorker is a faithful supporter of the Kennedys, who help to send him to Washington where he sponsors legislation to provide job training for non-English-speaking immigrants.

POLI. The Raza Unida Party is established on January 17 in Texas to bring greater economic, social, and political self-determination to Mexican-Americans in the state. The party presents candidates for nonpartisan city council and school board races in several cities, winning 15 seats, including two city council majorities, two school board majorities, and two mayoralties. The term *La Raza* refers to the concept first presented by Mexican writer and philosopher José Vazconcelos, who saw the people of Latin American as forming a new race, *raza cósmica,* which includes the blood of Africans, Europeans, and indigenous people.

POLI. Salvador Allende is elected president of Chile.

POPU. There are 93,292 Dominicans living in the United States.

1971

ARTS. In April, Cuban poet Heberto Padilla is arrested and forced to make a staged confession before the *Unión de Escritores y Artistas de Cuba*— Cuban Union of Writers and Artists, in which he accuses his wife, poet Belkis Cuza Malé, and friends of making counterrevolutionary statements and being critical of the revolutionary process. Padilla is placed under house-arrest and his books are banned; he is forbidden to publish his work. In 1980, with the help of Senator Edward Kennedy, Padilla is allowed to leave Cuba.

ARTS. Woody Allen releases the comedy *Bananas,* which makes fun of the concept of the banana republic and such strong rulers as Fidel Castro. The Puerto Rican actor and author Jacobo Morales spoofs Castro. The film is partially shot in Puerto Rico.

LIT. The novel *Y no se lo trago la tierra*, by Tomás Rivera, is published. It is an extraordinary narrative about a young boy and his migrant family. The work documents the discrimination experienced by Chicano farm workers in the Southwest. The author will become the Chancellor of the University of California. Dying at the age of 49, Rivera leaves in his files extensive accounts of the discrimination and belittlement Chicano academics suffer in university settings.

POLI. In Puerto Rico, the proindependence movement becomes the Puerto Rican Socialist party and aligns itself with the Cuban government.

POLI. The first Mexican-American treasurer of the United States is appointed by President Richard M. Nixon. Her name is Ramona Acosta Buñuelos.

SPOR. *Sports Illustrated* names Mexican-American Lee Trevino, the professional golf champion, Sportsman of the Year. Trevino is the only Latino ever awarded such a distinction in sports.

WORK. The United Farm Workers sign a pact with the Teamsters Union giving the latter jurisdiction over food-processing workers and the United Farm Workers jurisdiction over field workers.

WORK. Four thousand Mexican women workers go on strike at three pants factories in Texas, seeking the right to form a union.

1972

ARTS. Jo Raquel Tejada becomes a superstar under the name of Raquel Welch in the science fiction classic *Fantastic Voyage*. A sex symbol throughout the 1970s and early 1980s, she becomes a businesswoman, promoting her own designs of wines and cosmetics. She will portray a Mexican-American in the PBS series, *An American Family*, from 2000 to 2004.

CRIM. On July 17, three Cuban exiles are arrested at the Watergate Hotel in Washington, D.C. Their names are Virgilio González, Bernard Barker, and Eugenio Martínez. They have broken into the Democratic Party's National Headquarters with three other men to steal the files and records on candidate George McGovern's campaign for the presidency. The insignificant break-in will become a major scandal and will result in the resignation of

The Cubans of Watergate

"Three Cubans who gained unwanted notoriety in the 1970s were Bernard Barker, Virgilio González, and Eugenio Martínez, among the 'Watergate burglars' caught while breaking into Democratic Party headquarters to photograph documents for the reelection campaign of Richard M. Nixon. A year later, their actions brought down a presidency.

Why Cubans in the middle of a great American scandal? Most Americans thought of Watergate as proof of the manipulative and unlawful extremes to which Nixon and his aides would go to win reelection, a matter of domestic politics. To the Cuban burglars, the break-in was a continuation of the struggle against Castro. *El exilio*, distrustful of Democrats to begin with, was deeply worried that an ultraliberal administration under George McGovern would embrace the Cuban regime. Barker, González, and Martínez believed the Democratic files at the Watergate would help Nixon win a second term and prevent a McGovern presidency, which they saw as disastrous for the cause of Cuba."

Source: Alex Anton and Roger E. Hernández. *Cubans in America: A Vibrant History of a People in Exile.* New York: Kensington Books, 2002, p. 175.

President Richard Nixon, who had authorized the burglary. All the burglars and conspirators who worked with Nixon will serve reduced prison sentences except for the Cuban conspirators who, due to lack of resources and legal know-how, do not receive appropriate guidance in the legal process.

MED. Scholar Nicolás Kanellos founds *the Revista Chicano-Riqueña*, featuring works by Latinos from diverse backgrounds rather than concentrating on works written by authors from a specific ethnicity. The intent is to show Latino readers that they have a cultural heritage as valuable as anything from the United States and Europe.

POLI. Rafael Hernández Colón wins the election for governor of Puerto Rico. He wants to maintain the commonwealth status of the island.

POLI. The United Nations approves a resolution supporting self-determination and independence for Puerto Rico.

SOCI. The Puerto Rican Legal Defense Fund (PRLDEF) is founded by a group of Puerto Rican lawyers in New York. The fund challenges systemic discrimination. The group files a class action suit against the New York City Board of Education, demanding bilingual education in the classrooms.

SPOR. Roberto Clemente is the first Latino baseball player to reach 3,000 hits and the first Puerto Rican enshrined in the National Baseball Hall of Fame.

SPOR. Armando "Mando" Ramos, a Mexican-American, wins the World Boxing Congress championship. Ramos boxes only for nine years, but during that time he wins two world titles as lightweight.

1973

ARTS. The Nuyorican play, *Short Eyes*, by Miguel Piñero, wins the Obie and New York Drama Critics Circle Award for Best American Play of the 1973–1974 season. The play is a prison drama about a child abuser.

EDUC. Centro de Estudios Puertorriqueños is established at Hunter College, New York. The library becomes the center for Puerto Rican archives in the country.

MED. *The Bilingual Review* appears. Edited by Gary Keller, a literature professor at the City University of New York, the *Review* becomes a respected and recognized outlet for discourses on bilingual education. The success of the journal encourages Keller to found the *Bilingual Review Press*, three years later.

MILI. Cuban-American Mercedes Cubria wins the Legion of Merit for her service to the United

---

Bilingual Blues

"Supporters of bilingual education today imply that students like me miss a great deal by not being taught in their family's language. What they seem not to recognize is that, as a socially disadvantaged child, I considered Spanish to be a private language. What I needed to learn in school was that I had the right—and the obligation—to speak the public language of *los gringos*. The odd truth is that my first-grade classmates could have become bilingual, in the conventional sense of the word, more easily than I. Had they been taught (as upper middle-class children are often taught early) a second language like Spanish or French, they could have regarded it simply as that: another public language. In my case such bilingualism could not have been so quickly achieved. . . . Without question, it would have pleased me to hear my teachers address me in Spanish. . . . But I would have delayed . . . having to learn the language of public society."

Source: Richard Rodriguez. *Hunger of Memory: The Education of Richard Rodriguez.* Toronto: Bantam Books, 1982, p. 19.

States as a lieutenant colonel in the United States Army. She is the first Latina elected to the United States Army Intelligence Hall of Fame. During the October Crisis of 1962, she debriefed Cuban exiles and gathered intelligence information for the CIA.

OBIT. Baseball great Roberto Clemente dies in an airplane crash on January 1. Clemente is riding on a plane overloaded with food and medical supplies for the people of Nicaragua, who are recovering from a major earthquake.

POLI. The United Nations recognizes the right of the Puerto Rican people to choose their future as a nation. The U.N. also declares that Puerto Rico is an American colony.

REBE. On September 11, Chile overthrows Allende's regime with support from the CIA. As General Augusto Pinochet takes over the government, more than 300,000 Chileans flee the country to Cuba, México, Spain, and the United States.

WORK. The United Farm Workers Organizing Committee changes its name to the Farm Workers of America and becomes accredited by the AFL-CIO.

1974

CRIM. Omega 7, an anti-Castro Cuban terrorist group, is formed on September 11. The name refers to seven original members from different anti-Castro Cuban factions. The number of individuals actively participating in this group is fewer than 20. The group operates in New York, New Jersey, and Miami, Florida. The targets are representatives of the Cuban Government or any individual, organization, facility, or business that deals with the Communist government of Fidel Castro. The majority of Omega 7 attacks are bombings, shootings, and assassinations.

EDUC. Congress passes the Equal Education Opportunity Act to provide equality in all public schools by making bilingual education available. The act mandates that students who have trouble with the English language must be given programs and resources to help them master English.

EDUC. New York City provides bilingual education for students with limited English-language ability. It is the result of a lawsuit brought by the Puerto Rican Legal Defense Fund in 1972.

EDUC. Boricua College, a private institution, is established as a four-year college in New York City. It is created to attract and serve Puerto Rican students.

POLI. New Mexico elects Raul Castro as its first Mexican-American governor.

POLI. In New Jersey, a young politician named Bob Menendez is elected president of the Board of Education of Union City. The election helps this Cuban-American seek the post of mayor of the city 12 years later. In 1992, he will be elected to Congress. In 2006 he will be elected to the Senate.

RELI. Roberto Sánchez is appointed archbishop of the Catholic Church in Santa Fe, New Mexico, the first Mexican-American to hold such a position.

1975

ECON. Due to a recession in the United States, Puerto Rico's unemployment is more than 18 percent and the government borrows millions to balance its budget.

EDUC. The Hispanic Scholarship Fund is created specifically to assist Latinos who are already in college, providing grants of up $3,000 to help students taking at least 15 credits a semester.

LAWS. An amendment to the Voting Rights Act of 1965 makes bilingual ballots a requirement in areas where needed.

POLI. The United States returns to Puerto Rico the island of Culebra, a former Navy base used for naval maneuvers and target practice.

REBE. Puerto Rican nationalists, members of the *Fuerzas Armadas de la Liberación Nacional,* explode a bomb in Fraunces Tavern in New York City, killing 4 and injuring more that 50 patrons. The paramilitary group wants independence for Puerto Rico.

SOCI. The National Association of Latin Elected and Appointed Officials, NALEO, is formed in Washington, D.C., with the objective of promoting Latinos in all levels of government.

SPOR. Brazilian soccer star Pelé joins the New York Cosmos, hoping that his presence will increase the popularity of the game. In the 1980s the sport will increase in popularity in the United States, as Latinos are seen playing the games in public parks, and towns in the suburbs create leagues for youngsters.

1976

CRIM. On September 21, Chilean President Salvador Allende's former ambassador to the United States, Orlando Letelier, is murdered in Washington, D.C. The plot is designed by Chile's secret service and carried out by Cuban exiles, who believe they are helping the United States fight Communism and Fidel Castro.

LIT. Chicano author Rolando Hinojosa wins the prestigious literary award Casa de las Américas, from Cuba, for his novel *Klail City y sus alrededores*. He is the first Latino author to receive this honor. The novel depicts the lives of both long-term Chicano residents, whose ancestry dates back to Spanish colonial times, and recent arrivals from México.

MED. *El Herald* appears as the Spanish edition of the *Miami Herald*. It is an attempt at reaching the Cuban community. The community is critical of the *Miami Herald,* which they feel only reports news that is favorable toward Castro while reporting little on activities of Cuban-Americans.

POLI. In the United States, President Ford declares his endorsement for statehood for Puerto Rico. In November, Ford loses to Jimmy Carter. Carter will attempt to establish relationships with Cuba, but a larger presence of Soviet troops on the island in 1980 and the Mariel boatlift of the same year will derail the diplomatic efforts.

POLI. Carlos Romero Barceló is elected governor of Puerto Rico. He works to address economic issues on the island and to forego political discussions about Puerto Rico's commonwealth status.

He is also elected president of the National League of Cities, the first Latino to hold such a position.

POLI. In Argentina, General Jorge Rafael Videla overthrows President Isabel Perón, the third wife of the late President Juan Perón.

POLI. The Hispanic Caucus is formed in Washington, D.C., as a forum for Latinos in Congress and the Senate. The Caucus voices and promotes issues affecting Latinos. The Caucus offers scholarships to Latino college students and links Latino organizations and institutions serving the Latino community.

REBE. On July 26, to celebrate an anniversary of the Cuban revolution, Puerto Rican independence leader Filiberto Ojeda Ríos founds the Ejercito Popular Boricua with the objective of leading Puerto Ricans into an open rebellion against the local government and the United States. A year later, on January 3, the group, known as Los Macheteros, to honor the Puerto Rican peasants who had fought against U.S. Marines in 1898, plans a bombing campaign that is discovered by the police. After a half dozen bank robberies in Puerto Rico and attacks on military personnel, Los Macheteros rob a Wells Fargo truck in Connecticut on September 12, 1983, getting away with $7 million.

1977

SOCI. A group of young Cuban-Americans form the Antonio Maceo Brigade to visit Cuba, volunteer for work on the island, and attempt to create avenues of dialogue between Cuban exiles and Cubans on the island. The group invites young Puerto Ricans to join them on their trips to Cuba. The creation of the group causes conflict in the Cuban community, which sees the brigade as being supportive of the Castro regime. Later on, some of the members of the brigade will feel that the Castro's regime used them for their own political purpose.

1978

ARTS. The play *Zoot Suit*, by Luis Valdes, about the race riots that took place in Los Angeles during World War II, opens in that city. Meant to play for 10 days, the production runs for over a year before opening on Broadway and becoming a movie three years later. The play makes actor Edward James Olmos a respected and influential figure in Hollywood.

REBE. Two Puerto Rican proindependence youths are killed by police in El Cerro Maravilla, in Puerto Rico. The police officers believe the youths are planning to bomb a television antenna placed on the hill.

1979

ARTS. Cuban-American directors Leon Ichaso and Orlando Jiménez Leal release the film *El Super,* the moving story of a Cuban refugee who works as a building superintendent in New York City. Homesick for Cuba, *el super* dreams of moving to Miami where there is no snow. In one scene, his Puerto Rican friend tells him that both are in exile and cannot return home, regardless of political conditions, because they belong neither in the United States nor to the Caribbean. Raymundo Hidalgo-Gato portrays the lead role and his Puerto Rican friend is interpreted by Raynaldo Medina. The script is based on a play by Cuban-American playwright Ivan Acosta.

BUSI. Cuban-American exile Roberto C. Goizueta is appointed president of Coca-Cola. He introduces the slogan "Coke is it" (Coca Cola Slogans, Wikipedia, November 17, 2006). and makes the brand the best known in the world. He also introduces Diet Coke.

LIT. The collection of poetry *La Carreta Made a U-Turn,* by Tato Laviera, is published. In the volume, Laviera rejects Rene Marques's concept that to be Puerto Rican a person needs to be on the island; Laviera maintains that Puerto Ricans can be found in New York as well. Laviera becomes one of the best-known poets to write in Spanglish, using both English and Spanish, and will be awarded a Before Columbus Award.

MED. Arte Público Press is founded by Nicolás Kanellos. One of its first triumphs is the publication of the innovative novel *House on Mango Street* by the Chicana Sandra Cisneros. The novel, consisting of vignettes recalling the author's life in a poor neighborhood, will become part of the American literary canon in less than a decade.

RACE. Panamian Rod Carew is disturbed by racist comments made by the owner of the Minnesota Twins and forces a trade to the California Angels. In 1967, Carew was Rookie of the Year and from 1969 onwards, he had 15 consecutive seasons batting .300 and winning seven American League batting championships.

WARS. Civil wars in Central America force thousands of refugees to flee and to try to cross the border to the United States.

1980

LANG. The English Only movement emerges to oppose bilingual education and to require that

---

English Will Rock You

"When Mexican-Americans were asked in the National Latino Political Survey whether people residing in the United States should learn English, nearly 95 percent agreed that they should. Immigrants demonstrate their eagerness to learn English by crowding into low-cost English classes almost anywhere they are available.

. . . Some Americans understandably worry that their nation is becoming a Babel because so many people are speaking so many languages, but all the evidence shows that the primacy of English is not threatened by immigration. . . . Those who fear a polyglot future need to be patient and supportive while immigrants learn English. Those who dream of a multilingual society . . . need to recognize that it is not going to happen in the United States, ever."

Source: Roberto Suro. *Strangers Among US: Latino Lives in a Changing America.* New York: Vintage Books, 1999, p. 313.

people speak only English in public gatherings. The movement opposes the use of other languages besides English in printed materials funded by the national or local governments. The English Only advocates lobby their local officials to pass legislation making English the official language of the country. An early champion of the cause is Senator Samuel Ichiye Hayakawa, from California, who proposes in 1981 an amendment to the Constitution of the United States establishing English as the official language of the United States, though neither the Congress nor the Senate take action on the proposal.

LANG. The Mariel boatlift of April introduces a new term in Spanish and in English, *Marielito.* Since there is exaggerated information about the criminal background of the Cubans who participate in the boatlift, coupled with the initial rejection of the new exiles by the established exiles, who view themselves as socially superior, the term suggests a lower-class immigrant who is not competent within American society. Marielito specifically refers to a Cuban who arrives in the United States in 1980 as part of the boatlift.

LIT. Among those leaving Cuba in the Mariel boatlift are dozens of writers who are not allowed to publish in Cuba or have suffered persecution because their writing is considered antirevolutionary. These writers form a group known as the Mariel Generation, because they are united not by literary style but by their participation in the boatlift. There are some common characteristics in their works, including a critical view of the revolution and a rejection of American capitalism and materialism. The most famous of the writers in the group is novelist Reynaldo Arenas, who settles in New York City.

MIGR. The deteriorating economic conditions in the Dominican Republic push professionals and technical workers to seek employment in the United States.

MIGR. Between April 21 and September 26, over 125,000 Cubans flee the island as part of the Mariel Boatlift. The sudden flight is the result of a dispute between Fidel Castro and the Peruvian Government who refuses to return six exiles who are seeking protection in that country's embassy in Cuba. An angry Castro removes protection from the embassy and announces to the Cuban people that those wishing to leave the island could seek asylum in the embassy. In less than 24 hours, 10,000 Cubans crammed into the embassy. In April, Castro opens the port of Mariel, inviting Cuban exiles in Miami to travel to the island to pick up relatives. To discredit those leaving, Castro releases about 10,000 hard-core criminals and mentally ill people, forcing Cubans from Miami to take them with their families. Part of his plan is to create a negative image of Cubans in the United States, an approach that is somewhat successful.

OBIT. Luis Muñoz Marín dies on April 30. In the 1940s, he was president of the Puerto Rican Senate, economic commissioner, and chairperson

---

Castro Gives Cubans a Bad Name

"The Mariel boatlift has been popularly cast in a negative light. The Cuban government as well as the U.S. mass media exaggerated the presence of criminals, mental patients, prostitutes, and other misfits among the new exiles. Sensationalist stories and editorials about Marielitos' delinquent activities began to appear in the main U.S. newspapers. Brian De Palma's popular remake of "Scarface," which depicted Mariel exiles as vicious mobsters, pimps, and drug dealers, is one of the best known unflattering portrayals. . . . Contrary to widespread media reports, less than 2 percent of the Marielitos were serious criminals, although 25 percent had been imprisoned for various reasons, including . . . homosexuality and trading in the black market."

Source: Jorge Duany. "Mariel Boatlift." In *Cuban Encyclopedia: People, History, Culture.* Ed. Luis Martínez Fernández, et al. Westport, CT: Greenwood Press, 2003, pp. 585–86.

of the commission on the island's political status. In 1948, he was elected governor of the island. Choosing whether to promote full independence or to concentrate on an economic infrastructure that would improve conditions for all Puerto Ricans, he opted for instituting the commonwealth status, which allowed Puerto Rico to enact its laws—as long as they did not violate the American constitution—and to receive federal benefits and protection. He also initiated Operation Bootstrap to encourage the presence of American corporations on the island.

POLI. The Refugee Act of 1980 removes the definition of a political refugee as a person who is escaping from a Communist country, allowing refugees of other oppressive regimes to seek entry into the United States.

POLI. Ronald Reagan is elected president in November. He is one of the first presidential candidates to seek Cuban support in Miami. His visits to *La Esquina de Tejas*, a popular Cuban restaurant in Little Havana, is celebrated by Cuban-Americans throughout Dade County. Reagan's promise to fight communism encourages Cuban-Americans to campaign for his presidency, the beginning of electoral involvement for Cubans in the United States. Over 85 percent of Cubans in Florida vote for Reagan.

POPU. From the Dominican Republic, 148,135 settle in the United States. More than 65 percent choose New York City as their home.

SPOR. Boxer Roberto Durán, a native of Panama, wins the World Boxing Council welterweight title.

1981

BUSI. Fashion designer Oscar de la Renta, from the Dominican Republic, donates four years of service to the Boy Scouts to design a new uniform for the association.

POLI. Mexican-American Henry Cisneros is elected mayor of San Antonio, Texas, the first Latino to administer a large U.S. city. He receives international attention for his ability to develop the local economy and seek consensus within the

different racial constituencies in the city. The Democratic Party considers him a good vice-presidential candidate in the Walter Mondale campaign. His good looks, eloquence, and charm encourage politicians to consider him as a future presidential candidate, but family affairs and a publicized romance with another woman force Cisneros to withdraw from public life.

SOCI. In Florida, the Cuban American National Foundation is founded to support a nonviolent transition to a pluralistic, market-based democracy in Cuba and to seek the protection of human rights and basic freedoms in Cuba. The foundation establishes a lobbying presence in Washington, modeled on Israeli lobbyists, and promotes the embargo against Castro's government. Unlike other similar Latino bodies that promote the welfare of Latinos in the United States, the CANF concentrates on Cuban matters.

SPOR. Mexican-American Fernando Valenzuela, from the Los Angeles Dodgers, is named Rookie of the Year and Player of the Year, leading the league in strikeouts. He is believed to throw the best screwball in the game.

1982

EDUC. Eighteen Latino students from an East Los Angeles school take Advanced Placement calculus exams and pass. As teacher Jaime Escalante and his students celebrate the accomplishment, the Educational Testing Service concludes that the students cheated. Fourteen students retake the test and pass with the same high marks. The Bolivian-born Escalante becomes a celebrity. His motto is "Determination, Discipline and Hard Work Equals Success." In 1988, President Reagan will award him the Presidential Medal for Excellence in Teaching.

LIT. Colombian author Gabriel García Márquez receives the Nobel Peace Prize for Literature. Gabito, as he is affectionately called in South America, first achieved international fame with his novel *One Hundred Years of Solitude*, a retelling of Latin American history that is one of the most read books from Latin America in the United States. The novel will influence scores of American and Latino writers including Isabel Allende, Oscar Hijuelos, and Tony Morrison.

LIT. *House of Spirits*, a translation of the *La casa de los espiritos*, makes Isabel Allende a best-selling author in the United States. Allende, the niece of doomed Chilean president Salvador Allende, presents a history of her native Chile in a sweeping style that converts the book into a history of all Latin America. Allende becomes one of the world's most popular authors, and her novel serves as an introduction to Latin American literature and history for many American readers.

LIT. The publication of *Hunger of Memory: The Education of Richard Rodriguez* scandalizes the Latino community. In his memoirs, the Mexican-American author chronicles his separation from his family and Mexican culture as he becomes a gifted scholar and pursues studies in England and in the United States. A particular assertion that infuriates many Latinos is Rodriguez's criticism of bilingual education and affirmative action programs, proclaiming the need for disadvantaged students to enter the public arena by mastering English and assimilating into American culture.

1983

ARTS. The film *The Ballad of Gregorio Cortez* is shown on Public Television to great acclaim. The film is based on the true story of the unjust arrest of Gregorio Cortez, falsely accused of murdering a sheriff in 1901. Actor Edward James Olmos, who portrays Cortez, obtains the rights to the film and shows it in local theaters in Latino communities, often not charging for admission. Eventually, Embassy Pictures picks up the film for a wider release.

ARTS. The independent film *El Norte* wins international praise for its portrayals of a brother and sister from Guatemala who escape death at the hands of the paramilitary by making their way to El Norte, the United States. The film demonstrates how American media, through popular magazines and films, present the United States as a paradise, an image the refugees believe as they cross the border into "el norte." But in the United States, the brother, played by David Villalpando, and the sister, portrayed by Zaide Silvia Gutiérrez, encounter tragedy. The film also emphasizes diversity within the Latino community as a Mexican-American

worker denounces an illegal alien who is a contestant for his job.

SPOR. Right-handed pitcher Juan Marichal, from the Dominican Republic, is inducted into the Baseball Hall of Fame. Marichel played for the Boston Red Sox and Los Angeles Dodgers. Playing over 15 years, his career includes 243 victories and 142 losses.

WARS. On October 25 President Reagan authorizes Operation Urgency, citing the need to protect 500 American medical students living and studying in Grenada and to heed the request by the Organization of Caribbean States to help restore order on the island. American forces disembark in Granada and fight Cuban forces, who support revolutionary ruler Maurice Bishop. It is the first time in history that American forces fight against Cuban forces.

1984

ARTS. Mexican American Edward James Olmos creates one of the most enigmatic characters in television: the austere and mystical Lt. Castillo in the hit crime series *Miami Vice*.

CRIM. Eduardo Arocena, leader of the terrorist group Omega 7, is arrested and the group ceases to function. Arocena had participated in the assassination of two individuals who the group believed were cooperating or working for Fidel Castro in the United States. In Cuba, the media accuses Arocena of being a CIA agent.

MED. To compete with Spanish International Network, a group of independent Spanish stations in the United States form NETSPAM. In 1986, the new network became known as *Telemundo*. It produces soap operas recorded in Puerto Rico. In 2001, NBC purchased Telemundo.

1985

MED. Radio Martí, under the auspices of the Voice of America, begins broadcasting to Cuba. The short-wave station is managed and staffed by Cuban Americans. The primary purpose of the station is to present uncensored news to contest the misinformation offered to Cubans by the

Cuban media on the island. The station also includes music programs and soap operas.

1986

LAWS. The Immigration Reform and Control Act is passed by Congress. The act creates an alien legalization program granting legal status to illegal aliens who were in the United States prior to January 1982.

MED. As the Spanish International Network acquires more television stations throughout the United States, it premieres *Sábado Gigante*, probably the most popular variety show in the world. It is seen in the United States, Latin America, several European nations, and even in Asia. Because of federal restrictions not allowing foreign corporations to own television networks in the United States, SIN is sold to Hallmark, which changes the name of the network to *Univisión*.

POLI. Members of the Reagan administration sell arms to Iran to use the money to fund anti-Sandinista guerrilla warfare in Nicaragua. Two Cuban-American operatives work in the Caribbean and in Nicaragua making contacts for the administration and delivering weapons. They see their participation as an effort to end communism's global domination and to strike a blow against Fidel Castro.

1988

EDUC. The first Latino Secretary of Education, Dr. Lauro F. Cavazos, is appointed by President Ronald Reagan.

MED. *Hispanic* magazine is launched. A sleek publication, the periodical targets middle-class Latinos or Latinos aspiring to the middle class and higher. It is a mainstream attempt that emphasizes the cultural values of maintaining Latino roots while celebrating the accomplishments of Latino artists, politicians, and celebrities. With a circulation of 150,000, it attracts advertisements, the main source of revenue for a periodical.

MED. Cuban-American Daisy Fuentes is the first Latina video jockey to host both MTV, which broadcasts in English, and MTV Internacional, which broadcasts in Spanish. The statuesque Fuentes is featured in advertisements for cosmetics and diet/exercise programs.

MUSI. On March 18, more than 119,000 people form the largest conga line ever during the Calle Ocho festival. The festival, a musical celebration in a carnival atmosphere, attracts a million tourists and residents to an area in Miami known as Little Havana. The festival dates to 1927 when the Florida legislature approved a week's celebration of Miami pride in the neighborhood. The Cuban and Latin flavor of the 1980s change the

---

Becoming Dominican Americans

"One of the most obvious results of the immigrant experience for Dominicans is that the space of their physical and existential mobility increases tremendously. Their living space after migration encompasses both the native country and the North American mainland. They now can access a large mental habitat within which to configure their human identity. Their ampler sphere of experience entails an ability to harmonize English with Spanish, snowstorms with tropical rains, and merengue with rock or rap . . . it also entails the possibility of creating alternative models by rearranging the existing ones. Thus, there can be a Dominican young man who, though born in the United States, eats rice and beans and yearns to visit Santo Domingo in the summer, sitting right next to a middle-aged woman who has given up on Dominican food even though she came to this country only five years ago."

Source: Silvio Torres-Saillant and Ramona Hernández. *The Dominican Americans.* Westport, CT: Greenwood Press, 1998, p. 146.

mood of the festival to the largest and grandest block party in the world.

1989

POLI. Cuban-American politician Ileana Ros-Lehtinen becomes the first Latina elected to the U.S. Congress. She attacks the Cuban government for human rights violations and for failures to enact progressive changes within the government. The Cuban government describes her as "ferocious wolf in woman's clothing." The congresswoman will be reelected to eight terms.

WAR. In December, the United States invades Panama and arrests its ruler, General Manuel Noriega, who is trafficking drugs and has murdered opponents. He is shipped to the United States for a trial.

1990

ARTS. Cuban-American actor Andy Garcia receives Best Supporting Actor nominations for the Golden Globe Award and the Oscar for his role in

Congresswoman Ileana Ros-Lehtinen, a Cuban American. Ros-Lehtinen is one of only a handful of Latino women elected to national office in the United States. Courtesy of Congresswoman Ros-Lehtinen's office.

the film *Godfather III*. His good looks and acting abilities make him one of the few Latinos in Hollywood to achieve international fame and to be considered a leading man type rather than a character actor.

BUSI. The U.S. Post Office issues a stamp commemorating governor Luis Muñoz Marín.

LANG. There is intense discussion regarding the use of the terms "Hispanic" or "Latino" to describe people in the United States of Latin American descent or of Latin American birth. The latter term is in Spanish and it is commonly applied to people from Latin America rather than Spain. It is a term created by the community itself. "Hispanic" has been used since the nineteenth century in the United States to describe people descending from countries where Spanish is the dominant language and to indicate a connection to ancient Spain, called Hispania. The terms carry political connections. Many scholars maintain that "Hispanic" is conservative while Latino is more aggressive; the first term suggests assimilation into American culture while "Latino" does not.

LAWS. The Immigration Act of 1990 establishes preferred status for family-sponsored aliens and for professionals and individuals with unique talents and skills, such as athletes and performers.

LIT. The Rockefeller Foundation, the Andrew W. Mellon Foundation, the Ford Foundation, the Meadows Foundation, and the National Endowment for the Humanities sponsor the Recovery Project, under the direction of Latino scholar Nicolás Kanellos. The objective of the project is to uncover the literature that was produced in Spanish in the United States from the sixteenth to the twentieth century and to promote that literature. The effort helps to change the American literature curriculum in schools by placing more emphasis on early works by the Spanish conquistadores and early Cuban, Mexican-American, and Puerto Rican writers.

LIT. Cuban-American novelist Oscar Hijuelos wins the Pulitzer Prize for fiction for his best-selling novel *The Mambo Kings Play Songs of Love*. He is the first Latino to win this award. The novel, a vivid recreation of Latino nightlife in New York

City during the late 1940s and early 1950s, is the story of two brothers who are musicians and who experience a moment of fame when they appear on the television show *I Love Lucy.* The award solidifies Hijuelos as one of the major writers of the late twentieth century; the author is often compared to Charles Dickens for his detailed depiction of city landscapes.

LIT. Latino literature emerges as an important extension of American literature, with many Latino authors, such as Julia Alvarez, Sandra Cisneros, Richard Rodriguez, and Gary Soto, achieving name recognition as their works become part of the high school and college curriculum. This body of work reflects a strong preference for autobiographical novels and memoirs.

MIGR. The Employment Creation Investors Visa is created with the intent of allowing wealthy foreigners to obtain visas if they promise to invest between $500,000 and a million dollars in the United States. Critics call this controversial visa the "America for Sale" visa.

MUSI. Latino music proliferates over the airwaves, crossing over from Latino radio stations to the mainstream. Puerto Ricans Ricky Martin and Marc Anthony become idols of teenagers across the United States. The newcomers Christina Aguilera, whose father is from Ecuador and mother from Germany, and Colombian-American Shakira combine rap and Latin beat with sexuality that makes them popular fixtures on MTV. Though not a singer, Cuban-American Daisy Fuentes begins on the Spanish version of MTV and crosses

over to the mainstream as a music commentator and hosts of variety shows. She also becomes a top fashion model.

POLI. Antonia C. Novello, from Puerto Rico, is the first woman and the first Latina appointed by President George Bush as Surgeon General of the United States.

POLI. Puerto Rican José Serrano is elected to Congress, representing New York City. He entered politics in 1974 when he was an assemblyman in the New York State Legislature. He labors vigorously for the removal of American forces from the island of Vieques off the coast of Puerto Rico and opposes the designation of English as the country's official language.

POPU. The United States has 22,354,059 Latino residents, with 1,086,000 Puerto Ricans living in New York City.

WARS. Twenty thousand Latino soldiers participate in Operations Desert Shield and Desert Storm in Iraq out of a force of over 400,000.

WARS. A narco-war rages in Colombia. Thousands of Colombian seek asylum in the United States, but the American government is unwilling to grant visas because Colombia is a democratic republic and the would-be exile seekers are not persecuted by the government.

1991

BUSI. In New York City, 70 percent of all bodegas are now owned by Dominicans.

LIT. With the publication of *How the García Girls Lost Their Accents* Dominican-American Julia Alvarez emerges as a new voice in Latino literature, one that expresses the experiences of a character from the Dominican Republic rather than México, Puerto Rico, or Cuba. The autobiographical novel follows the lives of four sisters who immigrate as children to New York City from their nation because of their wealthy father's opposition to the dictatorship of Rafael Leónidas Trujillo.

1992

BUSI. Goya, a company which was first founded to serve Puerto Ricans, reaches $500 million in revenue. The company, now managed by Joseph Unanue, son of the founder, is targeting both American and Latino consumers, placing its products in American supermarkets while still serving the popular bodegas or Latino supermarkets in the barrios.

LEGE. Newspapers in Puerto Rico report the appearance of a vampire-like creature that targets small animals, killing them and sucking their blood. The occurrences were first reported in the 1970s in the town of Moca, where the creature was called El Vampiro de Moca. In the 1980s and 1990s multiple sightings occur of the creature, who is reported to look like a dog that can stand up, with fangs and in some cases, wings. The creature lives in an area near El Yunque rainforest, but expeditions do not find it. Soon sightings are reported in Miami and then California before the creature appears in México. By now, people are calling it the *Chupacabra*, the goat sucker.

LIT. *Dreaming in Cuba*, by Cuban-American Cristina García, is published. The novel describes Cuban history from the 1930s to 1980, when thousands of Cubans fled through the Mariel boatlift. It is an attempt to offer a variety of

perspectives on the Cuban revolution and to document the success of Cuban-Americans in the United States. The author emerges as the best-known Cuban-American writer of the 1990s.

MUSI. Dominican musician Juan Luis Guerra wins a Grammy award for his recording, *Bachata Rosa,* affording the musical form known as bachata a level of respectability. Bachata emerges from the countryside and poor neighborhoods of the Dominican Republic. The songs play on sexual themes that, until their acceptance in the Latino communities in the United States and throughout Latin America, were considered too vulgar for cultured people in the Dominican Republic.

MUSI. Tito Puente is inducted into the National Congressional Record for his contribution to Latin Jazz and salsa music. Puente is known for using a Caribbean type of drums called timbales. During the 1950s the Puerto Rican musician helped to make Afro-Cuban and Caribbean sound popular with mainstream audiences. By the 1970s, Puente had received six Grammy awards.

POLI. On October 23, President George Bush signs the Cuban Democracy Act, also known as the Torricelli Bill, banning foreign companies

Musician Tito Puentes, the king of Salsa, receives an honorary degree from Bloomfield College.

subsidized by American corporations from conducting business with Cuba. The act demonstrates the successful lobbying effort of the Cuban-American National Foundation. The president signs the act in Miami.

POLI. In November, Cuban-American Lincoln Díaz Balart, representing Dade County, Florida, is elected to the U.S. Congress. Because of his firm anti-Castro stance and support of the embargo, the media in Cuba accuse him of being part of the Cuban-American mafia. In the late 1990s Díaz-Balart will successfully expand the reception of SSI, also known as disability benefits, and food stamps to legal immigrants who were denied aid by the Welfare Reform Law of 1996. He will also write legislation to grant legal residency to thousands of immigrants in the United States, especially refugees from Central America.

POLI. Nydia M. Velázquez is the first Puerto Rican woman elected to Congress, where she advocates for unpaid family and medical leave, faster voter registration procedures, and social and economic programs for the elderly.

REBE. On February 4, Colonel Hugo Chávez attempts to overthrow the democratically elected government of Venezuela. The plot fails and Chavez is sent to prison for two years. Upon his release, he becomes a national figure and chooses to pursue the political process as an avenue to power.

WARS. The civil war in El Salvador ends in February when the Farabundo Martí National Liberation Front and the government sign a peace treaty.

1993

EDUC. The Hispanic College Fund is established to encourage Latino college students to major in business. The fund attempts to connect Latino business administrators and executives with Latino students as well as providing financial assistance.

LANG. The Puerto Rican legislature declares English and Spanish the official languages of Puerto Rico.

MUSI. Cuban-American composer and performer Gloria Estefan receives a star on the Hollywood Walk of Fame. She developed a fast Latin and rock-and-roll sound with repetitive conga rhythm. In 1985, her song "Conga" became an international hit.

POLI. A referendum on Puerto Rico's status shows an almost equally divided island, 48 percent for commonwealth and 46 percent for statehood. Only 4 percent want independence.

POLI. President Bill Clinton appoints Federico Peña to the post of Secretary of Transportation and Henry Cisneros to the post of Secretary of Housing and Urban Development, the first Latinos to hold such positions. He also appoints Norma

Cuban Americans in Miami. The initial wave of hundreds of Cubans who left the island in January 1959, after Castro's victory over Batista, led to a migration of nearly one million Cubans by the end of the twentieth century.

Puerto Rico's Incredible Vampire

"The single most notable cryptozoological phenomenon of the past decade is undoubtedly the Chupacabras . . . carcasses of goats, chickens, and other small farm animals, seemingly devoid of blood, began to be found near the Puerto Rican towns of Morovis and Orocovis. . . . The first sight [of the Chupacabras] . . . said to combine the features of a kangaroo, a gargoyle, and the gray alien of abduction lore. It was said to be hairy, about four feet tall, with a large, round head, a lipless mouth, sharp fangs, and huge lidless eyes. Its body was small, with thin, clawed, seemingly webbed arms with muscular hind legs. The hairy creature also had a series of pointy spikes running from the top of its head to its backbone. . . . The first major American sighting . . . took place in March 1996 in Miami, followed by others in Texas, Arizona, and other North American locations. . . . The International Society of Cryptozoology . . . feels that the Chupacabras folklore may comprise mixed traditions . . . [dating to Taíno mythology]."

Source: Loren Coleman and Jerome Clark. *Cryptozoology A to Z.* New York: Simon and Schuster, 1999, pp. 61–63.

Contú as Assistant Secretary for Civil Rights. The three appointees are Mexican-Americans.

RELI. After a lengthy court battle, the U.S. Supreme Court recognizes Santería as a religion with prescribed rituals, religious training for priests, santeros, and a code of conduct. Miami and New York City emerge as major centers of Santería practice. Santeria maintains that each person has a destiny that he or she must discover. Gods, called *orisha*, help individuals find their destiny. To stay in harmony with an orisha, the practitioner must bring food to the god at the altar. There are also animal sacrifices that must take place with speed and minimum pain to the animal. Santería also includes spiritual possession, when an orisha possesses a vessel for a short while with the objective of divination.

SOCI. The Cuban Committee for Democracy is organized to promote working for a peaceful transition to democracy in Cuba and to establish a diplomatic resolution of the longstanding conflict between Cuba and the United States. Members are Cuban intellectuals, professors, and writers. The organization also promotes political tolerance within the Cuban community, which tends to favor conservative views and support of the embargo.

1994

ARTS. Puerto Rican actor Raul Julia wins Emmy and Golden Globe awards for his portrayal of Brazilian environmentalist and activist Chico Mendes in the film *The Burning Season*. Julia worked on the film while battling cancer, succumbing to the disease on October 24. Julia was the memorable revolutionary in the film *Kiss of the Spider Woman* and charming eccentric Addams in the two popular *Addams Family* films.

EDUC. The CUNY Dominican Studies Institute is accredited on February 22. It is a research center of the City University of New York devoted to the production, the gathering, and dissemination of knowledge on Dominicans in the United States, the Dominican Republic, and elsewhere. The institute sponsors research projects covering areas that include education, migration, language, literature, history, economics, women's issues, politics, youth, cultural identity, sports, performing arts, and visual arts.

LIT. Puerto Rican Esmeralda Santiago publishes *When I Was Puerto Rican,* in which she recounts episodes from her childhood in Puerto Rico as well as from her migration experience. The first of 11 children raised by a single mother, Santiago describes in detail the hardships, but also the

World of Spirits

In the novel *Bless Me, Ultima*, a young child remembers the mysticism he experienced when he meets a healer named Ultima:

"Ultima came to stay with us in the summer I was almost seven. When she came the beauty of the llano unfolded before my eyes, and the gurgling of waters of the river sang to the hum of the turning earth. The magical time of childhood stood still, and the pulse of the living earth pressed its mystery into my living blood. She took my hand, and the silent magic powers she possessed made beauty from the raw, sun-baked llano, the green river valley, and the blue bowl which was the white sun's home. My bare feet felt the throbbing earth and my body trembled with excitement. Time stood still, and it shared with me all that had been, and that all that was to come. ...

The silent magic powers she possessed made beauty from the raw, sun-baked llano, the green river valley, and the blue bowl which was the white sun's home. My bare feet felt the throbbing earth and my body tremble with excitement. Time stood still, and it shared with me all that had been, and that all that was to come."

Source: Rudolfo Anaya. *Bless Me, Ultima.* New York: Time Warner Books, 1972, p. 1.

comforting community, that surrounded her poverty-stricken family. With them she moved to Brooklyn, New York, when she was 11 and battled her way into a school system that favored natives and English speakers. She would eventually attend the prestigious School of Performing Arts in New York City and graduate from Harvard University.

MIGR. From August 13 to September 13, the U.S. Coast Guard intercepts over 35,000 Cubans escaping from the island on homemade rafts known as *balsas*. The term *balsero* refers to a Cuban who reaches American shore on this flimsy vessel. A surprising number of balseros, 21 percent, are members of Cuba's Communist Party. They are well educated and live in cities.

MUSI. A Grammy Music Award is bestowed on Mexican-Texas-American singer Selena Quintanilla Pérez for the album *Selena Live*! Selena's music combines Mexican sounds and rhythms with Texan country-western melodies to create a Latino flavor. Selena becomes a sensation in México and is in the process of crossing over into mainstream American music culture when she is murdered on March 31, 1995 by one of her employees.

POLI. On November 4, 59 percent of the voters in California approve Proposition 187, which prohibits undocumented aliens from receiving public education and numerous other benefits, such as welfare assistance. Teachers and doctors are required to report suspected illegal alien activities in California. On November 11 a federal judge issues a temporary restraining order against it, explaining that the proposition exceeds state authority in the federal realm of immigration. In 1999, Governor Gray Davis upholds the judge's ruling and outlaws the proposition.

TRAD. The North American Free Trade Agreement, known as NAFTA, is approved by Congress. The agreement eliminates all tariffs between trading partners in Canada, México, and the United States. In the United States, labor unions oppose NAFTA out of fear that jobs will be lost to México. In México, the Zapatista National Liberation Army, composed of Mayas, leads a rebellion to protest NAFTA. They take over the southern city of San Cristóbal de las Casas and the towns of Ocosingo and Las Margaritas.

1995

MIGR. The "wet feet, dry feet" policy is established by President Bill Clinton. It is a revision of the Cuban Adjustment Act of 1966 that welcomed Cubans into the United States even when intercepted on the open sea. The new policy mandates the return of any Cubans caught at sea by the U.S. Coast Guard, hence the "wet-feet" designation. Those Cubans who make it to American soil are allowed to stay. The move angers Cuban-Americans, who see the new policy as a victory for Fidel Castro.

1996

LIT. Dominican-American Junot Díaz, who was raised in New Jersey, achieves critical recognition with his collection of short stories *Drown*, in which he explores the machismo culture of Latinos and the challenges encountered by young Latinos who live in a poor and urban environment.

MUSI. Paquito D'Rivera wins a Grammy in the category of Best Latin Jazz Performance. D'Rivera had left Cuba in 1979, settling in the New York/New Jersey area. His music combines Afro-Cuban rhythms with American jazz sounds.

POLI. On February 24, the Cuban air force shoots down in international water two civilian planes being flown by Cuban-Americans. The two planes are part of the operation *Hermanos al Rescate,* Brothers to the Rescue, which scouts the Caribbean Sea for Cuban balseros, rafters, and then alerts the U.S. Coast Guard so the rafters can be rescued. The bodies of the four Cuban-Americans are never found. An unrepentant Castro accuses the Cuban-Americans of violating Cuba's air space. The cockpit's recording reveals the planes were 12 miles away from Cuban waters.

POLI. In November, William Clinton is re-elected president of the United States with overwhelming support of the Latino community. In a surprising development, over 40 percent of Cuban-Americans in Florida support Clinton, a Democrat. The switch from the traditional preference for a Republican candidate may be the result of Clinton's support of the Helms-Burton Act, which sought to tighten the embargo by punishing foreign companies that invested in Cuban properties the revolutionary government had confiscated from private owners or American corporations. Clinton also appeared receptive to immigrants, while the Republican Party was identified with tough anti-immigrant postures. Subsequent political moves that Clinton would make, such as ending the political refugee status for Cubans and his decision to return Elian González back to Cuba, would place Cuban-Americans again in the Republican fold.

SPOR. Major League Soccer is created. The MLS has 10 teams and a roster of national and international players. Seven years later, the MLS will boast of 17 million fans attending games, with millions of Latinos as regular attendees. Major television networks broadcast matches but Spanish television, such as Univisión, offers the best coverage, often broadcasting games from México.

1996–1999

MIGR. More than 200,000 Colombians leave their country for the United States. The Colombian government has difficulty accepting the idea that Colombians are leaving because of economic distress and the violence plaguing the country.

1997

OBIT. Che Guevara's remains are exhumed and flown to Cuba, where he is buried in Santa Clara, the site of his victory over Batista's troops in 1958.

POLI. The U.S. Congress approves "Process Young" to allow Puerto Rico to develop plans to realize full self-government and to do so in consultation with the people of Puerto Rico.

1998

ARTS. The film *Selena*, a biography of the doomed Mexican-American singer, makes Jennifer Lopez an international sensation in the title role. The Puerto Rican actress receives a Golden

More Latino and American youth took to soccer in the 1990s, with the creation of the Major League Soccer and the showing of international games on the Univisión network.

Globe Award nomination for best actress and becomes a popular hip-hop and rap singer and dancer. Her physique is so admired that news articles report hundreds of girls who want to have plastic surgery done so that their anatomy will resemble Lopez's statuesque figure. Lopez, known as "J-LO," owns a clothing line as well. She is one of the first Latinas in Hollywood to become a mainstream entertainer.

MED. *El Nuevo Herald* appears as an independent paper in Miami, separating itself from its parent publication, *The Miami Herald*. Circulation soon reaches 70,000. The paper provides extensive coverage of events in Latin America as it tries to reach the diverse Latin American population of Miami.

MIGR. The Honduras Consulate in Alabama estimates that 140,000 Hondurans are settling in the New Orleans area, arriving first to help with the cleanup of Hurricane Mitch and staying to work in the construction and landscaping industries.

SPOR. Dominican-American Sammy Sosa hits 66 home runs. A player for the Cubs who is a consistent home-run hitter, Sosa earns $10 million a year. He becomes a favorite of Latino and American fans.

1999

BUSI. The Cuban- and Puerto Rican–owned Bacardí company, maker of the famous rum, purchases the wine firm Martini-Rossi, becoming one of the largest suppliers of alcoholic spirits in the world. The company's headquarters is based in Puerto Rico.

CRIM. The Latin Kings, a gang that originated in Chicago in the late 1940s and was originally composed of Puerto Rican youth, expands into

Miami skyline. Miami and Miami Beach have become thriving communities for Latinos. Photo by Daniel A. Figueredo.

the East Coast, Florida, and Texas urban centers. They are involved in drug trafficking.

HEAL. The Centers for Disease Control in Atlanta reports that 21 percent of reported AIDS cases in the country are Latinos.

LAND. In March, the U.S. Air Force accidentally kills a civilian in Vieques during target practice. Civilians from Puerto Rico and the United States protest on the island, aided by several celebrities like Puerto Rican singer Ricky Martin, Mexican actor Edward James Olmos, and Guatemala's Nobel Prize winner Rigoberta Menchú. The protests will continue for the next four years, prompting President George W. Bush to order that the military leave the island by May, 2003.

MIGR. On November 22, a boat carrying 14 refugees from Cuba capsizes off the Florida coast. Only three survive. One of them is a young child named Elian González. The boy is placed under the care of a great uncle. In Cuba, his father requests that the boy be returned. Castro meets with Elian's father and on December 2, he turns the situation into a political confrontation with the Cuban community in exile,

announcing in a speech that "Elian González will be returned." The Cuban relatives in Miami refuse to send the boy back to his father. In the United States, a court battle ensues, with the authorities concluding that the boy must be reunited with his father. In Miami, Cuban exiles perceive the event as a political ploy used by Castro to show his power in Latin America, caring little for the boy. On April 22 of the following year, a special police team, heavily armed, removes the young boy from his great uncle's care. The boy is returned to Cuba.

MUSI. The song "Living La Vida Loca" makes an international star of Puerto Rican performer Ricky Martin, whose handsome face graces the cover of teen magazines and is regularly seen on British and Japanese television. In the United States, the song remains at the top of the Billboard chart for nine weeks. Martin uses his fame to promote such political issues in Puerto Rico as the removal of the U.S. Navy from the island of Vieques.

POLI. On August 8 President Bill Clinton offers clemency to 19 Puerto Rican nationalists and former members of FALN, the Fuerzas Armadas de Liberación Nacional. The nationalists were in prison for exploding bombs throughout the

One Look at the Border

"The most invisible line that stretches two thousand miles along sand, yellow dirt dotted with scrub brush, and the muddy waters of the Rio Grande. Invisible, save for certain stretches near San Diego, Nogales, and El Paso, where the idea of the U.S.-Mexico border takes physical form through steel, chain links, barbed wire, concrete, and arc lamps that light the barren terrain at night. At these three crossing points—San Diego being the busiest port of entry in the world—the Border Patrol has cleared the land for miles around, so that the human figures who try to break the line stand in stark relief and cast shadows. The Border Patrol swallows as many shadows as it can."

Source: Rubén Martínez. *Crossing Over: A Mexican Family on the Migrant Trail.* New York: Metropolitan Books, Henry Holt and Co., 2001, p. 1.

United States in the 1970s. They are released on September 11.

POLI. On December 6, Hugo Chávez is elected president of Venezuela with 56 percent of the vote. An admirer and friend of Fidel Castro, he runs an anti-American campaign and an antipoverty program claiming the wealth of Venezuela is in the hands of a few families and that he plans to share that wealth with the marginalized people of his country. He is popular with many Latinos in the United States, but Cuban-Americans view him with skepticism, assuming Chavez will implement a dictatorship in his country. Like Simón Bolívar, Chávez believes in the unification of Latin America.

Twenty-First Century

2000s

ECON. Seventy-five percent of the income made by Latinos is spent on housing, food, transportation, and clothing. It is estimated that the purchasing power of Latinos in the United States is over $450,000,000 a year. Such figures encourage companies like Ford, Verizon, and Continental Airlines to promote their businesses in Spanish in the Latino media.

EDUC. Latino students represent a little less than 10 percent of the 10 million students attending college. More Latinas, about 60 percent, attend college than Latinos. Latino students prefer community colleges, where they tend to major in liberal arts, business, and health professions. The two-year program at community colleges also allows Latinos to enter the work force earlier than a four-year college will.

IMMI. It is estimated that there are between 10 and 12 million illegal aliens in the United States from Latin America. Nearly 85 percent of immigrants crossing the U.S.-Mexican border illegally are Mexicans.

IMMI. Ecuadorian authorities estimate that 100,000 and 250,000 Ecuadorians a year relocate to Guatemala with hopes of eventually reaching the United States. Many attempt an illegal crossing, paying up to $10,000 to be smuggled across Central America and México into the United States by a coyote, a smuggler of illegal aliens.

IMMI. Venezuelan sources and the U.S. Census report a migration of 120,000 to 150,000 Venezuelans to the United States, about 40,000 of which settle in Florida. The arrivals distrust President Hugo Chávez's regime. Many of the immigrants are young professionals and recent university graduates.

POLI. The Tomás Rivera Institute conducts a study demonstrating a growth of 40 percent in Latino voters registration and election participation. Certain political characteristics emerge: Mexican-Americans, Dominicans, and Puerto Ricans are more likely to support candidates from the Democratic Party, while Cuban-Americans tend to identify with the Republicans.

POLI. Sila M. Calderón is elected the first woman governor of Puerto Rico on November 7.

POPU. More than 35,305,818 Latinos live in the United States, with Mexicans or Mexican descendants numbering 20,640,711; Puerto Ricans, 3,406,178; and Cubans, 1,214,685. There are 764,946 Dominicans and 1,686,937 from Central America. Argentines account for 100,864, Bolivians 42,068, and Chileans 68,849. From Colombia there are 470,684, from Ecuador 260,559, and from Paraguay 8,769. There are 233,926 Bolivians, 18,804 Uruguayans, and 91,507 Venezuelans. There are over 60,000 that the U.S. Census describes as other South Americans or Hispanic/Latinos without specific national or ethnic information.

POPU. The Latino population is distributed throughout the country, with the largest congregation in the West at 44.7 percent. The Northeast is second with 14.1 percent. The Southeast claims 33.2 percent and the Midwest 7.9 percent.

POPU. There are more Spanish-speakers in the United States than in Cuba (11,141,997), the Dominican Republic (8,442,553), Nicaragua (4,812,569), Paraguay (5,585,828), and Puerto Rico (3,889,507).

REBE. On November 5, Puerto Rican protesters step on the top deck of the Statue of Liberty in New York and unfurl a Puerto Rican flag to protest American military presence in Vieques.

SETT. A new pattern emerges in the Latino community when new arrivals eschew traditional points of entry like Los Angeles, Newark, and New York to settle in the suburbs. Reports of high crime in urban areas encourages new immigrants to relocate to smaller towns not normally associated with Latino barrios. Since several Latinos rent large townhouses as a group, converting the dwellings into a format similar to boarding rooms, the residents of those communities are not always eager to welcome their new neighbors.

2000

ARTS. Puerto Rican actor Benicio del Toro wins an Oscar for Best Supporting Actor. He is also awarded a Golden Globe and a Screen Actors Guild Award for his portrayal of a Mexican police officer in the film *Traffic*.

MUSI. Recognizing the growing popularity of Latin music in the United States as well the marketing potential for Latino stars, Latin Grammy Awards are established in 2000. They air on CBS, the first a Spanish-language program carried on network television. Like the Grammy Awards, the Latin Grammys reward artistic and technical excellence in the recording arts.

2001

LANG. On January 3, New York congressman José Serrano proposes legislation to combat the English-only movement, which endorses a constitutional amendment to make English the official language of the nation, and to establish an English Plus initiative. His legislation encourages all U.S. residents to master English while conserving and developing the country's linguistic resources by maintaining skills in languages other than English.

TRAN. Two hundred sixty passengers, mostly Dominicans, die as an American Airlines jet crashes into a neighborhood in Queens, New York. At first it is suspected that it is an act of terrorism, but it is soon learned that the accident has occurred as a result of engine failure. One of the victims is Hilda Yolanda Mayol, who had survived the September 11 World Trade Center attack. She had worked at the restaurant Windows of the World, on top of the World Trade Center.

WARS. On September 11, four hijacked planes crash into the twin towers of the World Trade Center, the Pentagon, and a field in Pennsylvania.

Dreaming of Estados Unidos

"They come from many different nations, many different races, yet once here they are treated like a pack of blood brothers. In the United States, they live among folk who share their names but have forgotten their language, ethnic kinsmen who are Latinos by ancestry but U.S. citizens by generations of birthrights. The newcomers and the natives may share little else, but for the most part they share neighborhoods . . . where their fates become intertwined. Mexican-Americans and Puerto Ricans account for most of the native-born Latino population. They are the U.S.-made vessel into which the new immigration flows. They have been Americans long enough to have histories, and these are sad histories of exploitation and segregation."

Source: Roberto Suro. *Strangers Among US: Latino Lives in a Changing America.* New York: Vintage Books, 1999, p. 9.

At the World Trade Center the 2,726 known casualties include 388 Latinos. At the Pentagon, five of the victims had Spanish surnames.

2002

ECON. Latinos in the United States with families and relatives in Latin America send $30 billion to pay for housing, medicine, and education.

POPU. Political uncertainty in Venezuela propels approximately 126,000 Venezuelans into the United States. Mostly middle class, about 40,000 choose to stay in Miami where they set up businesses and stay in contact with family members in Venezuela.

2003

BUSI. Venezuelan Carolina Herrera opens four high-fashion stores in Florida, New York, Nevada, and Texas. In the 1980s, the Venezuelan-American designer was Jackie Onassis's favorite designer. With the Dominican Oscar de la Renta, Herrera is one of the most recognizable Latino names in the fashion industry.

IMMI. The September 19 edition of the major Ecuadorian newspaper *El Universal,* published in Guayaquil, reports that coyotes, smugglers of illegal aliens into the United States, advertise their service in the Ecuadorian press without repercussions from the Ecuadorian government.

OBIT. On July 16, salsa queen Celia Cruz dies of a brain tumor in Fort Lee, New Jersey. After leaving Cuba in 1960, Cruz settled in New York and then in New Jersey. In 1974, her long-play record, *Celia y Johnny*, recorded with Dominican musician and producer Johnny Pacheco, became a best-seller in the Latino community and throughout Latin America. In the 1980s, she was established as a superstar of Caribbean and salsa music and in 1990, she received a Grammy award for her recording *Ritmo en el corazón*. With the Puerto Rican Tito Puentes, she became one of the most recognizable Latino performers in the United States.

2004

ARTS. Puerto Rican performer Rita Moreno receives the Presidential Medal of Freedom from President George W. Bush. The award is one of two highest civilian awards given in the country and recognizes long-term contributions, in cultural and private endeavors, to the United States and the world. Rita Moreno is the only Latina to receive an Emmy, a Grammy, an Oscar, and a Tony award. She is also only the ninth performer to receive such distinctions.

BUSI. There are 2 million companies with more than three workers each owned by Latinos in the United States. The companies are in the fields of advertising, computing, food services, industrial equipment, and media.

From El Salvador, Long Walk to Liberty

"It was hard for Juana but she told Cruz [a physician at the hospital where she was] everything—how her parents and three sisters were murdered in front of her in one of the massacres by the army; her torture and rape by soldiers (she still remembered the metal taste of the rifle barrel they held in her mouth); being left for dead afterward, and knowing she was a dead woman if she stayed much longer in El Salvador. She described the walk through Guatemala, where thieves stole her rosary and most of her belongings, and the months it took to get through Mexico. She worked for a few weeks in a hotel in Acapulco, earning a little money by cleaning hotel rooms. She remembered one room with a closet full of beautiful men's suits and women's dresses, an open case of tequila, and dried vomit caked on the bathroom floor. She wondered how people could spew so much food from their bodies when she would go days wishing for a small scrap of tortilla to quell her hunger."

Source: Glenn Flores. "She Walked From El Salvador." *Health Affairs* 24, no. 2 (March–April 2005): 3.

Slippery Assimilation

"Because not all Hispanics are easily categorized as Hispanic, Hispanics experience varying levels of discrimination. . . . Hispanics who do experience discrimination are less likely to self-identify as American because this discrimination increases their awareness of their non-white status in the United States. . . . Hispanics who do experience discrimination are more likely to self-identify as Hispanic or Latino/a, because experiences of discrimination teach Hispanics that they are labeled as Hispanics or Latinos/as by others in the United States. . . . The fact that Hispanicity is associated with foreignness can also be seen in questions Latinos often get about their origins. Many U.S.-born Latinos and Latinas report that when they are asked where they are from, the answer California or Texas only begets the well-known follow-up: 'But, where are you really from?' . . . Hispanics who are viewed as white in the United States are less likely to face racial discrimination and more likely to follow a similar path of assimilation to that of Irish, Italian or Polish Americans. In other words, they will become Americans, perhaps with a symbolic attachment to their national origins. However, Hispanics who are perceived to be black in the United States are likely to face discrimination as other African-Americans do, and to develop an oppositional identity as African-Americans. On the other hand, those Hispanics who have the racial and cultural features that result in their being perceived as Hispanics are less likely to assimilate and adopt an identity as an American, and more likely to develop a hyphenated identity as Latino or Latina Americans."

Source: Tanya Golash-Boza. "Dropping the Hyphen? Becoming Latino(a)-American through Racialized Assimilation." *Social Forces* 85, no. 1 (September 2006). www.proquest.com. Accessed November 7, 2006.

BUSI. Two Spanish banks, Banco Bilbao Vizcaya Argentaria and Banco Santander Central Hispano, announce plans to open branches in California, Pennsylvania, and Texas with intentions of marketing to the 40 million Latinos in the United States.

HEAL. Over 93,000 Latinos have died of AIDS. According to the Centers for Disease Control, Puerto Ricans are more likely than other Latinos to contract the disease through injection drug use, while same-sex sexual relations are blamed for AIDS cases in the Mexican-American community.

IMMI. On January 8, President George W. Bush proposes a temporary worker program to allow immigrants to enter the United States for particular jobs. He also suggests the construction of a fence or a wall along the border and the swift deportation of anyone crossing the border illegally. The president proposes easier bureaucratic processes to obtain residency cards and to increase

the number of green cards issued to would-be immigrants from the current population of 140,000 to an unspecified number. He objects, however, to amnesty for illegal aliens.

MIGR. A pattern is developing in Puerto Rican immigration. There are now more than 300,000 Puerto Ricans in Orlando, Florida. They are middle class and professionals rather than poor rural workers as in the past. They choose Orlando because of the climate and the economic opportunities the area offers in education, and in the tourism and hospitality industries.

POLI. Representing Florida, Mel Martínez is the first Cuban-American elected to the Senate. Martínez is a Republican.

POPU. The Latino population reaches 41.3 million on July 1. The population is on the young side, with Puerto Ricans having an average age of 27 and Cubans an average of 41 years. Economically, the income for family households is lower than the non-Latino income, which is reported as $53, 993. The average Mexican-Americans household income is more than $34,000, and the average for Puerto Rican is more than $36,000. Cubans earn more than $45,000. Other studies suggest that Latinos are not ready for retirement, reporting only an average of savings of $5,000 for the post-work years.

SPOR. On June 5, Oscar de la Hoya becomes the first boxer in history to win world titles in 6 different weight divisions.

A Mexican restaurant near Philadelphia. Mexican restaurants can be found almost anywhere in the United States.

The Mexican-American de la Hoya is nicknamed "the Golden Boy" for his ability to win matches in the welterweight and lightweight categories, emerging basically unscathed from the fights. In the 1990s, he won several Olympic Medals for the United States. De la Hoya has fought in 42 fights, winning 38.

2005

ECON. *Hispanic Trends Magazine* reports that Latinos spend 20 percent more per week dining out at casual and family-owned restaurants, and fast-food and pizza restaurants than the general market.

The average amount spent per week on eating out is $71, compared to $59 for the general market.

MUSI. Puerto Rican singer Marc Anthony wins the Latin Grammy Award for his album *Amar Sin Mentiras*. A salsa performer popular in Latin America, in the late 1990s he began to record songs in English to cross over into the mainstream. He is also known for several roles in movies and television films, and his marriage to pop singer and actress Jennifer Lopez.

POLI. Within the Latino community there are divisions regarding the proposed immigration

---

A Dream of Colombia

"[For] most . . . Colombians there is a pervasive feeling that Colombia offers greater opportunities to satisfy emotional needs, such as ties to friends and family. The lack of emotional and social fulfillment in the United States is one of the major reasons that most of the Colombian immigrants yearn to return to the land of their birth some day. As one respondent said, 'This country [the United States] really offers many opportunities, more than are found in Colombia. However, I think all Colombians, like myself, miss the human warmth that we can have only in our country.'"

Source: Amparo Hoffman and Escala Zuleyman. "The Colombian Community in Metropolitan New York." *Migration World Magazine* 27, no. 4 (1999): 3.

reforms made by President George W. Bush. Even with Mexican-Americans two groups emerge: LULAC supports the president's initiatives, while the National Council of La Raza objects to the plan. Nevertheless, advocates for amnesty and ease on entry restrictions are making plans to protest against the immigration reforms. A year later, millions of Latino workers will take to the streets of large cities like Los Angeles and smaller cities like Trenton, New Jersey, to demand the right of illegal immigrants to remain in the United States.

REBE. On September 23, Filiberto Ojeada Ríos is killed in a confrontation with the FBI in Puerto Rico. He was an independence advocate and leader of a paramilitary group, known as Los Macheteros, intent on bringing independence to the island. The United States considers Los Macheteros a terrorist group. In 1961, Ojeada Ríos visited Cuba, where he was trained in intelligence-gathering techniques and urban warfare. It is rumored that he returned to Puerto Rico to spy on the American military. In 1976, he founded Ejercito Popular Boricua, known as Los Macheteros.

WORK. In October, crews of Latino workers flock to New Orleans to help rebuild the city in the aftermath of Hurricane Katrina. Many are Mexican and Central American workers who are legal visitors to the United States. Figures estimate that the Latino workers number in the hundreds. Many find temporary shelters in Protestant churches.

2006

IMMI. In the spring, thousands march throughout numerous cities in the United States, from Los Angeles to Atlanta, to ask the U.S. Congress to allow 11 million illegal aliens to stay in the country. In Washington, D.C., both the president and the Congress contemplate immigration reforms to control the flow of illegal aliens into the United States. Many immigrants feel that the desire to build a wall along the border between México and the United States, as recommended by President Bush and other Republican legislators, indicates discrimination since no similar effort is being proposed for the Canada-U.S. border. In places such as Dallas, over 500,000 immigrants participate in the march.

LAWS. The Immigration Reform Act stirs much discussion in the United States, reviving old arguments against immigration. Many maintain that immigrants are flooding the market for low-skilled workers, thus taking jobs away from legal citizens who are not college educated and have no training. In communities like Bogota, New Jersey, the mayor criticizes immigrants who do not speak English in public; his administration approves an ordinance prohibiting advertising in any other language but English.

LAWS. In Washington, D.C. Democrats and Republicans argue over a bill to reform the immigration act. The Democrats support amnesty for illegal aliens and Republicans oppose it, demanding stricter procedures to control the influx of illegal aliens into the United States. President Bush supports a middle ground while rejecting outright amnesty.

LAWS. On October 26, President Bush signs the Secure Fence Act, which authorizes the construction of hundreds of miles of additional fencing along the U.S.-Mexican border as well as the use

---

The Latinization and Gringonizing of the United States

"[Latino writer and scholar] Ilan Stavans . . . believes that the mainstream culture itself is being inexorably Latinized within a complex dialectic of transcultural exchange between old and new Americas. The rise of 'Latinos agringados' addicted to hamburgers and Friday night football, he asserts, is tendentially balanced by the emergence of 'gringos hispanizados' infatuated with chiles and merengue. . . . The result . . . will be a new hegemonic global culture."

Source: Mike Davis. *Magical Urbanism: Latinos Reinvent the U.S. City.* London: Verso, 2000, 2001, p. 23.

of technology to detect people crossing the border. Currently, legislation to reform the immigration act is still pending.

LIT. In June, the Board of Education in Miami bans a children's book titled *Vamos a Cuba*. According to Cuban-Americans the book provides erroneous information, complimentary to Castro, about life in Cuba. The criticism the Cuban-American community receives from non-Cubans reaffirms their beliefs that their concerns about Castro and Cuba are misunderstood and not accepted by non-Cubans.

MIGR. By August, it is estimated that 14,000 to 40,000 Latinos from México and Central America are settling in and near New Orleans, finding work in construction and with other companies still involved in cleaning up the aftermath of Hurricane Katrina. Earlier in the year New Orleans mayor Roy Nagging had expressed fear that the city would be overrun by Mexicans, but later on apologized for his comment.

POLI. During the first week in August thousands of Cuban-Americans celebrate in Miami the fact that Fidel Castro, who is recovering from intestinal surgery, is not ruling Cuba for the first time since January 1, 1959. The Cubans wave flags as cars blow horns and people shout: Viva Cuba Libre. By the second week, when it is clear that Castro is recovering and plans to return to power, the demonstrations quiet down while Senator Bob Menendez recommends that plans be made to help Cuba's transition from Fidel's rule to a democratic regime.

POLI. On November 7, Cuban-American Bob Menendez is elected senator. A year before, New Jersey Senator Jon Corzine had appointed Menendez to his position. The liberal Menendez is the only major Cuban-American politician to be a Democrat; his compatriots favor the Republican Party. He is known for his staunch opposition to the Castro regime, which makes him a favorite with Cuban-American voters.

GLOSSARY

Aguinaldos. Christmas carols; a popular form of holiday entertainment throughout Latin America but especially in Puerto Rico, where the practice started during Spanish rule in the seventeenth century.

Areyto. Art form used by the Taínos and Caribs in the Caribbean. It consists of musical narration, dance, and drama.

Aztecs. An ancient mesoamerican civilization located in what is now central and southern México. Also known as Mexicas.

Bachata. A dance that emerged from the countryside and poor neighborhoods of the Dominican Republic.

Balsa. A home-made raft made by Cubans seeking to escape the island. It is also a small boat.

Balsero. Cuban political refugee of the 1990s who reached the United States on a home-made vessel.

Bandido. A Mexican stereotype probably inspired by the exploits of Pancho Villa during the Mexican Revolution. The bandido has often been portrayed as a villain or a fool.

Barrio. A Spanish word meaning district or neighborhood.

Batu. An ancient form of volleyball played by the Taínos.

Bodega. Spanish grocery store; grocery store that sells products from Latin America and Spain.

Bohuti. A Taíno healer.

Borinquen. An ancient name for Puerto Rico.

Bracero. A program to attract laborers from México and other countries to work in agriculture and industry; bracero refers to brazos, arms.

Cacique. A Taíno or Carib chief; it also means local ruler.

Caiman. A Caribbean cocodrile.

Caló. A combination of Mexican street vernacular and English slang.

Camino Real. The Spanish Royal Highway connecting towns in Florida and the Spanish Southwest with each other and, during the 1600s, with México.

Caribs. Indigenous people from the Caribbean.

Casa de la Contratación. House of Contracts, which oversees all economic transactions in colonial Latin America.

Caudillismo. The practice of Caudillo rule, "the rule of the strong man."

Caudillo. A Spanish word meaning "strong ruler."

Cédula de Gracia. Royal Decree of Graces from Spain, which allowed immigrants to settle in the mountainous countryside of Puerto Rico.

Cemis or zemis. Spirits in ancient Taíno culture that protect villages and individuals.

Cenotes. Large wells or sink holes in Yucatán, México.

Chichén Itzá. Ancient Maya/Toltec city in Yucatán, México.

Chololatl. A word meaning "chocolate" in the Nahuatl language, which was spoken in ancient Central America and México.

Choteo. To make fun of a person who is powerful; to make fun of authority.

Ciboneyes. Oldest indigenous people in the Caribbean. It is also spelled Siboneyes and the people are also known as the Guanahatabey.

Compagnie de Saint Christophe. The Compagnie des Iles D'Amerique, and the Compagnie des Indes. Companies established by the French to colonize the Caribbean and steal islands away from the Spanish.

Comuneros. A group of citizens in Latin America who organized against Spanish rule during the colonial era.

Conga. A popular Cuban dance of African origins. Dancers form a long line and sway back and forth on the street to the beat of drums.

Conquistador. A Spanish conqueror of Latin America.

Conuco system. An ancient agricultural method used by the Taínos and Caribs of the Caribbean.

Coplas. Rhyming two-line songs sung by the Spanish. Love and homesickness were popular themes.

Corridos. Songs, with repetitive stanzas, that celebrate the courage of the Mexicans who oppose the growing American presence, as well as discrimination, in the southwest.

Cortés. The Spanish Parliament.

Criollos. People born in Latin America of Spanish parents.

Descamisados. The shirtless ones; term used by Evita Perón to refer, affectionately, to the poor of Argentina.

Día de Acción de Gracias. Thanksgiving Day. Some Latino residents of New Mexico still consider the high mass held by Juan de Oñate in 1598 the original Thanksgiving.

Diario. Spanish daily newspaper.

Encomienda. A form of slavery in Latin America forced on indigenous people by the Spanish.

Fufu. Mashed plantain cooked with lemon and garlic; a popular dish in Cuba. There are variations of the recipe throughout the Caribbean.

Generación del 30. The "1930 Generation" refers to Puerto Rican writers and intellectuals concerned with American influence on the island and the development of a Puerto Rican identity.

Gibaro or jibaro. A Puerto Rican peasant or farmer.

Gringo. A derogatory term used to refer to an American of non-Latino origins.

Grito. To cry out; it refers to a call to arms in several rebellions in Latin America during Spanish rule.

Guitarra latina. A Roman guitar introduced in Spain during the Roman empire.

Guitarra morisca. A Moorish guitar introduced in Spain during the Muslim invasion.

Haciendas. A compound of several large houses.

Hispania. Ancient Spain.

Hispanic. Cultural designation to refer to people from Spanish descent and the Spanish language.

Hispaniola. Present day Dominican Republic and Haiti.

Incas. An ancient civilization located in South America. At its height in the sixteenth century, the Inca empire extended from present-day Ecuador to central Chile.

La Noche Triste. The sad night. It refers to Cortés' first major defeat in his conquest of the Aztec or Mexica Empire.

La raza. Race; for Chicanos it refers to unity based on the knowledge that Mexicans descend from a great ancient civilization.

Latino. Term describing people of Latin American descent who have linguistic roots to the Spanish language.

Libreta. A Spanish word meaning "notebook." In nineteenth-century Puerto Rico the libreta system required that no plantation laborer could leave the plantation without the dates of return and departure marked in the plantation owner's libreta.

Los Macheteros. The Machete Wielders. A paramilitary group that attempted to bring revolutionary change to Puerto Rico and overthrow the American presence on the island.

Mambo. Dance created in Cuba during the late 1930s and early 1940s.

Maquiladora. A factory in México or on the México–U.S. border that assembles parts of a product that originates in another country.

Mariachis. The band and music that is so characteristic of Mexican culture. Mariachi is a small orchestra that consists primarily of guitars and violins with the guitarists also providing the vocal components.

Marielito. Cuban political refugee who arrived in the United States through the Mariel boatlift of 1980.

Mariposas. The butterflies; code name used by three sisters—Patria, Minerva, and Marita Teresa Mirabal—who in the Dominican Republic fought against the dictator, Rafael L. Trujillo.

Maroon. A community of run-away slaves. The term might originate from the Spanish *cimarrón*.

Maya. An ancient mesoamerican empire that occupied present-day México, Belize, and Guatemala. The Maya were one of the most advanced civilizations in the Western hemisphere before the European conquest and many Latinos today are their direct ancestors.

Memoria. A personal recollection of events during the conquest of Latin America and Spanish North America.

Merengue. A popular dance from the Dominican Republic.

Mestizo/mestiza. A person of mixed ancestry; usually a mix of European and indigenous ancestry.

Mexicanidad. A sense of being Mexican.

Mexicas. Ancient Latin American Civilization; also the Aztecs.

Mezquite. A mosque.

Mihrab. A center courtyard of a mesquite. The mihrab faces in the direction of Mecca.

Motecuhzoma. The last Aztec emperor. It is also spelled Montezuma.

Mulata/mulato. The offspring of a couple where one is of African descent, black, and the other of European descent, white.

Música tejana. A style of Mexican folk songs and Texan music that was influenced in the 1830s and 1840s by French, Irish, and German music, especially polkas and waltzes.

Muwassahas. Arabic poems introduced in Spain during the Muslim invasion.

Nahuatl. Language spoken by the Aztecs.

Niños Heroes. The heroic boys; Mexican cadets who fought bravely against American troops during the Mexican–American War of 1846.

Nosotros. A Spanish word meaning "we." In 1969, Ricardo Montalban and other Latino actors formed the organization *Nosotros* to confront stereotypical images of Latinos in television and film.

Nuyorican. A Puerto Rican born or raised in New York City who identifies more with the city than with the island of Puerto Rico.

Olmec. An ancient Latin American civilization.

Operation Pedro Pan. The largest exodus of unaccompanied minors in the history of the Americas. More than 14,000 children between the ages of 6 and 18 were sent alone to the United States from Cuba by their parents who feared communist indoctrination and rumored plans that the government would usurp parental custody.

Orisha. Afro-Cuban gods in the Santería religion.

Pachucos. Mexican Americans who, in the 1940s, wore the stylized Zoot Suits and spoke the street vernacular, Caló.

Periodiquitos. Free newspapers given away in bodegas; the papers emphasize Latino news and events.

Plena. Music from Puerto Rico.

Prensa. The Spanish press.

Quechua. Language spoken by the Incas. It is still in use.

Quetzalcoat. Feathered serpent god from whom the people of mesoamerica, including the Mexicas/Aztecs, Olmecs, and the Toltecs descended.

Ranchos. Ranches of hundred of acres owned by one family or several members of the same family.

Relación. A written account or report of events during colonial times.

Relajo. A noun describing a situation where people are making fun of powerful figures or governments. The expression is used in Cuba and Puerto Rico.

Repartimiento. Land and indigenous people rewarded to Spanish settlers during colonial times for their own use and profit.

Romance. Spanish folk song narrating the deeds of great heroes.

Rumba. A dance of Afro-Cuban origin, characterized by a back and forth style and hip motion.

Salsa. Music that evolved in New York City in the early 1960s. Its origins are the Cuban mambo, rumba, the son, and Puerto Rican music.

Santería. An Afro-Cuban religion largely practiced in New York City and Miami. In 1993 the Supreme Court recognized Santería as an official religion in the United States.

Santero. A Santería priest.

Sombrero. A wide brimmed hat worn by Mexicans, Tejanos, and other Latino men in New Mexico in the early nineteenth century.

Taínos. Indigenous people from the Caribbean.

Tamales. In ancient México, tamales were made of dough and rolled into corn leaves and filled with turkey or dog meat as well as chili and avocado leaves. Modern variations are popular today, with recipes changing from one Latin American country to another.

Tampeños. Descedants of the Cubans who settled in Ybor City, Tampa, in the late 1880s.

Tango. A type of sensous dance and romantic songs from Argentina.

Teatro bufo. A Cuban combination of blackface farce and vaudeville.

Teatro Campesino. Politically oriented theater in California that promotes the labor movement of migrant workers.

Tejanos. A Spanish word used in the early nineteenth century to refer to Mexican-Texans of Spanish descent.

Tenochtitlán. A great city of the Aztec empire, the site of present-day México City.

Tertulias. Literary salons, sometimes organized through a society, sometimes an informal gathering at a home.

Texians. Americans who sought independence from México during the mid-1830s.

Timbales. Afro-Caribbean drums played by musician Tito Puentes.

Toltecs. An ancient Latin American Civilization.

Tortilla. Similar to puff pastry, they are filled with green tomato and chili sauce. Tortilla also means omelet in Cuba, Spain, and other Latin American countries.

Tradición. Literary genre from Perú in which factual and fictional narratives are combined to depict a local event or a story with a moral.

Vaqueros. Spanish and Mexican horsemen of the Southwest; cowboys.

West-Indische Compagnie. Dutch West Indian Company that specialized in the slave trade.

Yucca. A tubular root used in the Caribbean for cooking.

Zarzuelas. Spanish musical comedies or melodramas.

Zéjel. Arabic poems introduced in Spain during the Muslim invasion.

Zoot Suit. Stylized suit consisting of a long blazer and baggy pants with colorful two-tone shoes. These suits were worn by Mexican American youths during the late 1930s and early 1940s.

BIBLIOGRAPHY

PRINTED SOURCES

Abalos, David T. *The Latino Family and the Politics of Transformation*. Wesport, CT: Praeger, 1993.

Acevedo, Ramón Luis. *Pachín Marín: poeta en libertad*. San Juan: Instituto de Cultura Puertorriqueña, Cuadernos de Cultura, no. 4 (2001): p. 46.

Allen, James Egert. *The Legend of Arthur A. Schomburg*. Cambridge, MA: Danterr, 1975.

Allende, Isabel. *The House of the Spirits*. Trans. Magda Bogin. New York: Knopf, 1985.

Anaya, Rudolfo. *Bless Me, Ultima*. New York: Time Warner, 1972.

Andrews, George Reid. *Afro-Latin America, 1800–2000*. Oxford: Oxford University Press, 2004.

Anton, Alex, and Roger E. Hernández. *Cubans in America: A Vibrant History of a People in Exile*. New York: Kensington Books, 2002.

Anzaldua, Gloria. *Borderlands: La Frontera; the New Mestiza*. San Francisco: Aunt Lute Books, 1987.

Appiah, Kwame Anthony, and Henry Louis Gates, Jr., eds. *Africana: The Encyclopedia of the African and African American Experience*. New York: Basic Civitas Books, 1999.

Augenbraum, Harold, and Margarite Fernández Olmos. *The Latino Reader*. New York: Houghton Mifflin, 1997.

Azuela, Mariano. *The Underdogs*. Pittsburg, PA: University of Pittsburgh Press, 1992.

Báez, Víctor, ed. *La Gran Enciclopedia de Puerto Rico*. San Juan: Puerto Rico en la Mano and La Gran Enciclopedia de Puerto Rico, 1981.

Bailey, Helen and Abraham P. Nasatir. *Latin America: The Development of Its Civilization*. Englewood Cliffs, NJ: Prentice-Hall, 1968.

Balroya, Enrique A., and James A. Morris, eds. *Conflict and Change in Cuba*. Alburqueque: University of New Mexico Press, 1993.

Berger, Thomas. *A Long and Terrible Shadow: White Values, Native Rights in the Americas, 1492–1992*. Vancouver: Douglas and McIntyre, 1992.

Bjarkman, Peter C. *Baseball with a Latin Beat*. Jefferson, NC: McFarland and Company, 1994.

Bonilla, Frank, Edwin Meléndez, Rebecca Morales, and María de los Angeles Tomes. *Borderless Borders: U.S. Latinos, Latin Americans, and the Paradox of Interdependence*. Philadelphia: Temple University Press, 1998.

Brown, Isabel Zakrzewski. *Culture and Customs of the Dominican Republic*. Westport, CT: Greenwood Press, 1999.

Butts, Ellen, and Schwartz, Joyce R. *Fidel Castro*. Minneapolis: Lerner Publications, 2005.

Cancel, Mario R. *Segundo Ruíz Belvis: el procer y el ser humano (una aproximación crítica a su vida)*. Bayamón: Editorial Universidad de América, 1994.

Canizares, Raul. *Cuban Santeria: Walking with the Night*. Rochester, VT: Destiny Books, 1999.

Cardona, Luis Antonio. *A History of the Puerto Ricans in the United States of America.* Bethesda, MD: Carreta Press, 1995.

Carrasco, David. *Moctezuma's Mexico: Visions of the Aztec World.* Boulder: University Press of Colorado, 1992.

Carrasquillo, Angela L. *Hispanic Children and Youth in the United States.* New York: Garland Publishing, 1991.

Castañeda Salamanca, Felipe. *El indio, entre el bárbaro y el cristiano: ensayos sobre filosofía de la conquista en Las Casas, Sepúlveda y Acosta.* Bogotá, Colombia: Ediciones Uniandes, Departamento de Filosofía: Alfa-omega Colombiana, 2002.

Chase, Gilbert. *The Music of Spain.* New York: Dover Publications, 1959.

Chasteen, John Charles. *Born in Blood and Fire: A Concise History of Latin America.* New York: W.W. Norton, 2001.

Chávez, Fermín. *Eva Perón: sin mitos.* Buenos Aires: Ediciones Theoría, 1996.

Chavez, Linda. *Out of the Barrio: Toward a New Politics of Hispanic Assimilation.* New York: BasicBooks, 1991.

Chávez Candelaria, Cordelia, Arturo J. Almada, and Peter J. García, eds. *Encyclopedia of Latino Popular Culture,* 2 vols. Westport, CT: Greenwood Press, 2004.

Cocco De Filippis, Daisy. *Para que no se olviden: The Lives of Women in Dominican History.* New York: Ediciones Alcance, 2000.

Coleman, Loren, and Jerome Clark. *Cryptozoology A to Z.* New York: Simon and Schuster, 1999.

Coll y Toste, Cayetano. *Folk Legends of Puerto Rico.* Trans. José L. Coll y Toste. Vivas and Ulises Cadilla [s.i.]: Trans Caribbean Airways, [n.d.].

Colón, Jesús. *The Way It Was and Other Sketches.* Houston: Arte Público Press, 1993.

Conde, Yvonne M. *Operation Peter Pan: The Untold Exodus of 14,048 Cuban Children.* New York: Routledge, 1999.

Cortés, Eladio, and Barrea-Marlys, Mirta. *Encyclopedia of Latin America Theater.* Westport, CT: Greenwood Press, 2003.

Crassweller, Robert D. *Trujillo: The Life and Times of a Caribbean Dictator.* New York: Macmillan Company, 1966.

Crosby, Alfred, Jr. *The Columbian Exchange: Biological and Cultural Consequences of 1492.* Westport, CT: Greenwood Press, 1972.

Cuevas Zequeira, Sergio. *Manuel de Zequeira y Arango y los albores de la cultura cubana.* Habana: "Tipografía Moderna" de A. Dombecker, 1923.

Davis, Mike. *Magical Urbanism: Latinos Reinvent the U.S. City.* London: Verso, 2000.

De La Torre, Miguel. *Santería: The Beliefs and Rituals of a Growing Religion in America.* Grand Rapids, MI: Wm. B. Eermands Publishing, 2004.

Del Rio, Daniel A. *Simon Bolivar.* New York: Bolivarian Society of the United States, 1965.

Dent, David W. *The Legacy of the Monroe Doctrine: A Reference Guide to U.S. Involvement in Latin America and the Caribbean.* Westport, CT: Greenwood Press, 1999.

Díaz del Castillo, Bernal. *The Discovery and Conquest of Mexico.* New York: The Noonday Press, 1956.

Dold, Gaylor. *Dominican Republic Handbook.* Chico, CA: Moon Publications, 1997.

Falola, Toyin. *Key Events in African History.* Westport, CT: Greenwood Press, 2002.

Fernández, Roberta. *In Other Words, Literature by Latinas in the U.S.* Houston: Arte Público Press, 1994.

Fernández, Ronald, Serafin Mendez Mendez, and Gail Cueto, eds. *Puerto Rico Past and Present: An Encyclopedia.* Westport, CT: Greenwood, 1998.

Fernández Méndez, Eugenio. *Luis Muñoz Rivera, hombre visible.* San Juan: P. Biblioteca de Autores Puertorriqueños, 1982.

Ferrer Canales, José. *Martí y Hostos.* Río Piedras: Instituto de Estudios Hostosianos, Universidad de Puerto Rico, San Juan: Centro de Estudios Avanzados de Puerto Rico y el Caribe, 1990.

Figueredo, D. H. *When This World Was New.* New York: Lee and Low Books, 1999.

Foster, David William, ed. *Handbook of Latin American Literature.* New York: Garland Publishing, 1992.

Foster, Lynn V. *A Brief History of Mexico,* rev. ed. New York: Checkmark Books, Facts-on-File, 2004.

Fuentes, Carlos. *The Buried Mirror: Reflections on Spain and the New World.* New York: Houghton Mifflin, 1992.

Galasso, Norberto. *Perón.* Buenos Aires: Colihue, 2005.

Galván, Manuel de Jesús. *Enriquillo: leyenda histórica dominicana, 1503–1533.* Santo Domingo, República Dominicana: Ediciones de la Fundación Corripio, 1990.

Gann, L. H., and Peter J. Duignan. *The Hispanics in the United States: A History.* Boulder: Westview Press, 1986.

García, Cristina. *Dreaming in Cuban.* New York: Knopf, 1992.

García, Mario T. *Mexican Americans: Leadership, Ideology and Identity, 1930–1960.* New Haven, CT: Yale University Press, 1989.

García Márquez, Gabriel. *One Hundred Years of Solitude.* New York: Harper Perennial, 1970.

George, Alice L. *Awaiting Armageddon: How Americans Faced the Cuban Missile Crisis.* Chapel Hill: University of North Carolina Press, 2003.

Gerónimo, Joaquín. *En el nombre de Bosch.* Santo Domingo, República Dominicana: Editora Alfa Omega, 2001.

González Echevarria, Roberto. *The Pride of Havana: A History of Cuban Baseball.* New York: Oxford University Press, 1999.

González López, Emilio. *Historia de la civilización Española.* New York: Las Americas Publishing, 1970.

Greenbaum, Susan D. *More Than Black: Afro-Cubans in Tampa.* Gainesville: University Press of Florida, 2002.

Güereña, Salvador, and Vivian M. Pisano. *Latino Periodicals: A Selection Guide.* Jefferson, NC: McFarland and Company, 1998.

Henderson, John S. *The World of the Ancient Maya.* Cornell University Press, 1981.

Henriques, Affonso. *Perón, Evita, and Their Comedians: A Study of How Dictatorships Operate.* Pompano Beach, FL: C.B. Correa, 1999.

Hernández, Carmen Dolores. *Puerto Rican Voices in English.* Westport, CT: Praeger Publishers, 1997.

Hernández, Ramona, and Luis Rivera Batez. *Dominican New Yorkers: A Socioeconomic Profile.* New York: CUNY Dominican Studies Institute, Dominican Research Monograph Series, 1995.

Hernández González, Heriberto. *Félix Varela: retorno y presencia.* La Habana: Imagen Contemporánea, 1997.

Hijuelos, Oscar. *The Mambo Kings Play Songs of Love.* New York: Farrar, Strauss, Giroux, 1989.

Hijuelos, Oscar. *Our House in the Last World.* New York: Persea Books, 1983.

Hoffman, Amparo, and Escala Zuleyman. "The Colombian Community in Metropolitan New York." *Migration World Magazine* 27, no. 4 (1999): 3–7.

Hoyt, Edwin P. *The Alamo: An Illustrated History.* Dallas: Taylor Publishing Company, 1999.

January, Brendan. *Fidel Castro: Cuban Revolutionary.* New York: Franklin Watts, 2003.

Kandell, Jonathan. *The Capital: The Biography of Mexico City.* New York: Random House, 1988.

Kanellos, Nicolás. *Herencia: The Anthology of Hispanic Literature of the United States.* Oxford: Oxford University Press, 2002.

Kanellos, Nicolás. *The Reference Library of Hispanic Americans,* 3 vols. Detroit: Gale Research, 1997.

Kanellos, Nicolás, and Helvetia Martell. *Hispanic Periodicals in the United States: Origins to 1960. A Brief History and Comprehensive Bibliography.* Houston: Arte Publico Press, 2000.

King, John, ed. *The Cambridge Companion to Modern Latin American Culture.* Cambridge: Cambridge University Press, 2004.

Koslow, Phillip. *Centuries of Greatness: The West African Kingdoms, 750–1900.* New York: Chelsea House, 1995.

Kullen, Allan S., comp. *The Peopling of America: A Timeline of Events That Helped Shape Our Nation.* Beltsville, MD: Portfolio Project, 1992, 1993, 1994.

Kurland, Gerald. *Fidel Castro, Communist Dictator of Cuba.* Charlotteville, NY: SamHar Press, 1972.

El Laúd del desterrado, ed. Matías Montes-Huidobro. Houston: Arte Público Press, 1995.

Lockwood, Lee. *Castro's Cuba, Cuba's Fidel: An American Journalist's Inside Look at Today's Cuba in Text and Picture.* New York: Macmillan, 1967.

Loza, Steven. *Tito Puente and the Making of Latin Music.* Urbana: Universtiy of Illinois Press, 1999.

Marqués, René. *La Carreta: drama puertorriqueño.* Río Piedras, Puerto Rico: Editorial Cultural, 1983.

Marrin, Albert. *Empires Lost and Won: The Spanish Heritage of the Southwest.* New York: Atheneum Books for Young Readers, 1997.

Martínez, Rubén. *Crossing Over: A Mexican Family on the Migrant Trail.* New York: Metropolitan Books, Henry Holt and Co., 2001.

Martínez Fernández, Luis, et al. *Encyclopedia of Cuba: People, History, Culture.* Westport, CT: Greenwood Press, 2003.

McCullough, David. *The Path between the Seas: The Creation of the Panama Canal.* New York: Simon and Schuster, 1977.

Morison, Samuel Eliot, ed. and trans. *Journals and Other Documents on the Life and Voyages of Christopher Columbus.* New York: The Heritage Press, 1963.

Moss, Joyce, and George Wilson. *Peoples of the World: Latin Americans.* Detroit: Gale Research, 1989.

Musacchio, Humberto. *Milenios de México: Diccionario Enciclopédico de México.* México, D.F.: Diagrama Casa Editorial, 199.

Novas, Himilce. *Everything You Need to Know about Latino History.* New York: Plume Books, 1994.

Nueva Enciclopedia de Puerto Rico, ed. José A. Toro Sugrañes. Hato Rey, Puerto Rico: Editorial Lector, 1994.

O'Toole, G.J.A. *The Spanish War: An American Epic, 1898.* New York: W.W. Norton and Co., 1984.

Padura, Leonardo. *José María Heredia: la patria y la vida.* La Habana: Ediciones Unión, 2003.

Pérez Firmat, Gustavo. *Life on the Hyphen: The Cuban-American Way.* Austin: University of Texas Press, 1994.

Pérez Firmat, Gustavo. *Next Year in Cuba.* New York: Anchor Books, 1995.

Pessar, Patricia R. *A Visa for a Dream: Dominicans in the United States.* Boston: Allyn and Bacon, 1995.

Prago, Alberto. *The Revolutions in Spanish America: The Independence Movements of 1808–1825.* New York: MacMillan, 1970

Press, Petra. *Fidel Castro: An Unauthorized Biography.* Chicago, IL: Heinemann Library, 2000.

Ramírez Morillo, Belarminio. *Joaquín Balaguer: la escuela del poder: su biografía, su pensamiento, su obra.* República Dominicana: Ediciones del Instituto de Formación, 1999.

Randel, Don, ed. *The New Harvard Dictionary of Music.* Cambridge, MA: The Belknap Press of Harvard University Press, 1986.

Reyes, Luis, and Peter Rubie. *Hispanics in Hollywood: An Encyclopedia of Film and Television.* New York: Garland Publishing, 1994.

Rodríguez, Richard. *A Hunger of Memory: The Education of Richard Rodríguez.* New York: Bantam Books, 1992.

Rogziński, Jan. *A Brief History of the Caribbean From the Arawak and the Carib to the Present.* New York: Meridian Book, 1992.

Ruíz Belvis, Segundo. *Informe sobre la abolición inmediata de la esclavitud en la Isla de Puerto-Rico.* Madrid: Establecimiento Tipográfico de R. Vicente, 1870.

Santiago, Esmeralda. *When I Was Puerto Rican.* New York: Random House, 1993.

Shorris, Earle. *Latinos: A Biography of a People.* New York: Avon Books, 1992.

Stavans, Ilan. *Spanglish: The Making of a New American Language.* New York: Rayo, 2003.

Suro, Roberto. *Strangers Among US: Latino Lives in a Changing America.* New York: Vintage Books, 1999.

Taube, Karl A. *Aztec and Maya Myths.* London: British Museum Press and University of Texas Press, 1995.

Thomas, Piri. *Down These Mean Streets.* New York: Vintage Books, 1997.

Torres-Saillant, Silvio, and Ramona Hernández. *The Dominican Americans.* Westport, CT: Greenwood Press, 1998.

Varela, Félix. *Jicótencal.* Houston: Arte Público Press, 1994.

Villaverde, Cirilo. *Cecilia Valdés.* Trans. Helen Lane, ed. Sibylle Fischer. New York: Oxford University Press, 2004.

Wagenheim, Kal, and Olga Jimenez Wagenheim, eds. *The Puerto Ricans: A Documentary History.* Princeton: Markus Weiner, 2002.

Wedel, Johan. *Santería Healing: A Journey into the Afro-Cuban World of Divinitie Spirits, and Sorcery.* Gainesville: University Press of Florida, 2004.

Weisman, Alan. *La Frontera: The United States Border with Mexico.* New York: Harcourt Brace Jovanovich, 1986.

West-Durán, Alan. *African Caribbeans: A Reference Guide.* Westport, CT: Greenwood Press, 2003.

Wilford, John Noble. *The Mysterious History of Columbus: An Exploration of the Man, the Myth, the Legacy.* New York: Alfred K. Knopf, 1991.

Williams, Eric. *From Columbus to Castro: The History of the Caribbean.* New York: Vintage Books, 1984.

Williamson, Edwin. *The Penguin History of Latin America.* New York: Penguin Books, 1992.

Wyden, Peter. *Bay of Pigs: The Untold Story.* New York: Simon and Schuster, 1979.

Ximenez de Sandoval, Felipe. *Cristobal Colón: Evocación del Almirante de la Mar Oceana.* Madrid: Ediciones Cultura Hispanica, 1963.

Zamora, Lois Parkinson, and Wendy B. Faris, eds. *Magical Realism: Theory, History, Community.* Durham, NC: Duke University Press, 1995.

Zeno Gandía, Manuel. *The Pond.* Trans. Kal Wagenheim. Princeton, NJ: Markus Wiener Publishers, 1999.

WEB SITES

The Americas. www.cemaweb.library.ucsb.edu/cema_index.htmllobalexchange.org/countries/americas/cuba/profile/history.html. This Web site offers a chronology for all Latin American countries; click on the country of choice.

California Ethnic and Multicultural Archives. cemaweb.library.ucsb.edu/cema_index.html. This site contains a wealth of non-book materials on the Latino experience, especially Mexican-Americans, Chicanos.

Center for Latin American Studies. clas.georgetown.edu. Presented here is information on Colombia, Mexico, and Venezuela.

Center for Puerto Rican Studies. www.centropr.org. This is the "center" for the study of Puerto Ricans in the United States. The Center is housed in Hunter College Library, New York City.

Center for U.S.–Mexico Border. usmex.ucsd.edu/research/research_governance_intl_links.php. This site contains material on Mexico–U.S. border studies.

Cuban Heritage Collection. www.library.miami.edu/umcuban/cuban.html. The best archival source for Cuban history.

Embassy of Colombia. www.colombiaemb.org/opencms/opencms. This site is an excellent source about Colombians in the United States.

Escritores Dominicanos. www.escritoresdominicanos.com. This site is dedicated to writers from the Dominican Republic; it is in Spanish.

Fast Facts About U.S. Hispanic Catholics. www.feyvida.org/research/fastfacts.html?gclid=CPOw7t-TzIgCFQ-ZHgod_jLIJw. Statistical information is presented in a user-friendly format on this site.

Hispanic Americans in Congress. www.loc.gov/rr/hispanic/congress/. Biographies of Latino elected officials are collected on this site.

Hispanic Businesses. www.hispanicbusiness.com/news/newsbyid.asp?id=48865. This site contains information on business and economics.

Hispanic Population in the United States. www.census.gov/population/www/socdemo/hispanic.html. Latino/Hispanic profiles are presented on this site.

Hispanic Reading Room/Library of Congress. www.loc.gov/rr/hispanic/. This site contains vast materials on Latinos.

Hispanics in the Military/Pew Hispanic Center. pewhispanic.org/reports/report.php?ReportID=17. The history of Latinos/Hispanics in the U.S. Armed Forces is presented here.

Latino Religion in the U.S.: Demographic Shifts and Trends. http://www.facsnet.org/issues/faith/espinosa.php. This site presents articles and studies of religion in Latino communities.

League of United Latin American Citizens. www.lulac.org/. LULAC's home page contains valuable information on business, education, and politics.

National Association for Bilingual Education. www.nabe.org/. Educational, political, and cultural information on bilingual education in general is presented here.

Office of Minority Health: Hispanic or Latino Population. www.cdc.gov/omh/Populations/HL/HL.htm. This site profiles Latino health and ten diseases that affect Latinos the most.

Status and Trends in the Education of Hispanics. nces.ed.gov/pubs2003/hispanics/. This site presents a profile of education in the Latino population.

U.S. Census. www.census.gov/. The U.S. Census Bureau's statistics, profiles, and news.

United States Hispanic Chamber of Commerce. www.ushcc.com/. A business and education related site for the Hispanic community.

The World Fact Book. www.cia.gov/cia/publications/factbook/geos/co.html. This site presents general information on all countries of the world.

FILMS

Around the World in Eighty Days. United Artists, 1956.

The Ballad of Gregorio Cortez. PBS/Embassy Pictures, 1984.

Ben-Hur. Metro Goldwyn Mayer, 1925.

The Bronze Screen. Questar, 2004.

The Buried Mirror, 5 vols. Sogetel, 1991.

Conquistador. PBS Home Video, 2001.

Dangerous When Wet. Metro Goldwyn Mayer, 1953.

Frenchman's Creek. Paramount, 1944.

Giant. Warner Brothers, 1956.

House of Spirits. Avid Home Entertainment, 1993.

Latin Lovers. Metro Goldwyn Mayer, 1953.

El Norte. CBS/FOX, 1984.

Remember the Alamo. PBS and Paramount, 2004.

Stand and Deliver. Warner Brothers Home Video, 1988.

U.S. Mexican War. PBS Home Video, 1998.

Viva Zapata. 20th Century Fox, 1952.

West Side Story. United Artists, 1961.

INDEX

Abolitionist Society, 57
Abubéquer-Aben-Tofail, 7
Adams, John Quincy, 43, 44, 52
Adonis (Carthaginian deity), 4
Aguilera, Christina, 116
Aguinaldo puertorriqueño (poetry collection), 51
Aguirre, Francisco, 92
Aguirre, Horacio, 92
AIDS epidemic, 128
Alabama, 19
The Alamo, 42, 49
Albermarle, Lord, 34
Alexander IV (Pope), 11
Algarin, Miguel, 95
Alhambra (in Granada), 8
Alianza Hispano-Americana, founding of, 62
Allende, Isabel, 113
Allende, Salvador, 105, 108
Alta California, 40, 51, 55
Alvarez, Julia, 117
Álvarez, Luis, 104
"Always in My Heart" (song), 85
American Civil Liberties Union, 82
American Federation of Labor, 78
American Tropical mural (Siqueiros), 80
Los amores de Ramona (Gonzáles), 73
Anacaona (Taíno princess), 14
Anaya, Rudolfo, 120
Andrew W. Mellon Foundation, 115
Anthony, Marc, 116, 129
Antigua, 28
Apache Indians, 28, 35
Areyto art form, 3
Argentina, 6, 7, 14, 51, 75, 77, 96, 99; colonists proclaim independence, 42; founding of, 19; Quechua

language, 7, 8, 27; tango music of, 83
Arizona, 20
Armijo, Antonio, 46
Arnaz, Desi, 68, 83, 84
Arnaz y de Acha, Desiderio Alberto, III, 71
Arocena, Eduardo, 113
Arrelano, Tristán de Luna, 21
Arrendondo, Joaquín de, 43
Arriola, Andrés de, 30
Ashford, Bailey K., 66
Astarte (Carthaginian deity), 4
Atahualpa (Inca emperor), 19
Ateneo Puertorriqueno, founding of, 59
Auraco Indians, 24
Austin, John, 47
Austin, Moses, 43
Austin, Stephen, 45, 48
Las aventuras de Don Chipotes o cuando los pericos mamen (Venegas), 77
Avilés, Juan, 93
Ayerra Santa Maria, Francisco de, 27
Aztecs, 2, 5, 7, 8, 17, 21
Azuala, Mariano, 70
La Azucena (journal), 58

Baal (Carthaginian deity), 4
"Babalu" song (Lecuona), 84
Badillo, Herman, 102
Bahamas, 11
Balaguer, Joaquin, 103
Ball, Lucille, 68, 82
The Ballad of Rocky Ruiz (Ramos), 85
Balseros, 120
Bancroft, Hubert Howe, 59
Barceló, Antonio R., 81
Barceló, Carlos Romero, 109
Basilica Menor de Santa María, 15

Bastidas, Rodrigo e, 13
Battle of Bull Run, 57
Battle of Pensacola, 33
Battle of Refugio, 49
Battle of San Jacinto, 50
Battles, 4
Batu (ball game), 4
Bay of Pigs invasion, 98
Beat Generation, 105
Belaval, Emilio S., 78
Belize, 5, 6
Belpre, Pura, 80
Belviz, Segundo Ruíz, 58
Bering Strait, 1
Betances, Ramón Emeterio, 55, 58
Bilingual Review (ed. Keller), 107
Bithorn, Hiram, 85
"Black Legend," 13
Bless Me, Ultima (Anaya), 120
Bobadilla, Francisco, 13
Bodegas (grocery stores), 76, 82, 94, 97, 98, 101, 116, 117
Bogotá, founding of, 19
Bohuti (Taíno healer), 3
Bolivar, Simón, 36, 40, 43, 45, 46–47, 72, 124
Bolivia, 8, 21, 42, 43, 102, 103, 125
Bonaparte, José, 41
Bonaparte, Napoleon, 41, 42
Bonilla, Francisco Leyva de, 23
Border Patrol, 75
Bosch, Juan, 102
Bowie, Jim, 48, 49, 50
Bracero Program, 86, 91, 94, 100
Brevísima relación de la destrucción de las Indias (Las Casas), 13
Brooklyn, New York, 43, 58, 89, 101, 120
Brothers to the Rescue *(Hermanos al Rescate)* operation, 121

Buccaneers (pirates), 28
Buenes Aires, Argentina, 23, 36
Bull Run, Battle of, 57
Burgos, Julia de, 70, 92
Burton, Maria Amparo Ruiz de, 60
Bush, George W., 127, 128, 130, 131
Bustamante, Anastasio, 46, 47

"The Caballero's Way" (O'Henry), 67
Cabello y Robles, Domingo, 36
Cabeza de Baca, Ezequiel, 71
Cabeza de Vaca, Alvar Nuñez, 10, 18, 20
Cacique (Taíno chief), 3
Cadiz junta, 42
Calderón, Juan Rodriguez, 41
California: colonization of, 36; Communist Party, 78; drafting of state constitution, 54; establishment of printing press, 47; Foreign Miners Tax, 54; Gold Rush, 46, 55; LULAC, 87; prohibition against bullfighting/cockfighting, 55. *See also* Alta California
California Nueva (New California), 40
California Vieja (Old California), 40
The Californian (newspaper), 47
Camino Real (royal road) construction, 28
Campos, Pedro Albizu, 82, 88, 89, 102
Capablanca, José Raúl, 76
Carew, Rod, 110
Caribbean settlers: African Slaves, 25; Taínos, 25; whites, 25
El Caribe (newspaper), 74
Carlos IV (King of Spain), 41
Carnegie, Andrew, 64
Carranza, Emilio, 77
Carranza, Venustiano, 70, 71
Carthage city, 2
Carthaginians, 2, 3, 4
Caruso, Enrico, 87
Casa de la Contratación (House of Contracts), 14
Castorena, Juan Ignacio María de, 31
Castro, Fidel, 75, 92, 93, 95, 98, 99, 100
Castro, Raul, 108
Cathedrals, 14, 15, 18, 19
Cather, Willa, 51
Catholicism, 15, 18, 19, 21, 22, 26, 31, 32, 45, 57, 83
Caudillismo (rule of the strong man), 48, 51
Cavazos, Lauro F., 114

Cecilia Valdés o La Loma del Ángel: novela de costumbres cubanas (Villaverde), 59
Celts, 2
Cenotes (sink holes), 6
Central America, 2, 5, 14, 18, 42, 56, 58, 68, 77, 110, 118, 125, 130
Centro Cívico Cultural Dominicano (NYC), 100
Cervantes (Saavedra), Miguel de, 25
Chac (Mayan deity), 1
Chacón, Eusebio, 62
Chapultepec Castle, 52
La charca (Gandia), 55, 62
Charles V (King), 16
Chavez, Cesar, 88, 100
Chavez, Hugo, 118, 124
Chewing gum. *See* Sapodilla tree
Chicano, term usage, 98
Chichen Itzá (city), 5
Chile, 7, 16, 20, 24, 46, 53, 61, 108; Magellan's sighting of, 17; Quechua language, 8; warship dispatched to San Francisco, 54
Chocolate, 5, 6
Cholera epidemic, 47, 55
Christianity, 4, 7, 83
Cibola (Seven Cities of Gold), 18, 19
Cisneros, Sandra, 110
Civil Rights Act (1965), 101
Civil Rights Commission (NYC), 93
Civil War (United States), 53, 57
Clemente, Roberto, 103, 107, 108
Clinton, Bill, 118, 123–124
Cofresí, Roberto, 45
Colombia, 7, 13, 18, 23, 33, 37, 43, 46, 67, 116; Bogotá's founding, 19; colonists proclaim independence, 43; establishment of, 43; founding of Santa Maria la Antigua del Darién, 18; Quechua language, 8
Colón, Miriam, 102
Colon, Rafael Hernández, 107
Columbus, Christopher: death of, 15; enslavement of Taínos, 13; Hispaniola arrest, 13; modern perspective on, 11; ships of, 10; successful voyage, 9; as symbol of capitalism/repression, 11
Comentarios reales (Vega), 25
Compagnie de Saint Christophe, 27
Compagnie des Iles D'Amerique, 27
Compagnie des Indes Occidentales, 27
Confederación de Trabajadores Generales, 84

Confederación de Uniones Obreras Mexicanas, 76
Conquistadores, 14, 24, 39
Constitution of 1812 (Spain), 41, 42
Continental Congress, 36
Contra dance music, 61
Conuco planting system, 2
Coppinger, José, 43
Cordero, Andres, 95
Córdoba, Hernandez de, 15
Córdoba city, 7, 8
Cordova, Arturo De, 86
Coronado, Francisco Vázques de, 20
Corridos (songs), 54
Cortes, Gregorio, 58
Cortés, Hernán, 11, 16, 17
Cortes, Renaldo, 58
Cortina, Juan Nepomuceno, 45, 56
Cortina War, 56
Corzine, Jon, 131
Cos, Martín Perfecto de, 48
Costa Rica, 22, 42, 56, 58, 64
Council of Indies, 17
Counting system, 5
Court of Private Land Claims, 61
Cowboys, 39
Crockett, David, 49
Crusada Para la Justicia, 103
Cruz, Celia, 127
La cuarterona pla (Rivera), 57
Cuauhtlahtoatzin, Juan Diego, 18
Cuba, 11, 14, 19, 31; abolition of slavery, 60; Bay of Pigs invasion, 98; British occupation of Havana, 33; establishment of Free Masonry, 33; Operation Pedro Pan, 98; Polk's purchase of, 53; rebellions of, 42; and slavery, 43; war of independence from Spain, 63
Cuban Adjustment Act, 103
Cuban American National Foundation, 112, 118
Cuban Committee for Democracy, 119
Cuban Democracy Act, 117–118
Cuban Missile Crisis, 100
Cuban Revolutionary Party *(Partido Revolucionario Cubano),* 62
Cuban Union of Writers and Poets, 105
Cubria, Mercedes, 107–108
Cuéllar, Diego Velásquez de, 15
CUNY Dominican Studies Institute, 119
"The Curse of Capistrano" (McCulley), 72
Cuzco (city), 9

The Daily Worker (Communist news-paper), 75
La Dama de Eche (Lady of Eche), 2
Dancing in Cuba (García), 117
Davila, Félix Córdova, 71
Davis, Jefferson, 53
De León, Alonso, 29
Death Comes to the Archbishop (Cather), 51
Declaration of Independence, of Texas, 48
Degeteau, Federico, 66
Deities: Carthaginian, 4; Mayan, 1; Táinos, 2, 3
Del Rio, Dolores, 76
Desperate Generation writers, 87
Diario Las Americas newspaper, 92
Díaz, Porfirio, 46, 59, 69
Díaz del Castillo, Bernal, 11, 23, 28
Dickinson, Susana, 49
Diego, José de, 67, 71
Dominican Republic (Hispaniola), 11, 13, 51, 100–101, 111
Don Quijote. See El ingenioso Hidalgo Don Quijote de la Mancha
Down Argentine Way, 82
Down These Mean Streets (Thomas), 103
Drake, Francis, 20, 23
D'Rivera, Paquito, 121
Duarte, Juan Pablo, 51
Duprey, Ana Roque, 67
Dutch West India Company, 27

Economic Development Adminis-tration (Puerto Rico), 91
Ecuador, 7, 42, 43, 63, 116, 125, 127
La Edad de Oro (children's magazine), 60
Ejercito Popular Boricua, 130
El Salvador, 18, 45, 118, 127; estab-lishment of United Provinces of Central America, 42; invasion of, 56; request for United States an-nexation, 45
Emeterio, Betances, 55
Employment Creation Investors Visa, 116
Encomienda system (slavery), 11, 14
The End of Trujillo (Galindez), 94
England, 26, 28, 32, 34, 38, 45, 72, 113
English Only movement, 110–111
English Plus initiative, 126
Enriquillo (Taíno chief), 16
Entremés (Llerena), 19
Epiphany Day, 79

Equal Education Opportunity Act, 108
Ermita de la Virgen de Monserrate (shrine to Virgin Mary), 28
Espanza, Gregorio, 49
Estefan, Gloria, 118
Esteves, Luis, 72
Estrada, Noel, 71
Ethnic diversity, 27
Eugenio María Hostos Community College, 104
Euro-American traders, 46
Exploratory Travels through the Western Territories of North America (Pike), 41

Facundo Civilización y barbarie (Sarmiento), 51
Fair Employment Practices Act, 84
Falkland Islands, 35, 36
Fannin, James Walker, 49
Federación Libre de los Trabajadores, 66, 84
Federal Relations Act (Puerto Rico), 89
Federalist Party (Puerto Rico), 64
Feliciano, José, 104
Ferdinand (King of Spain), 9, 11, 13, 14
Fernández, Antonio Manuel, 86
Fernos-Murray Bill, 96
Ferrer, José, 89
Filibustering, 54
Finlay, Carlos J., 59–60
First Battalion of U.S. Infantry in Porto Rico, 65
Flores, Irving, 95
Florida, 3, 8, 15, 16, 17, 18, 19, 26, 32, 34, 35, 36, 37, 39, 52, 86, 112, 125
Ford Foundation, 115
Foreign Miners Tax (California), 54
The Four Horsemen of the Apocalypse (Ibánez), 74
France: naval blockades, 51; v. Great Britain, 31, 32; v. Prussia, 32
Franciscan missions/missionaries, 25, 40
Fredonia, Republic of, 45
Free Masons, 33
Freedom Airlift, 102
French and Indian War, 32
French Revolution, 71
Fuentes, Daisy, 114
Fuerzas Armadas de Liberación Na-cional (FALN), 123–124

Fufu (mashed plantain), 33
Fulang Chang and I (Kahlo), 82

La Gaceta de México newspaper, 31, 43
La Gaceta de Puerto Rico newspaper, 41
Galíndez, Jesúsde, 94
Gálvez, Bernardo de, 33, 36
Gandia, Manuel Zeno, 55
Garcia, Andy, 115
García, Cristina, 117
Garcia, Eduarda Mansilla de, 59
Garciá, Fabian, 63
La Garcia de Texas newspaper, 39
Garcilaso de la Vega, 25
Gardel, Carlos, 81
Gautier, Felisa Rincón de, 93
Georgia, 18, 19, 26
Ghana, 1
El gibaro (Alonso), 53
Gil, Emilio Portes, 79
Giralt, Ramón Power y, 42
Godfather III movie, 115
Goizueta, Roberto C., 110
Gold Rush, 46, 53, 54, 55
González, Adalberto Elías, 73
González, Elian, 123
González, Henry B., 99
González, Pancho, 77, 88
Gramática y pronunciación en Timucuan (Pareja), 26
Granada, 7, 8, 56, 113
La grandeza mexicana (Mexican Great-ness), 25
Grant, Ulysses S., 53
Great Basin Desert, 45
Great Britain, 28, 30, 37, 70; occu-pation of Havana, 33, 34; U.S. declares independence from, 36; v. France, 31, 32; v. Spain, 32, 36
Great Depression, 77
Griffith, W., 70
El Grito de Dolores rebellion, 42
Guadeloupe, 11
Guale Inidans, 26
"Guantanamera" song, 55
Guatemala, 5, 6, 64, 93, 113, 125; establishment of United Provinces of Central America, 42; founding of, 17; invasion of, 56
Guerra, Juan Luis, 117
La Guerra Gaucha movie, 85
Guerrero, Vicente, 43, 46
Guevara, Ernesto "Che," 77, 93, 102, 103, 121

Guía confesional in las lenguas Timucuan y Castellana (Pareja), 26
Guitar, 14, 54, 65

El Habanero newspaper, 45
Haciendas, 40
Haiti, 3, 13, 38, 51
Harmar, Archer, 63
Harvard University, 19
Havana, Cuba, 17, 21, 23, 33, 34, 39
Hearts of the West (O'Henry), 67
Hebrew alphabet, 3
Hemingway, Ernest, 86
Henríquez y Carvajal, Francisco, 67
Henry, Patrick, 36
Hernández, Rafael, 77
Hernández v. Texas case, 93
Herrera, Carolina, 127
Hidalgo, Miguel, 42
Hijo de la tempestad (Chacón), 62
Hijuelos, Oscar, 115
Hinojosa, Rolando, 109
Hispanic, term usage, 74, 97
Hispanic Caucus, 109
Hispanic College Fund, 118
Hispanic magazine, 114
Hispanic Scholarship Fund, 108
Hispanic Young Adult Association, 89
Hispaniola (Dominican Republic, Haiti), 28; arrest of Columbus, 13; Columbus introduces sugar cane, 11; encomienda system (slavery), 14; Núñez Cabeza de Vaca sails from, 18
Hispano, term usage, 74
La historia de Nuevo México (Villagra), 26
History of Arizona (Bancroft), 59
History of California (Bancroft), 59
History of Nevada, Colorado, and Wyoming (Bancroft), 59
Honduras, 5, 6, 17, 42, 56, 122
Hoover, Herbert, 80
House of Spirits (Allende), 113
House on Mango Street (Cisneros), 110
Houston, Sam, 49, 50
How the Garcia Girls Lost Their Accents (Alvarez), 117
Hoya, Oscar de la, 129
Huerta, Victoriano, 69
Human sacrifices, 6
Humaná, Antonio Gutiérrez de, 23
Hunger of Memory: The Education of Richard Rodriguez (Rodriguez), 113
Hurricane Katrina, 130

I Love Lucy, 90, 116
Ibáñez, Vicente Blasco, 74
Iberia/Iberians, 2, 7
Ice age, 1
Immigration Act (1917), 71
Immigration Act (1924), 75
Immigration Act (1990), 115
Immigration and Nationality Act (1952), 91
Immigration Reform and Control Act, 114
Impelliteri, Vincent R., 90, 93
Incas, 1, 7, 25, 36; building city of Cuzco, 9; Quechua language, 8
Los infortunios de Alonso Ramírez (Siquenza y Gongora), 29
El ingenioso Hidalgo Don Quijote de la Mancha (Cervantes), 25, 26
Institute of Culture (Puerto Rico), 93
International Ladies Garment Worker's Union (ILGWU), 101
Isabella (Queen of Spain), 9, 11, 13, 14
Iturbide, Agustín de, 44, 45
Itzamna (Mayan deity), 1
Ix Chel (Mayan deity), 1

Jackson, Helen Hunt, 73, 76–77
Jackson, Thomas "Stonewall," 53
Jamestown settlement, 25
Jefferson, Thomas, 36, 40, 46
Jesuits, 35, 37
Jicoténcal (Varela), 45
John Paul II (Pope), 18
Johnson, Lyndon B., 101, 103, 104
Jones Act, 71
Juárez, Benito, 40, 55, 57
Julia, Raul, 119

Kahlo, Frida, 82
Kanellos, Nicolás, 39
Kansas, 20
Kearny, Stephen W., 51
Keith, Minor, 58
Kennedy, John F., 98, 99, 101
Khrushchev, Nikita Sergeyevich, 100
Kineo, Eusebio (Father), 31
Klail City y sus alrededores (Hinojosa), 109
Korean War, 90
Kukulcan (Mayan deity), 1–2

Laguerre, Enrique A., 78
Lam, Wilfredo, 86
Lamento Borincano (Hernández), 77–78

Languages: English Plus initiative, 126; Nahuatl, 8, 16, 18, 27; Quechua (Incas), 7, 8, 27; Semitic, 3; Spanglish, 97; Spanish, 4
Las Casas, Bartolomé de, 10, 13, 15, 21
"De Las Margaritas" (song), 52
Latin, term derivation/usage, 73–74
Latin America, 1, 2, 4, 7.8, 14, 16, 21, 22, 28, 33, 35, 39, 48, 66, 73, 79, 112, 125, 129
Latin Grammy Awards, 126, 129
Latin Kings gang, 122–123
League of United Latin American Citizens (LULAC), 78, 87, 93, 130
Lebrón, Lolita, 95
Lecuona, Margarita, 84
Lee, Robert E., 53
Lesser Antilles, 27
Lewis and Clark expedition, 40
Lima, Peru, 19
Lindbergh, Charles, 77
Lindsey, John, 103
Literary Currents in Hispanic American (Ureña), 82
Llerena, Cristóbalde, 20
Long, James, 44
Lopez, Jennifer, 121–122, 129
López, Narciso, 53, 56
Los Angeles, 37
Losoya, Toribio Domingo, 49
L'Ouverture, Toussaint, 40
Lozano, Ignacio, 69, 75
Luque, Adolfo, 72
Lust for Life (movie), 91

Machado, Gerardo, 75
Madero, Francisco, 69
Madrid, Treaty of, 28
Magellan, Ferdinand, 16
Malintzin (Princess), 16
Malvinas/Falkland Islands, 35, 36
The Mambo Kings Play Songs of Love (Hijuelos), 115
The Man and the City television show, 91
Manhattan Chess Club, 76
Manifest Destiny doctrine, 39, 47, 54, 56
Marcantonio, Vito, 89
María Candelaria movie, 85
Mariachi bands/music, 54
Mariel Boatlift, 111
Marín, Muñoz, 96, 101, 111
Marín, Pachín, 63
The Mark of Zorro silent film, 73

Maroon slaves, 32

Marqués, René, 92

Marquez, Gabriel Garcia, 64, 112

Marti, José, 55, 59, 60, 61

Martial (Spanish poet), 5

Martin, John Bartlow, 100

Martin, Ricky, 116, 123

Martinez, José, 50–51

Martínez, Rafael C., 95

The Martyrs of the Alamo (Griffith), 70

Maximlian of Habsburg, 57, 58

Mayan Civilization, 1, 2, 5, 6, 15, 21, 22

Mayflower Compact, 26

Mayol, Hilda Yolanda, 126

McClellan, George B., 53

McCulley, Johnston, 72

McKinley, William, 51, 63, 66

Meade, George Gordon, 53

Meadows Foundation, 115

Menchú, Rigoberta, 123

Menendez, Bob, 108, 131

Menendez, Francisco, 32

Mérida, founding of, 21

Mesoamerica, 2

Mexican American Legal Defense and Education Fund (MALDEF), 104

Mexican American Political Association (MAPA), 98

Mexican-American War, 51, 52, 54, 60

Mexican Americans, as second-class citizens, 52–53

Mexican Greatness (La grandeza mexicana), 25

Mexican Indians, 42

Mexican Revolution (1910), 46, 69, 779

Mexican-Spanish cowboys, 39

El Mexicano (newspaper), 43

Mexicas. See Aztecs

México, 2, 5, 7, 8, 14, 17, 18, 20, 21, 22, 40, 42, 45, 47

México City, 2, 4, 7, 8, 16, 17, 18, 19, 25, 26, 37

Miami, Florida, 102, 114, 130

Miraculous crucifix of our Lord of Esquipulas, 42

Miralles, Juan, 36

Miranda, Francisco de, 33

El Misisipi (community newspaper), 39

La Missión de Santa Isabel, 26

Missions: Franciscan missions, 40; La Missión de Santa Isabel, 26; Luis

de las Amarillas, 33; Nuestra Señora de Loreto, 31; San Antonio, Texas, 31; San Pedro de Athuluteca, 26; Tucson, Arizona, 31

Monroe, James, 44, 47

Monroe Doctrine, 44, 47

Montalban, Ricardo, 89, 104

Montaner, Rita, 78

Montejo, Franciso de, 18

Montez, Maria, 85

Moors: enslavement of, 10; v. Spain, 7

Morelos, José Maria, 42

Moreno, Mario (Cantinflas), 93

Moreno, Rita, 99, 127

Morgan, Henry, 28

Motecuhzoma (Emperor), 9, 16, 17

Motecuhzoma wars, 14

Murieta, Joaquín, 46, 55

El Museo del Barrio (NYC), 104

Music: of Argentina, 83; contra dance music, 61; of Latin America, 84; *Mariachi* bands, 54; *musica tejana,* 65; of slaves, 31; in Spanish Americas, 14; of Texas, 65

Muslims, 7, 8, 9

Nahuatl language, 8, 16, 18, 27

Narváez, Pánfilo de, 17, 18

National Council of La Raza, 130

National Endowment for the Humanities, 115

National Latino Political Survey, 110

National Republic Party, 67

Nationalist Party (Puerto Rico), 95

Native Americans, 10; Apache Indians, 28, 36; Mexican Indians, 42; Pueblo Indians, 28, 31; Zapoteca Indians, 40

Navarro, José Antonio, 48, 49, 50

Navarro, Ramon, 75

Nevis, 11

New Laws, 21

New Mexico, 20, 26

New York City: Centro Cívico Cultural Dominicano, 100; cholera epidemic, 47; Civil Rights Commission, 93; *El Museo del Barrio,* 104; Porto Rican Democratic Club, 74; Puerto Rican Brotherhood of America, 75; Puerto Rican Day Parade, 96; Puerto Ricans v. Blacks, 76

New York Sun (newspaper), 59

Newspapers: *The Californian,* 47; *El Caribe,* 74; *The Daily Worker,* 75; *Diario Las Americas,* 92; *La Gaceta*

de México, 31, 43; *La Gaceta de Puerto Rico,* 41; *El Habanero,* 45; *New York Sun,* 59; *El Nuevo Herald,* 122; *La Opinión,* 75; *El paso del norte,* 70; *Porto Rico Progress,* 69; *La Prensa,* 69; *San Juan Star,* 99; *La Voz de Puerto Rico,* 57

Nicaragua, 56, 64, 68, 71, 81, 84, 92, 99, 108, 114, 126; establishment of United Provinces of Central America, 42; founding of, 17; Marines end occupation, 8

Nicot, Jean (French diplomat), 25

Nicotiana Tabacum (tobacco), 25

Niña (Columus's ship), 10

Nixon, Richard M., 104, 106

Niza, Marcos de, 19

La Noche Triste (the sad night), 17

El Norte independent movie, 113

North American Free Trade Association (NAFTA), 120

Novela de la Revolución Mexicana novels, 73

Novello, Antonia C., 116

Nuestra America, Our America (Martí), 61

Nuestra Señora de Loreto mission, 31

El Nuevo Herald newspaper, 122

Nuyorican Movement, 98

Nuyorican Poets Café, 105

Ocios de Juventud (Calderón), 41

Oglethorpe, James, 32

Oklahoma, 20

The Old Guide: Surveyor, Scout, Hunter Indian Fighter, Ranchman, Preacher: His Life in His Own Words (Policarpo), 63

Olmecs, 2

Olmos, Edward James, 113, 123

Oñate, Juan de, 23, 24

One Hundred Years of Solitude (Marquez), 64, 112

Onís, Luis de, 43

Operation Bootstrap, 112

Operation Desert Shield, 116

Operation Pedro Pan, 98

Operation Urgency, 113

La Opinión newspaper, 75

The Orden Hijos de América, 74

Orozco, José Clemente, 80

Ortíz, Prudencio Unanue, 81

Otero, Miguel Antonio "Gillie," 56, 63

Ottoman Empire, 9

Ovando, Nicolás de, 14

Pacheco, Johnny, 101
Pacheco, José Antonio Romualdo, Jr., 47, 59, 63–64
Padilla, Heberto, 105
Palma, Tomás Estrada, 67
Panama, 15, 64, 67; attacked by Drake, 22; attacked by Morgan, 28; colonists proclaim independence, 42
Pantoja, Antonia, 86, 99
Papal Bull (1494), 11
Paraguay, 19, 125, 126; colonists proclaim independence, 42; rebellion against Spain, 31
Pareja, Francisco, 26
Paris, Treaty of, 66
Partido Popular, founding of, 79
Partido Revolucionario Cubano (Cuban Revolutionary Party), 62
Partido Unionista de Puerto Rico, 67
El paso del norte newspaper, 70
Pastry War, 51
La Paz, Bolivia, 21
Peña, Federico, 118
Pensacola, Florida, 33
Peralta, Pedro de, 23, 24
Pérez, Selena Quintanilla, 120
Perez and Martina: A Portorican Folk Tale (Belpre), 80
Péron, Eva, 87, 91
Péron, Juan Domingo, 87
Pershing, John J., 71
Personal Memoirs of John N. Sequín (Seguín), 61
Perú, 1, 2, 6, 7, 18, 20, 22, 36, 43, 60, 111
Pez, Andrés de, 29
Pierce, Franklin, 53, 56
Pike, Zebulon, 41
Pineda, Alonso Álvarez de, 16
Piñero, Miguel, 107
Pinta (Columus's ship), 10
Piracy, 29
Pizarro, Francisco, 18, 19, 20
Plains Indians, 23
Platt, Orville, 66
Platt Amendment, 65
Poesías, 41
Policarpo, José, 63
Political activism, 39
Polk, James K., 51, 52, 53, 54
Pomerian War, 32
Ponce de León, Juan, 9, 15, 17
Ponce de León, Juan, II, 23
Popé (Pueblo medicine man), 29
Porto Rican Democratic Club, 74
Porto Rico Progress newspaper, 69

Porto Rico Steamship Company, 68
La Prensa (newspaper), 69
Printing press, 37, 41, 47
Proyecto para la abolición de la esclavitud en Puerto Rico (Belviz), 58
Pueblo Indians, 28, 31
Puente, Tito, 117
Puerto Rican Brotherhood of America, 75, 76
Puerto Rican Community Development Project (PRCDF), 103
Puerto Rican Day Parade (NYC), 96
Puerto Rican Herald (newspaper), 65
Puerto Rican Legal Defense Fund (PRLDEF), 107, 108
Puerto Rican Traveling Theater, 45
Puerto Rico, 3, 11, 15, 17, 22, 23, 25, 27, 38; abolishment of slavery, 59; and Christmas carols, 40; declared a province, 41; Economic Development Administration, 91; established as American territory, 74; Federal Relations Act, 89; Federalist Party of, 64; first books of, 41; Institute of Culture, 93; libreta system, 53; Nationalist Party, 95; right to declare independence, 42; schools for underprivileged children, 42; settled by Corsicans, 43; trading of sugar, 43; and United States Navy, 44
Punic Wars, 4

Quechua language (Incas), 7, 8, 27
Queen Anne's War, 31
Quetzelcoat (feathered serpent god), 2
Quinn, Anthony, 91

Railroads, 58, 63, 64
Ramona (Jackson), 73, 76–77
Ramos, Manuel, 85
Raza Unida Party, 105
Reagan, Ronald, 112, 113
Recovery Project, 115
Recuerdos de viaje (Garcia), 59
Refugee Act (1980), 112
Refugio, Battle of, 49
El Regimen del solitario (Zaratoza, Avempace de), 7
Reily, E. Mont, 74
La relación (Cabeza de Vaca), 20
Relación de meritos (Martinez), 50
"Remember the Alamo," 49
Republic of Fredonia, 45
Republican Party, of Puerto Rico, 67
Reverse discrimination, 105
Revolutionary War, 33, 35, 36, 41

Riggs, Francis E., 81
Ríos, Filiberto Ojeda, 109, 130
Rivera, Alejandro Tapia y, 57
Rivera, Diego, 79
Rivera, Luis Muñoz, 63–64, 67
Rivera, Tomás, 106
Riverside neighborhood (Miami), 97
Rockefeller Foundation, 115
Rodriguez, Richard, 113
Roman Empire, 4, 5, 6
Roman-Iberian culture, 4
Roosevelt, Franklin D., 81
Roosevelt, Teddy, 68, 78
Roque de Duprey, Ana, 71
Ros-Lehtinen, Ileana, 115
Royal Decree of Graces, 43
Roybal, Edward Ross, 98

Sages civilization (Guatemala), 6
Samana Cay island (Watling's Island), 11
San Antonio, Texas, 4, 48
San Cristóbal Ecatepec, 43
San Jacinto, Battle of, 50
San Juan Star (newspaper), 99
San Pedro de Athuluteca mission, 26
Sánchez, Alberto E., 101
Sandinista Movement, 99
Santa Anna, Antonio López de, 45, 46, 47, 50, 51, 55, 57, 58, 59, 61
Santa Fe Trail, 44
Santa María (Columus's ship), 10
Santa Maria del Darien, 15
Santa Maria la Antigua del Darién, 18
Santeria religious ceremony, 72, 83
Santiago, Esmeralda, 119
Santo Domingo, 14, 40
Sapodilla tree, 48
Sarmiento, Domingo Faustino, 51
Schomburg, Arthur, 58
Secure Fence Act, 131
Seeger, Pete, 55
Seguín, Juan Nepomuceno, 60, 61
Selena (movie), 121–122
Semitic languages, 3
Seneca (Roman-Spanish philosopher), 5
Sequin, Juan, 49
Serra, Junipero, 35
Serrano, José, 116, 126
Seven Cities of Gold (Cibola), 18, 19, 20
Seven Years' War, 32, 35
Sherman, William T., 53
Short Eyes play (Piñero), 107
Sierra Nevada mountains, 45, 55

Siguenza y Gongora, Carlos, 29
Siqueiros, David, 80
Slaves/slavery: abolished in Cuba, 60;
    abolished in Puerto Rico, 59; and
    Abolitionist Society, 57; daily life
    description, 26; defense of St. Au-
    gustine, 32; and filibustering, 54;
    introduced by Columbus, 11; and
    music, 31; rebellions in Cuba, 42;
    shipping to America, 25; shipping
    to Caribbean, 16
Smith, Jedediah S., 45, 46
Smith, John, 20
Sor Juana Inez de la Cruz, 28, 30
Sores, Jacques de, 21
Sosa, Sammy, 122
Soto, Hernando de, 19
South America, 1
South Carolina, 18, 19, 32
Soviet Union, 100
Spain: Bolivar's fight against, 43;
    capture of Málaga, 10; colonists
    proclaim independence, 42;
    Constitution of 1812, 42; estab-
    lishment of Royal Tobacco Fac-
    tory), 31; expulsion of French
    from, 43; founding of Mérida,
    21; McKinley declares war
    against, 63; Muslims expelled, 9;
    siege of Granada, 10; and Treaty
    of Madrid, 28; v. Apache Indi-
    ans, 36; v. Great Britain, 32, 36;
    v. México, 16, 42; v. Moors, 7,
    10; v. Visgoths, 6; Venezuela's re-
    bellion against, 33; withdrawal
    from Texas, 20; worries about
    Jefferson, 40
Spanish American Youth Bureau, 86
Spanish Civil War, 82
Spanish-Cuban-American War, 51,
    54, 66, 70
Spanish Inquisition, 17
Spanish International Network, 113
Spanish language, 4
Spanish Trail, 46
The Squatter and the Don (Burton),
    60
St. Augustine, Florida, 25, 28, 31,
    32
St. Croix, 11
St. Kitts, 11
St. Patrick's Cathedral (NYC), 18,
    19
Stahl, Agustín, 66, 71
"Story of a Woman" essay (La
    Deana), 53
Suárez, Oscar González, 96

Sugar cane, 11
Supply routes, 26

Taínos, 2, 3, 4, 5, 11, 13, 15, 16, 21,
    25
Tamales, 7
Tampeños, 65
Taylor, Zachary, 53
Teatro bufo (Cuban art form), 73
Tejada, Jo Raquel (Raquel Welch),
    106
Tejanos, 41, 42, 43, 44, 45, 46, 47,
    48, 49, 50, 57, 59, 61
Tejanos rebellion, 43
El Telegrafo de las Floridas newspaper,
    39
Telemundo tv network, 113
Tennessee, 19
Tenochtitlán city (México City), 7,
    8, 16; annexation of Tlatelolco,
    10; attacked by Cortés, 17
Teotihuacán city, 4
Tertuilias, 39
Texas, 16, 18, 20, 29, 31, 38, 42, 46,
    54, 66, 127; avenging the Alamo,
    50; Declaration of Independence
    of, 48, 58; founding of, 33; Spain's
    withdrawal, 30; v. México, 42, 47
Texian rebellion, 48
Thomas, Piri, 103
Tijerina, Reies López, 103
Tlatelolco city, 10
Tlaxcala city, 16
Tobacco *(Nicotiana Tabacum),* 25, 31
Toltecs, 1, 2, 6, 7
Toro, Benicio del, 126
Torre, Miguel de la, 45
Tortillas, 7
Tortugas island, 28
Tower, Horace M., 74
Trade Union Unity League, 78
Tras la tormenta la calma (Chacón),
    62
Travis, William, 41, 49
Treaty of Guadalupe Hidalgo, 52,
    53
Treaty of Madrid, 28
Treaty of Paris, 35, 66
Trevino, Lee, 106
La Trinitaria secret society, 51
Troya y Quesada, Silvestre de Balboa,
    25
*The True History of the Conquest of
    New Spain* (Díaz del Castillo),
    23, 28
*A True Relation of Such Occurrences and
    Accidents of Noate as Hath Happened*

*in Virginia Since the First Planting
    of That Colony* (Smith), 20
Trujillo, Rafael, 94
Tugwell, Rexford Guy, 84
Túpac Amaru II, 36

United Farm Workers, 100, 108
United Provinces of Central America,
    42
United States: Continental Congress,
    36; declaration of independence
    from Great Britian, 36; and El
    Salvador's annexation, 45; filibus-
    tering tactic, 54; increasing Latino
    population, 54–55; Mexican-
    American War victory, 52; and
    Puerto Rico, 44; purchase at Cuba,
    53; trade with Spanish Caribbean,
    41; v. Soviet Union, 100; warnings
    by Mexican government, 51
Universidad Autónoma de Santo
    Domingo, 19
Universidad de México, 2
Ureña, Henriquez, 67, 82
Uruguay, 42, 125

Valdes, Luis, 109
Valdiva, Pedro de, 20
Valentino, Rudolph, 61, 74
Valenzuela, Fernando, 112
Varela, Félix, 45, 47
Vásquez de Ayllón, Lucas, 18
Velázquez, Diego, 57
Velázquez, Loreta Janeta, 57
Velez, Lupe, 82, 86
Venegas, Daniel, 77
Venezuela, 12, 32, 33, 40, 84, 118,
    124; colonists proclaim indepen-
    dence, 42; political uncertainty,
    127; rebellion against Spain, 33
Vespucci, Amerigo, 9, 12, 13, 14
Viceroyalty of Perú, 20
Villa, Pancho, 69, 71, 75
Villagra, Gaspar Pérez de, 26
Villaverde, Cirilo, 59
Virgin Islands, 11
Virgin Mary, 27, 28
Virgin of Guadalupe, 18, 19, 42
Visgoths v. Spain, 6
Viva Zapita (movie), 91
Vivar, Rodrigo Díaz de (El Cid), 7
El viviente hijo del vigilante (Abubéquer-
    Aben-Tofail), 7
Vizcarrondo, Julio L., 57
Voting Rights Act (1965), 108
La Voz de Puerto Rico (newspaper),
    57

Walker, William, 56
War of Jenkin's Ear, 32
Warrior civilization (Mayas, Toltecs),
  6
Wars/battles: The Alamo, 49; Battle
  of Pensacola, 33; Battle of Refu-
  gio, 49; Battle of San Jacinto, 50;
  Caribs v. Táinos, 5; civil, of
  Incas, 18; Cortina War, 56;
  French and Indian War, 32;
  Mexican-American War, 51, 54;
  of Motecuhzoma, 14; Pastry
  War, 51; Pomerian War, 32;
  Punic Wars, 4; Queen Anne's
  War, 31; Revolutionary War, 33;
  Seven Years' War, 32; Spain v.
  Moors, 7; Spain v. Visgoths, 6;

Spanish-Cuban-American War,
  51, 54, 66, 70; Texas indepen-
  dence, 48
Washington, George, 36
Watergate scandal, 106
Watling's Island (Samana Cay island),
  11
Welch, Raquel (Jo Raquel Tejada),
  106
West Side Story movie, 98–99
When I Was Puerto Rican (Santiago),
  119
The White Rose poem (Martí), 62
White settlers, 25
Wilson, Woodrow, 70, 71
World Trade Center, 126–127
World War I, 54

World War II, 54

Ybor, Martinez, 60
Ybor City, 60
Yellow fever, 60
Yucatán, 5, 6

Zamoranao, Agustín Vicente, 47
Zapata, Emilano, 71
Zapoteca Indians, 40, 58
Zaratoza, Avempace de, 7
Zavala, Adina de, 57
Zelaya, José Santos, 68
Zoot Suit play (Valdes), 109
Zorba the Greek (movie), 91
Zumarraga, Juan, 18

About the Author

D.H. FIGUEREDO is director of the Library and Media Center at Bloomfield College. He is editor of *Encyclopedia of Caribbean Literature* (Greenwood 2006) and co-editor of *Encyclopedia of Cuba* (Greenwood 2003). He has taught Latin American literature at Montclair State University and Bloomfield College, and regularly contributes to *Booklist, Multicultural Review*, and other publications.